My Turn At Bat:

The Story of My Life
by TED WILLIAMS

with JOHN UNDERWOOD

SIMON AND SCHUSTER
New York

EC '69 | | 8 5 9

FOURTH PRINTING

SBN 671-20228-6
LIBRARY OF CONGRESS CATALOG CARD NUMBER: 78-75869
DESIGNED BY RICHARD C. KARWOSKI
MANUFACTURED IN THE UNITED STATES OF AMERICA
PRINTED BY MAHONY & ROESE, NEW YORK
BOUND BY AMERICAN BOOK-STRATFORD PRESS, NEW YORK

To Beverly, Lori, DeeDee, Leslie and John . . .
and to Ted The Kid himself,
who (God help him) always calls 'em as he sees 'em

J. U.

Two sections of illustrations will be found starting on pages 97 and 209.

part one

I'm glad it's over. Before anything else, understand that I am glad it's over. I'm so grateful for baseball—and so grateful I'm the hell out of it as a player. This business of managing the Washington Senators might yet prove a terrible mistake, but it's a new course and I'm excited about it. I certainly do not have a youth wish. I mean, I wouldn't go back to being eighteen or nineteen years old, knowing what was in store, the sourness and the bitterness, knowing how I thought the weight of the damn world was always on my neck, grinding on me. I wouldn't go back to that for anything. I wouldn't *want* to go back. I've got problems now. I've always been a problem guy. I'll always have problems. But I'm grateful that part of my life is over.

I wanted to be the greatest hitter who ever lived. A man has to have goals—for a day, for a lifetime—and that was mine, to have people say, "There goes Ted Williams, the greatest hitter who ever lived." Certainly nobody ever worked harder at it. It was the center of my heart, hitting a baseball. Eddie Collins used to say I lived for my next turn at bat, and that's the way it was. If there was ever a man born to be a hitter it was me. As a kid, I wished it on every falling star: Please, let me be the hitter I want to be.

I remember the first time I saw Carl Yastrzemski, a youngster in the Red Sox batting cage a few years ago, and how much he reminded me of myself at that age—I mean he positively *quivered* waiting for that next pitch. And I have to think there was nobody who had any more opportunity than I did, along with the God-given physical attributes and the intense desire. Almost always the first at the ball park, almost always the last to leave. I'm talking about from a kid on. I have to laugh now at my last five or six years in Boston, how I just wanted to get in and get out, to beat the crowds, to get it over with.

I should have had more fun in baseball than any player who ever lived. I played in what I think was baseball's best-played era, the years just before World War II, and then the real booming years, 1946 through the early 50's. We were always fighting for a pennant, we played before the biggest crowds. I won batting championships and home run championships and Most Valuable Player awards, and when it was all over I made the Hall of Fame. I had people around who encouraged me—a real hitter's manager like Joe Cronin, who would sit around the clubhouse for hours talking hitting, and I always loved that, and Joe McCarthy, who in my mind was the best of managers.

I played before the greatest fans in baseball, the Boston fans, and I know what you're going to say about *that:* Old Teddy Ballgame loved those fans, all right. He spat at them and made terrible gestures and threw a bat that conked a nice old lady on the head one day, and he never tipped his hat to their cheers. And you would be right. But there came a time when I knew, I *knew*, they were for me, and how much it meant to me, and I will get into that later. As for tipping my hat, I did my first year, but never afterward. I couldn't, not if I played another twenty years. I just couldn't. I was fed up for good with that part of the act.

Certainly baseball doesn't owe me anything, a not too well educated, not particularly smart guy who played probably the only game in which he could excel. And *to* excel, to participate, to see things, to have a few material things, I'm grateful for all that. I think at the same time I've taken a lot of undue abuse. My twenty-two years in baseball were enjoyable, but many times they were unhappy too. They were unhappy because I was in a shell an awful lot. I felt a lot of people didn't like me. I did things I was ashamed of, and sorry for, and yet know in my heart I would do again under the circumstances, because that was me. I felt— I *know*—I was not treated fairly by the press, and I'm not going to go soft on that now. And I'm not going to say the Boston management did not deserve part of the blame for those bad relations, because it did, especially when I was a young player, when I needed and should have had some protection, some common meeting ground to head these things off before they got worse, which they always did.

Oh, I hated that Boston press. I've outlived the ones who were really vicious, who wrote some of the meanest, most slanderous things you can imagine. I can *still* remember the things they wrote, and they still make me mad: How I was always trying to get somebody's job—the manager's, the general manager's, the guy's in the radio booth—and I never coveted another man's job in my life. Or how I didn't hit in the clutch, and yet drove in more runs per time at bat than anybody who ever played this game except Babe Ruth, and got on base more times per at-bat than anybody *including* Babe Ruth. I was a draft dodger. I wasn't a "team" man. I was "jealous." I "alienated" the players from the press. I didn't hit to left field. I took too many bases on balls. I did this, I did that. And so on. And so unfair.

I remember the time I broke my elbow in 1950. I'd had one of my best years in 1949. I batted .343, I hit 43 home runs, I drove in 159 runs, I was voted Most Valuable Player in the league, and gee, we missed winning the pennant on the very last day. I had started 1950 like it was going to be an even better year for me. I felt great. Then in the All-Star game, first inning, Ralph Kiner hit one deep into left center in Comiskey Park. I ran a long way and caught it and crashed the fence with my elbow. I didn't know then how serious it was. The elbow swelled up and there was pain, but I played seven more innings and even got a single in the fifth inning to put the American League ahead, 4–3. Later they X-rayed and found I had broken thirteen little chips off the head of the radius, and they were talking about taking out the whole thing, which would have finished me for good, but they managed to make a repair.

This *has* to be the greatest disappointment of my career, because as time went on and my arm never completely came around, I knew I would never again be the hitter I was. It was two months before I played again. I could barely straighten the elbow. To this day I have trouble with it. But the Red Sox were anxious for me to get started because we were hot in the pennant race. I went back into the lineup. It was a mistake because I wasn't ready. For two weeks I hit like an old woman. I was miserable. I wanted to play, but I wasn't doing the club any good. We lost in the last week to the Yankees, and do you know what they wrote in Boston? They wrote, "The Red Sox do better without Williams." That's the kind of writers they were.

There's no doubt, of course, that things got started and grew worse partly because of my temperament, because of my emotional, explosive nature. I have never been regarded especially as a man with great patience. Certainly as a young player I had none at all with myself. I was impetuous, I was tempestuous. I blew up. Not acting, but *re*acting. I'd get so damned mad, throw bats, kick the columns in the dugout so that sparks flew, tear out the plumbing, knock out the lights, damn near kill myself. *Scream.* I'd scream out of my own frustration.

There was the time in Minneapolis. I've still got the scars on my wrist. It was 1938, the year before I went up to the Red Sox, and to appreciate how intense I was you have to remember that it was a year any nineteen-year-old kid ballplayer would love to have had. I led the American Association in everything—runs, average, RBI's, homers, everything. I had a wonderful manager, Donie Bush, who put up with me. The town was mine, and I loved it.

Anyway, Lloyd Brown was pitching for St. Paul, a tough little pitcher with a good curve. I got him to 3 and 1 in the first inning, bases loaded, short right-field fence. Now he has to come in with the fast ball. He does. Right there. Perfect. If I'd gotten that much more bat on the ball it would have gone 440 feet, but I hit just under it, and popped it up, and the St. Paul first baseman reached over the boxes and made a hell of a play. Boy, I'm mad now.

I go back to the bench, this little wooden bench, little crackerbox dugout in Minneapolis, and I'm so mad I don't know what to do. I sit down and here's this big water cooler right there next to me. About half full of water. And I just can't contain myself. *Whoomph, kerr-rash.* I hit it with my fist. They must have thought a cannon had gone off in the dugout. It just exploded. Blood's flying, glass, everything. Well, I was lucky I didn't cut my hand off. There was one cut that went pretty deep and just missed a nerve. You don't have to cut very much there to do real damage. I could have ended my career before it started. As it was it wasn't even bad enough to take me out of the game. But that shows you how intense I was.

I was never able to be dispassionate, to ignore the things people said or wrote or implied. It just wasn't in me. In my heart I don't believe I am any more sensitive to criticism than a lot of athletes, but I am certainly in the upper bracket of sensitivity, maybe the top 3 per cent. In a crowd of cheers I could always pick out the solitary boo. I don't mean to say that criticism affected my hitting, because the boos always seemed to have the reverse effect. My last real outstanding season was in 1957, when as an old man pushing forty I hit .388. I spent the season being mad at the world for one reason or another. I don't think I said two words to the Boston writers all year. That hardly made life pleasant.

I read recently where Joe DiMaggio said that he felt the Yankees always tried to win without him. There had never been anything written like that, he just sensed it. So Joe's got to be a sensitive guy too. And there he was in New York with the grandest press support in the world—because the Yankees won.

And there I was in Boston, where there must be more newspapers per capita than any place in the world, with writers vying for stories, all trying to outdo the others, all trying to get a headline, all digging into places where they had no business being. They—one of them—sent a private detective to San Diego in 1942 to find out if I really did support my mother. They went out into the street to take a "public opinion" poll on my parental qualifications in 1948 when I happened to be in Florida fishing when my daughter Bobby Jo was born—*prematurely*. That type of thing.

Well, I had been a fresh kid. I did a lot of yakking, partly to hide a rather large inferiority complex. When somebody asked a question, I answered it. Never very coy, never very diplomatic. As a result I would get myself in a wringer. I'd say to myself, damn, I wish I hadn't said that, or said it that *way*, and sure as hell when I pick up the paper it's even worse than I thought.

There were people, friends of mine, even writers in other cities who I liked, always telling me to try harder, and I'll tell you a story. I was demonstrating fly casting at the Sportsman's Show in New York one year, something I still do, because if I didn't make it as the greatest hitter I'm not far from being the greatest fly caster. This was one year Jim Thorpe was on the program. Right off I was carried away with Thorpe. He looked the part of the big Indian—not the big, *big* Indian, but a *big* Indian. Boy, just one look and you knew he had it. He was about sixty-five then, and I was so impressed with how quiet and attentive he was, how he would listen to people. Here's Jim Thorpe, all-time all-time, and he'd listen to anybody. He'd smile and he'd laugh and he'd listen.

Well, Thorpe had played some in the big leagues, and somebody told him, "Look, you can help Williams. He's getting into trouble with the press, charging around like he does, and you can give him some advice. He looks up to you." So about the sixth day of the show, Thorpe took me aside for a heart-to-heart on how I should try to get along with the press.

He said, "You know, they can make it awful miserable for you, but they can make it easier for you too. It's better to get along with 'em." He kept going on in this real easy way, and then we started talking about hitting.

I said, "How long did you play in the big leagues, Jim?"

"Oh, five-six years."

"How good a hitter were you?"

"I was a pretty good hitter. Everybody said I couldn't hit the curve ball, but I hit .327 one year."

I can see I'm getting him stirred up a little bit now.

He says, "The writers were always saying I couldn't hit the curve, and not only that, one of them wrote one day, 'And Thorpe isn't very good for the team, either.' " I could see this bothered Thorpe an awful lot.

"You know," he says, "I thought about this a long time, that I wasn't a team player. And one day this writer comes into the clubhouse. I went right over to him and told him, 'I don't think that was a very fair article. I'm hitting .323. I must be hitting *something*, if I can't hit a curve ball. But the thing that really hurts me is you say I'm not a team man. I'm a little upset with that.' "

Well, if you ever met Jim Thorpe, you would realize that if he was upset a little bit, he was *upset*. So he says to this writer, "What do you think you would do if somebody wrote something like that about you?"

And Thorpe said the writer answered, "Well, I guess I'd punch him in the nose."

Thorpe smiled that big Indian smile and says, "So I punched him in the nose, and down he went." We both laughed like hell. I don't advocate going that far, of course, and I never laid hands on anybody myself, but that does not mean I was never tempted.

Certainly there were great disappointments in my life: the pennants we did not win in 1948 and 1949, when we had good teams that people thought were better than they were; the 1946 World Series that we lost and in which I did so poorly; the two service hitches that took four and a half years out of the heart of my career—the second time when I was thirty-four years old. I blamed that one on the unfair draft laws and the "gutless" politicians, and got myself in a wringer for saying it. I still think the draft laws are lousy. And I'll tell you another thing I've not mellowed on—my dislike for the very word "politician." Maybe you could stretch a point and say that 1 per cent of them are all right. Certainly I am convinced of Richard Nixon's abilities.

It's true that a guy can't be completely bitter about being in two wars if he's been lucky enough to live through a close call or two, which I was. And the guys I knew as a pilot in the Marine Corps were just great. I have to feel lucky and grateful too for having played twenty-two years without being seriously injured, permanently injured. I think of Harry Agganis, a guy who wouldn't quit despite doctor's warnings. I cried in Washington the day they held his memorial service.

And Herb Score. His tragedy struck me harder than anything that happened during my career. Score was going to be a *great* pitcher. You talk about Sandy Koufax. Koufax didn't come into full bloom until he was twenty-seven or twenty-eight years old. At twenty-three Herb Score won twenty games and was striking out everybody. By the time he was twenty-eight he would have won 150 games. And then he got hit in the eye with that line drive in Cleveland, and just like that his career was over.

I say Score. Maybe, now, Tony Conigliaro will be as great a tragedy. At twenty-two Conigliaro had already hit 104 home runs for the Red Sox. I don't believe anybody had ever hit so many so young. Good power, aggressive, a talented guy. Then *he* gets hit by a pitch, and it looks as if he may be through too. He's trying to come back now. If he doesn't make it, Boston has lost a standout player.

Look. I have said that hitting a baseball is the single most difficult thing to do in sport, and one of the factors that make it so is the danger involved, and the jeopardy you put yourself in every time you go to bat. Now, I said you have to be lucky. I went to bat over 7,000 times in the big leagues. I probably averaged four pitches a time at bat, because I made them pitch to me. That's 28,000 pitches. Plus all the bases on balls that don't count as official at-bats.

Add batting practice, my three years in the minor leagues, playing from the time I was nine or ten years old, and I have to think it adds up to 200,000 pitches, and the only time I came close to serious injury except for my elbow was the time Bill Zuber hit me in the head with a pitch in Minneapolis. A slight concussion. I was out three days and I remember how I gritted my teeth and dug in the next time I played and vowed these sons of bitches weren't going to scare *me*. Nevertheless, the threat of a crippling injury is always over you.

I will never forget the day I hit Lou Brissie with a line drive. It was 1946, and he had come out of the service a great war hero with part of his leg blown off. He had to wear an aluminum plate. We opened the season in Boston and gee, Brissie looked good. A fine arm, sneaky fast. He was beating us 4–2 in about the seventh inning when I hit a ball back to the box, a real shot, *whack*, like a rifle clap off that aluminum leg. Down he goes, and everybody rushes out there, and I go over from first base with this awful feeling I've really hurt him. Here's this war hero, pitching a great game, and they don't know if the rest of the leg's been knocked off or what.

I'll never forget Brissie. He sees me in the crowd, looking down at him, my face like a haunt, and he says, "For Chrissakes, Williams, *pull* the damn ball!" Well, he was all right and I remember the next time we played he threw me everything inside, making sure I did pull, and I hit one out of the park. As I was trotting around he yelled, "You don't have to pull it *that* far, Williams." Brissie was a great guy.

So you have to be lucky to last, and you have to have the

opportunity, and I think I was fortunate to grow up in Southern California, where it is always warm and a boy can stretch the baseball season to his own dimensions. I have an old yellow picture somewhere of me in a Buster Brown haircut, when I was about nine years old. It was right at that time I really got interested in playing ball.

San Diego was a smaller town then, about 100,000, and I can remember what a big day it was when the *Shenandoah*, the big dirigible, flew over, and seeing Lindbergh at the stadium. I always admired Charles Lindbergh, the hero that he was, the terrible tragedy he had to live with, his great obsession to be alone despite the important things he did, to keep his life free from the limelight. A man I admire. But the day I'm talking about is the day I got my first barbershop haircut. My mother had been giving me those Buster Brown jobs, I used to have fights over my hair, and I remember how happy I was about that new haircut and how that very day I marched down to the playground thinking, Gee, here I am, playing ball without all that hair to worry about.

We lived in a little $4,000 house on Utah Street my mother had gotten through the kindness of the Spreckles family, a prominent family in San Diego. My mother was going to pay them back, but I don't think she ever did. The North Park playground was a block and a half from my house. It had lights and we could play until nine o'clock at night.

I was there all the time. Play, play, play, *play*. Horseshoes, handball, a game called "Big League," where all it took was two guys, a bat and one of those ten-inch softballs with the high seams. With those seams you could make the ball do anything—curve, drop, screwball, knuckleball— and we'd play against the backstop of the softball field, where there was a screen with a bar across the middle. If you hit above the bar it was a triple, below it a double. A groundball past the pitcher was a single. Hit the bar and if the other guy didn't catch it coming off it was a home run. We'd play Big League by the *hour*.

The only sport I didn't particularly like was basketball because the ball always seemed four sizes too big. I was too frail for football. I suppose I played pretty good tennis, but I used to cut the ball and break the strings on the racket and when I had to get a couple replaced the bill came to thirty-five cents and my mother said I'd better find something less expensive.

I thought I was pretty good at marbles until one day this kid cleaned my bag. He was putting four in against my two for a while and he still cleaned my bag—agates, immies, puries, everything. After about twelve I didn't mess with marbles. The kid's name was Chuck Moran. During World War II he became a big contractor there in San Diego and, gee, right after the war he was in Mexico City and crashed his plane off the end of the runway, killing himself and one of his children.

I used to play pinochle with Chuck's father. His father was from back East, and we'd sit on the porch and play and he'd tell stories about seeing Joe Wood and Walter Johnson and some of the great players of the day. He told about seeing Walter Johnson pitch an exhibition against an all-Negro all-star team at a little park in New Haven where you were so close you could hear the players talking. He said in the first inning one of the Negro players got up and called out to Johnson, "Mr. Johnson, I sure heard plenty about that fastball. You throw it, Mr. Johnson, and I'm gonna hit it right out of this park." And he did, and the game ended 1–0.

Hearing that story, I thought to myself, What's this he's feeding me? I knew Mr. Moran used to cheat at pinochle, so any kind of story like that was suspect as far as I was concerned. Six or seven years later I finally met Walter Johnson in Washington. What an impressive man. Big, lean, strong-looking, soft-spoken. A very gentle man. I remembered Mr. Moran's story and I couldn't help asking. "I've got a friend in San Diego who says he saw you pitch against this Negro team in New Haven, and he said in the first inning one of the players . . ." and Johnson began nodding his head. "That's right," he said. "That sure is right. He hit that ball a mile."

My mother was gone all day and half the night, working the streets for the Salvation Army. I didn't see much of my dad. He had a little photographic shop on Fifth Avenue downtown, taking passport pictures and sailors with their girls, and he wouldn't get home until nine, ten o'clock. These were depression years, and we had a housekeeper I think we paid seven or eight dollars a week, I forget exactly, but none of them lasted long and they were all lousy, couldn't get a job anywhere else, the bottom of the barrel, and I remember being ashamed of how dirty the house was all the time.

The city water tank was right there, and it was four blocks to my grammar school. In the fifth and sixth grades I'd fix my own breakfast—orange juice was cheap in California then and I must have drunk a ton of orange juice— and I'd be at school waiting when the janitor opened up. I was always the first one there so I could get into the closets and get the balls and bats and be ready for the other kids. That way I could be first up in a game we played where you could bat as long as somebody didn't catch the ball, and maybe I'd only hit twice before I was out, but it was worth getting to school early, because hitting was the fun.

Then at lunch I'd run home and get a cloth or a sackful of potatoes, fried potatoes, that was my lunch, run all the way there and all the way back so I could get in another fifteen minutes of ball. I mean, that's the way I always was. I don't know how it was possible for anybody to have the desire to play, or the chances to satisfy that desire, as much as I had.

I was always tall and thin, taller than most of the kids but awfully thin. I wasn't exactly a weakling but I didn't have much strength. My mother used to get notes from the school nurse: "This boy's underweight. His tonsils need checking." Years later somebody wrote that I gave my lunch money away to kids who needed it more than I did, but I didn't have money to give away. If I had any extra it was going for a milk shake or something because I was always trying to gain weight.

From the time I was twelve years old I was a malted milk hound. Malted milk with eggs. When I started playing professionally, and could afford it, I'd have four or five a day. I'd like to know just how many calories I put away in those years. I look at myself now, when a dish of ice cream means another notch in the belt, and I have to think that that skinny skeleton body belonged to somebody else. When I signed with the San Diego Padres of the Pacific Coast League at seventeen, in 1936, the paper said I weighed 155 pounds. I was six foot three. I read that and I thought, Boy, if I only did weigh 155. I was actually 148 pounds, and those seven extra pounds sounded like forty to me. I was forever telling myself, You got to have bigger arms, you got to put on weight.

I pitched when I was a kid because there was more action there and I played first base and the outfield, and there were opportunities year-round and all around San Diego. I was on the junior high team, Horace Mann Junior High, and then the American Legion Padre Serra "Fighting Bob" Post team, and the sandlot teams in the summer. Good sandlot teams. We challenged the Navy teams off the *Lexington* and the *Saratoga*, which were tied up in San Diego Harbor. We'd warm up with their balls and maybe drop a few in the ash can when nobody was looking, and go back later to get them. Or a broken bat that wasn't too bad. They'd leave them, because if anybody had equipment and plenty of it, it was the Navy.

I had a picture of Babe Ruth on my wall, but my mother always made more of that than I did. Somebody would ask her, "Who was Ted's idol?" and she'd tell them Babe Ruth. Everybody knew Babe Ruth. The fact was I didn't have an idol. Cotton Warburton was more a hero to me then, a San Diego boy playing football at USC, 140 pounds, running zigzag up the damn field.

I wasn't really concerned about Babe Ruth. It was 3,000 miles to New York and that seemed like three and a half months to me. I wasn't thinking about being a Yankee or anything else. I followed the big leagues, but I wasn't all the time digging into the sports pages, memorizing the averages, listening to games on the radio. I was out *doing* it. That's all I cared about. If there was any player I thought about imitating it was Bill Terry. He was having big years for the Giants then, and when I'd be playing, or just swinging a bat, I'd say to myself, OK, Terry's up, last of the ninth, two men on, two-two count, Giants trailing three to one—announcing the game the way kids do—here's the pitch . . . Terry *swings* . . . And I'd treat myself to another home run.

I imagine you come to a point eventually when you realize that you have ability, that your eyes are good, that your reflexes are good. Wilbur Wiley was my first real boyhood pal. He's in real estate in San Diego now. His dad was a streetcar conductor. Wilbur had a job delivering the *Evening Tribune* and when he'd get through about an hour before dark we'd go to the playground, just the two of us, and hit, hit, hit, and throw, throw, throw.

Wilbur was a little smaller than me, but a little better and a little stronger. We'd play with however many balls we could round up and a bat that was taped up good. We'd hit three or four and go chase them and hit some more. We hit pepper by the hour. A great game, pepper. At the Red Sox camp in recent years I'd see these guys playing volleyball, of all things, and pepper makes ten times more sense for a baseball player. Well, we'd always tell one another when we were going to throw a curve, and the day came —one of those ten days you remember in your life—the day came when I said to Wilbur, "Throw anything you want. Don't tell me, just see if I can hit it," and I remember how well I hit the ball that day.

The playground director was a man named Rodney Luscomb, and Rod Luscomb was my first real hero. A big, blond rugged-looking guy, six foot three, 200 pounds plus, who had played at the University of Arizona with Hank Leiber. Leiber wound up with the Giants and helped them win a pennant as a rookie the same year Joe DiMaggio broke in with the Yankees, but the best Rod Luscomb could do was the California State League. After that he wound up at the playground, a real good athlete who just wasn't quite good enough to excel in any one sport, kind of a frustrated big leaguer. To me he was great.

I know when I walked up to that rostrum in Cooperstown the day they inducted me into the Hall of Fame Rod Luscomb was one of the people on my mind, one of the people I felt made it possible. That should tell you something about how much a coach can mean to a kid. I think coaches at that level, and on into high school, where the hours are long and there isn't much remuneration, I think they are special people, dedicated and selfless people who

22

have a kid in the palm of their hands during the most impressionable years of his life. A lot of times they're more of an influence than the parents. I think they do a great job, even when they're tough. They have to be special people.

Rod Luscomb was ten or twelve years older than me, but he loved to be out there with the kids and you would think he was getting ready for pro ball himself the way he'd go at it. We'd play Big League, or we'd go to the diamond and pitch to each other. Throw hell out of the ball. Him working on me, me working on him. We had the field marked off in our minds so that we knew what was a hit and what wasn't, and we'd play regulation nine-inning games, sometimes just the two of us.

I'm sure that during this time the little game between the pitcher and the batter was coming to light for me. It's so important, the real crux of baseball, and so many hitters seem to miss it. You're not playing the Cincinnati Reds or the Cleveland Indians, you're playing that pitcher—Johnny Vander Meer, Bob Feller, Bob Lemon, whoever he is—and he's the guy you concentrate on. There's a lot more to it than just remembering if you struck out on a curve ball the last time up.

We'd play those games, Lusk and maybe Wilbur Wiley and the Tallamani boys, eight brothers and *all* of them good ballplayers, and I'd probably get to bat a hundred times a day. Today they have the Little League, all regimented and tailored down, and maybe a boy will get to bat *four* times a day. It has to make a difference. I'm not debunking the little leagues, because their purpose is not to groom kids for professional ball. They're for kids to play in a safe, organized manner, and I'm for them. They actually make a pretty good proving ground for the young pitcher because he's in there in game-type surroundings all the time, learning about situations he will have to cope with for the next twenty years if he becomes a pro. I think if you checked you would find that the majority of big league players who started in the little leagues are, or were, pitchers. But little leaguers don't get enough hitting time.

I tagged after Rod Luscomb almost every day of my life for the next six or seven years, hanging around like a puppy waiting for him to finish marking the fields or rolling the diamond. A couple times I skipped my last class at school just to get there early, but Lusk got wise and made me cut it out. I was so eager to play, and hitting a home run off Rod Luscomb in those makeshift games was as big a thrill for me as hitting one in a regular game. We played for blood. And we'd argue, boy, we'd argue. I was always the kind of kid who spoke his mind, just blurted it out, without thinking of the consequences or what anybody might think.

A lot of the stuff probably sounded like bragging. The funny thing was *I* never thought I was the best player around. I know I wasn't. Roy Engle, who lived down the street, was better than I was, and a kid named Ted Gray, whose mother worked for the Salvation Army too. Both were bigger, stronger guys. I wasn't a home run hitter then. I wasn't strong enough—the biggest bag of bones you ever saw. But I could dream.

I used to tell Rod Luscomb, "Listen, Lusk, someday I'm going to build myself a ball park with cardboard fences. Then I'm going to knock every darn one of them down with home runs." Then I'd look at my skinny arms and wonder how in hell I was ever going to do *that*. I mean I *always* worried about having muscles. After a while Rod got me doing pushups to build myself up, and for as long as I can remember, even when I was nearing forty, I was still doing fifty or a hundred fingertip pushups a day.

For those seven years I don't suppose I missed a day at the North Park Playground. Except Saturdays. Saturday was for other things. I had a friend who had a .410 shotgun and on Saturday mornings we would hike down to Mission Valley to hunt jack rabbits. We'd be up before dawn, walk three miles there, tramp around another four or five miles, then walk the three miles back. We didn't do much shooting, actually, because shotgun shells cost money and we didn't have much. The two greatest presents my mother ever got me were a Bill Doak fielder's glove, *the* glove for kids in San Diego those days (I think it was named for some old third baseman), and my first shotgun, a Model 12 Winchester. So we'd hunt the morning away, then walk back in time to hear the USC games on radio Saturday afternoon. On Saturday night we'd listen to Benny Goodman. Swing bands were the thing then. I still prefer swing to anything else.

About this time I was developing a taste for fishing. It is probably true that when you don't have much of a home life, and you're a kid, you just naturally search for things to do, but whatever gets a man interested in fishing is a good thing as far as I'm concerned. Anybody who knows me knows of my passion for fishing—out on the Miramichi River in New Brunswick before breakfast, casting for Atlantic salmon, still out there after dark, 500 casts later, when everybody else has gone to supper.

I can stand at the bow of my boat for hours on the Florida Keys, hot sun beating down, just standing there waiting for that first tarpon strike of the day, watching for the first ripples of an advancing bonefish, and even as the time slips by the excitement and anticipation never wane. I sit at my tackle bench past midnight tying flies, making sure they're exactly right. It relaxes me. I used to tie flies during the season, come in after a game all taut and nervous, tie a few flies and, boom, right to sleep. You can draw whatever psychological conclusions you want: Fishing is a loner's sport, a loner gravitates to fishing to escape the realities of the world, the pressures around him, all that crap I've heard and read all my life. The fact remains I love to fish, period.

I think I got the chance to cultivate these interests because I lived in a small town, which San Diego was then, and in a small town you're not as insulated. You get to know people, you know your neighbors. I probably got interested in guns because the best shot I ever saw was Johnny Lutz, who lived right across the street from us. He'd shoot a rifle against the Marines, trap and skeet against the pros, a pistol with the best. During the war he got paralysis of some kind and it crippled him for life and I remember how sad I was hearing about that. In a big city I might not have gotten to know Johnny Lutz.

The first fishing I ever did was with a guy named Chick Rotert. Chick lived next door. He was a local game warden for a while, and he had a couple fingers shot off in World War I. As far as I was concerned he was great. He'd go for bass in the lakes around there and he'd come home with pictures—six, seven-pound bass, nice bass—and I was just fascinated as I could be. So he took me and eventually I got myself a $3.95 Pflueger-Akron reel and a Heddon bamboo rod. Just a straight bamboo rod. I practiced casting until I knew what I was doing, standing on the porch in the evenings, maybe waiting for my mother to come home, casting into the yard or out to the street. So I got some bass, not very big, and then Mr. Cassie took me surf fishing.

Mr. Cassie lived across the street. His first name was Les, but I never called him anything but Mr. Cassie. A wonderful man, tall with white hair, and he wore glasses. He did the maintenance work at the high school, fixing the desks and the lights and things. His son Les, Jr., is the principal at one of the high schools in San Diego now and he was a buddy of mine. Mr. Cassie loved to fish, but his boys didn't care much for it, they didn't want to go, but *I* wanted to go, so he'd take me. We'd make up two or three Calcutta rods, and on Friday nights he'd drive us up to Coronado Beach. We'd get there in time to catch the tide, fish all night for croakers and corbina, fish until maybe five in the morning. We'd wade in almost to our waists, get soaking wet, but I didn't care. Surf casting was great fun and after a while I could cast as far as anybody on the beach. Then at five we'd head back.

Mr. Cassie had an ulcer and all he could eat was graham crackers, chocolates and milk. That was his lunch. It must not have been very appetizing, because after I had finished mine he would give me his. I'd eat anything in those days. Then I'd go to sleep. I must have been lousy company, because I always conked out on him on the ride back.

I loved Mr. Cassie. The nicest, dearest man. He gave me a fountain pen when I graduated from high school, the only present I got. I remember he took his vacation and drove me down to spring training the second year I was with the Red Sox. All the way from San Diego to Sarasota. I promised him if I ever got in a World Series he was going to see it, and when we won the pennant in 1946 I sent him the tickets, tickets for him and Mrs. Cassie, and they came. When Mr. Cassie died I felt as bad as when my own father died.

During this time, of course, my mother had me out with the Salvation Army, marching with the band, and oh, how I hated that. I never wore a uniform or anything, but I was right at that age when a kid starts worrying about what other kids might think, especially a gawky introverted kid like me, and I was just so ashamed. Today I'd be proud to walk with those people, because they are truly motivated, but then I'd stand behind the bass drum, trying to hide so none of my friends would see me. I had been "dedicated"

27

to it by one of my mother's superiors. I guess the dedication didn't take. The thing was I had to go so damn often. I just hated it.

My mother was strictly Salvation Army. As a result, strictly non-family. Her maiden name was Venzer, she was part Mexican and part French, and that's fate for you; if I had had my mother's name, there is no doubt I would have run into problems in those days, the prejudices people had in Southern California. She was not a big woman. She was short and lithe, with one of those infectious Eisenhower smiles. She joined the Salvation Army in 1904 as a little girl, graduated from the Army's training college in Chicago and was in it until she died in 1961, and she probably set records for selling *War Cry* and giving her time to the cause. She would campaign right down into the seamiest sections of San Diego, and across the border into Tijuana, going into jails to minister to people and even into the red light districts if she thought she could get a contribution. Just a tireless worker, smiling all the time and God-blessing people and being generous. She even played the cornet.

They called her the Angel of Tijuana, and Salvation May, and I think she made lieutenant in the Army before she got busted to a non-com for marrying outside the service. She met my dad when she was on duty in Honolulu. You have to give her a lot of credit, but the thing a kid remembers is that he never saw his mother or father very much. Many nights my brother, Danny, and I would be out on that porch past ten o'clock waiting for one of them to come home. I was maybe eight at the time, and Danny was six. I know the neighbors must have thought it was terrible for us, but kids don't think in those terms. They think about getting inside and getting something to eat. You don't think of yourself as being "deprived" as a kid unless someone tells you you are. A lot of times I'd take the opportunity to practice my casting into the neighbors' yards.

Whenever anybody ever wrote about my dad they seemed to delight in calling him a "wanderer" or a "deserter of the family," but that's a lot of bull. He stuck it out with my mother for twenty years, and finally he packed up, and I'd probably have done the same. My mother was a wonderful woman in many ways, but gee, I wouldn't have wanted to be married to a woman like that. Always gone. The house dirty all the time. Even now I can't stand a dirty house. She was religious to the point of being domineering, and so narrow-minded. My dad smoked, usually a pipe, and she didn't like that and never stopped complaining about it. I remember one time he came home sick, he'd been drinking wine or some of that lousy beer, and God, you'd think it was the end of the world the way my mother carried on. My mother had a lot of traits that made me cringe.

My dad and I were never close. I was always closer to my mother, always feeling I had to do right by her, always feeling she was alone, and knowing for years afterward how hard she had worked with nothing to show for it. I loved my dad, it wasn't that I didn't love him. But he didn't push very hard. He was just satisfied to let things go as they were.

He was a quiet man. He never smiled much. He had straight black hair, not curly like mine. I get that from my mother. He was not much for sports. He had more of a flair for the military. He had run off and joined the Army when he was sixteen and was in the Philippines with the Fourteenth Cavalry during the Spanish-American war. They used to write that he was in Teddy Roosevelt's old outfit, but I'm not so sure. I've got pictures of him: a little guy, posing behind a horse that was lying down, getting ready to shoot over the horse, and another of him at attention, standing real straight with a bugle slapped against his side. He was Welsh and English. People liked my dad.

I remember he had a sword, a big saber he used to let me swing, and he always liked to shoot guns and ride horses. Later he became a U.S. marshal in San Diego, the best job he ever had, his biggest claim to fame. It was kind of a political appointment because he had done something for Governor Merriam when Merriam got elected. Strings were pulled.

I don't know where I got my size, because neither one of them was big. Years later I used to kid my dad when we walked together: "Come on, Shorty, let's keep up." I had uncles on both sides who were pretty big, but I was much the biggest in my family. I'm not even sure where I got my name. The birth certificate reads "Teddy Samuel Williams." I never did like that "Teddy," so I always signed my name "Theodore." The "Samuel" was for my mother's brother, who was killed the last day of World War I. My dad didn't take much interest until I got to the point where baseball contracts were being offered me, then he kind of liked to be in the act. In the real crises of my life he never once gave me any advice. He eventually got a job as a prison inspector in Sacramento, and after that he opened another little photography shop in San Francisco. Like I say, if there hadn't been other people around me taking an interest, people like Mr. Cassie and Rod Luscomb, I am sure things would not have worked out as well as they did.

I know Danny suffered because of it. I have to think poor Danny had a tormented life. He wasn't an athlete. He threw an orange at somebody one time and just throwing the orange broke his arm. They found out he had leukemia in the bone marrow and with any kind of violent movement, *snap*, a bone would go. Danny was always more interested in cars and other things, the kind of guy who always wanted a motorcycle and never got it. He hung out with an altogether different bunch, and I suppose a lot of people thought he was surly and mean, but I have to think he was just terribly tormented.

I know he was a thorn in my mother's side, always getting into scrapes. Nothing really serious, but one jam after another—piling up traffic tickets, maybe stealing a bicycle, or owing money on a truck and trying to clear out without paying. Rod Luscomb took a loaded revolver away from him one time. For me, respecting authority was no problem, not then or now. I never got into jams with the police or anything. But some guys have absolutely no respect for authority, and Danny was one of them. He was not about to make any concessions to my mother's way, either, so he went with my dad.

There wasn't the closeness between us there should have been. I regret that. After I left for pro ball, I never saw much of him. He used to use my name for things, and I'd have to bail him out, which was unpleasant for both of us. My being in the public eye probably made it tougher for him. He never had too many advantages. He never had the outlets for expression I did. His life was just an existence. He died tough. I got his little pistol. I always thought he would shoot himself because he suffered so much.

Certainly my baseball and my trying to please my mother always gave me something to occupy my time. My mother sent me to YMCA camp one summer, and Art Linkletter was one of the counselors. I didn't realize it until he mentioned it on his show one time. He said, "There was a guy in our camp who wasn't always on his best behavior," something like that, talking about me. Well, the only thing I can

31

remember about that camp was that I had a dollar for the week and it was stolen from me the first day, and the camp was down in a gully where the rain could settle.

The only other thing I remember is that I peeled potatoes until I couldn't peel the bastards any more. Gee, I peeled potatoes all the time. I must have been there on a work scholarship. I think of that camp, and I think of the boys' camp I've got now in Lakeville, Massachusetts, where they get good food, and where they don't do as much work, and where they get all kinds of coaching, nice diamonds, plenty of balls and bats. How times have changed.

I wasn't a good student. In fact I was a lousy student. The best grades I got at Hoover High were in history, and the reason was I liked it. I always took subjects I wouldn't have a lot of homework in. I took shop. I was lucky I didn't cut my fingers off. I wish I had then the inquisitive mind I have now. I feel like I've missed so much, and I'm always hammering away at myself trying to catch up. I bought a set of Encyclopaedia Britannica the other day, and I know I'm going to be into those books all the time. Art Linkletter might remember me as a brash kid, and I probably popped off a lot, but I always held so much inside.

I never went out with girls, never had any dates, not until I was much more mature-looking. A girl looked at me twice, I'd run the other way. You see pictures of me as a kid—gaunt. Nervous. Gee, I bit hell out of my nails, right down to the quick. Even later, when I first started signing autographs, I'd hold my head down.

Mostly they were a pretty rough bunch of boys around my neighborhood, older guys who drank beer and at least talked about going to Tijuana for women. Things like that scared me to death. I'll never forget one kid giving us a pretty vivid account of the treatment he had to go through for v.d. and boy, that scared me. I never drank. I never smoked. I was embarrassed about my home, embarrassed that I never had quite as good clothes as some of the kids, embarrassed that my mother was out in the middle of the damn street all the time. Until the day she died she did that, and it always embarrassed me, and God knows I respected her and loved her.

I suppose the first strong influence I had to continue in baseball, to make it my life's work, was my coach at Herbert Hoover High in San Diego, a wonderful man named Wos Caldwell. He is a professor of architecture now at the University of Florida. I still see him occasionally in the spring, and I still call him "coach." I had entered Herbert Hoover as a tenth grader. It was a new school, only 800 or 900 kids, about half the enrollment of the big established high school downtown. I was actually a block inside the bigger school's territory, but I felt I had a better chance to play on a team just starting out and I managed to get in.

Wos Caldwell tells the story that on my first day out, as a tenth grader I guess, I hit a couple balls on the cafeteria roof and the janitor came running out and made us change diamonds. What I remember is the switch Wos used to have. He was always after me to run faster, and he'd start me at home plate, let me get halfway to first base, then come after me with that switch. Usually he caught me between first and second and was hacking my butt the rest of the way. I'll never forget one day I hit a ball they say went 450 feet, between the right and center fielders. I fell down rounding second, and I fell down rounding third—a big skinny kid, all arms and legs—and I got thrown out at home plate.

Certainly the more I matured the more speed I picked up, but I was never as fast as I would like to have been or as slow as I looked. I remember going to the Red Sox camp in Sarasota in 1938, riding the train with Bobby Doerr and Babe Herman. Herman was out of the big leagues then, but he had been a fine hitter with the Dodgers. For two days and two nights we talked nothing but hitting. I asked him what he thought was the most important factor, and I didn't think at the time he understood my question, because he said, "Legs." *Legs*, I said to myself. Gee, what a dumb guy.

Well, what Herman was talking about was speed, and it is important to a hitter. I know I envied speedy guys like Willie Mays and Mickey Mantle, all the leg hits they got. But I know I was as fast as Ruth ever was, or Greenberg ever was, or Gehrig ever was, and I have to think I wasn't put on earth to steal bases. You can't do it all. So what happens? One year I led the league in hitting and RBI's and I got criticized by a writer who refused to vote for me in the Most Valuable Player poll. He said, "What the hell, the guy didn't even steal a base." In an average year, Greenberg probably stole one base, and maybe DiMaggio got three or four.

Here is the irony of the conservative base runner: The most embarrassing moment of my career occurred in a 1–0 game we lost in Washington. I hit a triple in about the fifth inning and Jake Early, the Washington catcher, picked me off third. I couldn't remember the last time that had happened, but the next time up I hit another triple, in the ninth inning, and I'm taking another lead in my customary style, what John Updike called "ponderous and menacing, like an attacking goose." And damn if Early doesn't pick me off again. The most embarrassing thing that ever happened to me. I slid into that base, and I knew I was out, and I could have *crawled* back to the dugout.

As a pitcher-outfielder, I batted .583 and .406 my last two years in high school, .430 for the three years, and I got this big offer of five dollars a Sunday to play for the Texas Liquor House team, which was owned by Walter Church. He had a bunch of service stations and this liquor house in

San Diego. I was excited because there were a lot of good players on the team, and because five dollars was a lot of money. I came home and told my mother about the money, and she said that was fine. "Who will you play for?" "Uh, the Texas Liquor House." If I had said Murder, Inc., I wouldn't have been turned down any quicker.

By this time, however, the scouts were coming around. Roy Engle was the catcher on the team and he and I were the big players. Roy and I are still close. He comes all the way from California every summer to coach at my boys' camp in Lakeville. Piles his family into a trailer and drives all the way across the country, spends two and a half months there and drives back. He was a fine athlete, and the scouts were after both of us. I remember seeing Herb Bennyhoven of the Cardinals sitting way out in the outfield, looking at me with field glasses, and Detroit sent a scout named Marty Krug. Krug watched my last game in high school. I didn't hit well that day, and we lost. Like I say, I did not cut an imposing figure at 6 foot 3, 145 pounds, even with all the stuff I was eating trying to put on weight. One time we went to Pamona for a doubleheader and people who remember those things say I started out with a shortcake and a malted milk, then mowed down thirteen ice cream bars and eleven bottles of pop before the doubleheader was over and we were back home. After Marty Krug watched me he came and sat with my mother, they talked and that night she was in tears. He had told her I had a lot of good moves, but I was so scrawny a year of professional baseball would kill me. Literally kill me.

In those days they had graduation in June and graduation in February. I was due to graduate from high school in February, but my baseball eligibility had been completed in June. So that summer I went to a St. Louis Cardinals tryout camp in Fullerton with Herb Bennyhoven. People always wonder about ballplayers—what if the Tigers had gotten DiMaggio? What if Musial had signed with the Yankees? The players wonder too, but fate usually makes the course.

The Cardinals were always a speed team. The old Gas House Gang. They loved speed. If you couldn't run the Cardinals didn't even want to look at you. So what happens? The week I was going to try out I was playing in a sandlot game and got hit in the thigh with a pitch. Really thunked. Gee, I thought it had torn my leg off. All black and blue, and sore. I could hardly move for a couple days, and when I got to the camp there must have been 350 kids there trying out. They put big numbers on our backs, mine was something like 346. There were so many kids wanting to be Cardinals they had to number you. The big star of the camp was the guy they called the Mad Russian, Lou Novikoff. He was a bit older than most of us, and he could hit the ball out of sight. Well, if I couldn't run fast when I was healthy, that sore leg made me look like I was anchored. I was discouraged, I didn't hit particularly well, and they hardly gave me a look.

I eventually did get an offer from the Cardinals, but they would have probably sent me to Oshkosh or Peoria or someplace, because they had a huge farm system then and you could get lost. By that time Bill Essick of the Yankees had come around. I'd hit a home run that broke a store window, and my mother thought Essick was the store owner.

"I know why you're here," she said. "It's because of that home run."

And he said, "Yes, ma'am, that's right."

Essick was as anxious as anybody to get me. I'll never forget what he said: "Ted, if I didn't think you were going to be a New York Yankee, I'd never sign you." Maybe he said that to everybody, but that sure impressed me. I think he offered $200 a month, and a $500 bonus if I made the team at Binghamton, New York, but the story is my mother asked for a $1,000 bonus and Essick refused.

I don't know if that $1,000 actually stood between me being a Yankee or not. I know years later Joe Cronin said to me, "I think you'll regret not having played in Yankee Stadium. You'd be a great hero in New York. There are eleven million people there, and no matter how good things are in Boston it won't be one-tenth what you would get in New York. Yankee Stadium was built for a left-handed batter." I got the feeling maybe Joe had wished he had played in New York, but I have to say I'm not sure I ever felt that way.

There were other parks I would have preferred to play in. Like Detroit. I saw the ball better there. I hit fifty-four home runs in Detroit, more than any other park I played in on the road. I never saw the ball well in Yankee Stadium, although I averaged .305 there. I hit like a son of a gun in St. Louis—.399. My ten-year average in Philadelphia was .353.

Los Angeles of the Pacific Coast League wanted to sign me. They were the Angels then, a good club, and I might have signed, but by this time my dad was in the act. He had never seen me play too much, but he could see I was getting an awful lot of attention and he got the idea I was the second coming of Ruth. He started buying me steaks on the days of my sandlot games. Just what I needed, eat a steak at twelve thirty with a game coming up at two. Something to slow me down even more. But I was pleased he was interested so I ate the steaks.

Anyway, as my spokesman he made up his mind he didn't like the Los Angeles manager, Truck Hannah. Hannah was a great big old tough catcher who had played with the Giants, and when my dad went down to talk to him Hannah said, "Where's the kid?"

Dad said, "He's not here."

Hannah said, "Well, for crying out loud, go *get* him, he's the one I'm interested in."

My dad didn't like his attitude.

So finally I went and worked out with the San Diego team, and by now the pressure's on pretty good for me to sign with San Diego. It was a new team. It had been moved to San Diego from Hollywood the year before and everybody was getting civic-minded about the San Diego Padres. A few of the politicians got into it, talking to my mother, and my mother liked the idea because she wanted me close to home. So I signed with the Padres in 1936, first for my mother's sake, second because when I signed for $150 a month they said they would pay me for the whole month of June, though this was on the twentieth of the month. That was my bonus. Part of the agreement my mother got out of them was they wouldn't sell or trade me, even to a big league team, until I was twenty-one. They eventually broke that agreement.

The San Diego manager was an old spitball pitcher named Frank Shellenback, a big good-looking German with about eight kids. He was a wonderful, wonderful man, a man I respected as much as any I've known in baseball. I don't mean to say he was all out for young ballplayers. He wanted to win, and there were some real established stars in the Coast League. Shellenback later coached for the Giants and he knew players. But I was just happy to be there, to travel with the team on the train, going places I'd never been, to have new balls to hit, new uniforms. I could order bats. Hillerich and Bradsby paid me fifteen dollars to endorse a bat, which meant I could have all I wanted. I'd get a box of used balls to take home with me, take them out to the playground for extra batting practice, and after I had hit them until the covers were off I'd ask for more. Shellenback thought I was selling them or something, because he came out to the park one day to see what I was up to.

On the road my roommate was Sid Durst, who had played with the Yankees during Babe Ruth's days, and he said I woke him up at six A.M., yelling and jumping on the bed and swinging at imaginary pitches and telling him how great it was to be young and full of vigor. Maybe I did those things, I don't remember. Certainly I was having the time of my life and my pleasure was bound to be spontaneous. I boiled with enthusiasm. I was always in front of mirrors with a rolled-up piece of paper, or a pillow, or *any*thing, studying my swing. I wanted to be stylish, I wanted to look good, I wanted to *see* how I looked, how I swung at low balls, fast balls, high balls. I was forever thinking, I want to be able to hit *any* ball out of the park. Well, that's a kid thinking. When you get older you realize you shouldn't be thinking that way.

Eventually, Shellenback let me get up as a pinch hitter and I took three strikes, right down the middle, petrified. After that I pitched batting practice until one Saturday night we got ten runs behind in the sixth inning of a game with the Angels at Wrigley Field in Los Angeles. With a doubleheader coming up Sunday, Shellenback was desperate for a pitcher. Eddie Mulligan was one of our coaches and I heard Shellenback say to Mulligan, "Damn it, Eddie, who am I going to put in there? I'm using up all my pitchers." When he went out to the coaching line I moved in beside Mulligan. "Tell him to put me in, Eddie. I can pitch. I'm ready." Mulligan looked at me, then smiled, and when Shellenback came in he suggested it. Shellenback nodded and told me to go down and warm up. He didn't have much choice, actually.

So I warmed up, then he let me pinch-hit. Boom, a double. A rally starts and by the time the inning is over, we've got five runs. So I go out and hold them an inning, and then I get to bat again. Boom, another double. Now we've whittled it down to 11 to 12, something like that, and Shellenback's got a *good* relief pitcher working in the bullpen. I go out to pitch again, and the first four guys in the next inning score runs. Shellenback's out there like a flash to pull me out, and the way he tells it I kind of shrugged and said, "Skip, I think you've got me playing the wrong position." He put me in left field for the rest of the game and I was there the rest of the year.

I never had so much fun. Those first train trips, into Seattle and Portland, seeing the natural beauty of the Northwest, and into Los Angeles, and signing for my meals in the hotels. We were allowed $2.50 a day, and I was eating everything in sight. When we got to Oakland, Bill Lane, who owned the club, a tough, gruff old guy, called to me in the clubhouse. "Hey, kid come over here." Real raspy voice.

He says, "You're heading the list."

"Heading the list? What list?" I knew I hadn't done anything too exciting.

He said, "The over-eaters list. You're allowed $2.50 a day, you know."

I said, "Well, I just can't eat on $2.50 a day." I was just starting to grow good. I said, "Take it out of my check."

That kind of slowed him up and we let it go at that, but he never did take it out of my check. He knew he wasn't paying me very much. I put on ten pounds a year for the next two years. Eddie Mulligan was worried all the time I was going to get an ulcer the way I shoveled it in.

I hit .271 in forty-two games that season and the next year I hit .291 and twenty-three home runs, despite my first real slump, a stretch where I went 0 for 18. I suffered through that one. A slump always follows a familiar pattern. When you first start going bad, you just try harder. Then you press, which means you do things unnaturally. Then you imagine you're getting all the tough breaks and you start feeling sorry for yourself.

At this time something happened that really jacked me up, and it stuck with me because it's a clue to the kind of encouragement a young player needs. Certainly it has been a reminder for me in my dealings with young hitters like Yastrzemski and Rico Petrocelli. Lefty O'Doul was the San Francisco manager. I'd seen him hit the year before, watching him from the fence, his line drives zinging into right field. My first real look at an all-time great. The only thing that keeps O'Doul out of the Hall of Fame today is that he didn't play in the big leagues quite long enough. He deserves to be in there. I was seventeen. I went right up to him bold as brass and started questioning him about hitting, something I would do from then on with every good hitter I ever met.

I said, "Mr. O'Doul, what should I do to become a good hitter?"

He said, "Kid, the best advice I can give you is don't let anybody change you." Wasn't that a nice thing for an all-timer to tell a young kid?

So now I was in this slump, feeling down, and I happened to pick up a paper in the Pickwick Hotel in San Francisco. The headline says, "Williams Greatest Hitter Since Waner." At first I wondered who the Williams was that it was talking about. I just kept looking at it. Actually the story said O'Doul had called me the best left-hand hitter to come into the league since Paul Waner. Something like that. You know that had to pick me up.

That winter—December 1937—I was sold to the Boston Red Sox. The purchase price was supposed to have been $35,000 and San Diego was to get two players, Dominic

D'Allessandro, an outfielder, and Al Niemiec, an infielder. I read about that for the first time in the paper too and I was sick. The Red Sox didn't mean a thing to me. A fifth-, sixth-place club, the fartherest from San Diego I could go. I sure wasn't a Boston fan. I might have been a New York Giant fan, with Mel Ott and Arky Vaughan and those guys, or a Detroit fan, with Greenberg and Charley Gehringer, but *Boston*. Then Eddie Collins came to visit us.

Collins was the general manager of the Red Sox at the time. He was a frail-looking little guy with a real nice, friendly face, big wide eyes and a big nose and mouth. In his day he had been the greatest second baseman in baseball. I remember he had big hands, big heavy fingers for a little guy. He had seen me hitting batting practice the year before when he came out to look at Bobby Doerr and Georgie Myatt on our club. The Red Sox had a working agreement with San Diego and they had an option on Doerr and Myatt.

Collins was there watching us hit and I must have been swinging pretty good that day, because when he went to Bill Lane, the owner, he said, "Bill, I'm going to pick up the option on Doerr, but not on Myatt. In the meantime, I want you to tell me about that left-hand hitting outfielder you got."

Bill Lane didn't even know who Collins was talking about. I wasn't playing then, I'd only been up that one time. Lane said, "Oh, you mean *Williams*. Hell, he's just a kid out of high school. He's only seventeen. Give him a few years." But Collins got him to agree to give the Red Sox an option on my contract.

So he came to the house, and the only decent chair we had was an old mohair thing that had a big hole you could see the springs through. We covered the hole with a five-cent towel and that's where Collins sat. And gee, he was an awfully nice, kindly man. Right away you had to love Eddie Collins.

He said the Red Sox were on the move. Since Mr. Tom Yawkey had taken over they were spending a lot of money building the team. They had Jimmy Foxx and Lefty Grove, Doc Cramer, Joe Vosmik, Wes Ferrell, and now young Bobby Doerr was there and established at second base. He said the Red Sox would give me a two-year contract, $3,000 for the first year, $4,500 for the second. I was making $200 a month with the Padres.

I thought to myself, Gee, he wants to give me all this money, and here I'm only hitting .290 and I could do so much better. What if I'd been hitting .320?

My mother and dad had been hearing stuff, though, and they still wanted that thousand dollars. They needed it. My father began pressing him a little bit and I left the room. That kind of thing always embarrassed me, any kind of hang-up over money. Somebody would shortchange me and I'd just ignore it, even when it was obvious. I didn't want any fuss. Today, somebody shortchanges me a nickel I let them know. Well, they finally put it to him straight: a $1,000 bonus.

Collins said he couldn't do it, not without checking with Tom Yawkey. Mr. Yawkey balked at first. He'd been spending a lot of money and he had to cut down sooner or later. Evidently Collins was persuasive. He always had a way with Mr. Yawkey. He was supposed to have said, "Mr. Yawkey, we've *got* to have this kid." I'm not sure my mother ever got the $1,000, but my understanding was she did.

I was ten days late getting to camp at Sarasota that spring. I had to borrow $200 from the bank to make the trip. They used to write that I came to camp with the clothes on my back and two bucks in my pocket, but that was an exaggeration. I had a trunk, like everybody else had in those days—you didn't travel with two or three suitcases, you used a trunk, even if you only half filled it.

It was the year of the big California flood, and the trains were out, everything was out, and Bobby Doerr had to get a couple of ham radio operators together to get through a message for me to meet him in Imperial Valley for the ride south. When I finally got into the dressing room in Sarasota, everybody else was on the field and Johnny Orlando, the clubhouse boy, says, "Who are you?"

"Ted Williams."

"Oh, well, The Kid has arrived, eh. You dress over there with the rookies, Kid."

I am still "The Kid" to Johnny Orlando, even now, and to everybody else who was around me then. Orlando says he followed me outside that first day, sensing something would happen. My shirttail was hanging out. It was too small, and the first guy I ran into said, "Stick your shirttail in, Busher, this is the big leagues." I gave him a sassy answer, then I asked Orlando, "Who's that smart guy?"

"That's Joe Cronin. He's the manager."

I lasted about a week. I remember writing home, telling how impressed I was with the Red Sox, how smooth Lefty Grove was, the smoothest, prettiest left-handed pitcher I had ever seen. And Jimmy Foxx with all those muscles, hitting drives that sounded like gunfire. *Kerr-rack*. A hell of a lot louder than mine sounded. They took pictures of me feeling Foxx's muscles. Mr. Yawkey had paid a lot of money to get Foxx and Grove from the Athletics. Connie Mack was trying to get the A's in the black, attendance was down, and he was selling away a lot of the talent that had won him pennants. Grove was an original. He was supposed to have been the only player who ever called Mr.

Mack "Connie" to his face. Mr. Mack called him "Old Man Mose." Grove's middle name was Moses. The story was they were always having contract fights. One year Mack agreed to pay Grove $20,000 and $500 for every game he won over twenty. Grove won thirty-one games. He couldn't get Mack to give him the same contract again.

Grove was a moody guy, too, a tantrum thrower like me, but when he punched a locker or something he always did it with his right hand. He was a careful tantrum thrower. He smoked those real big cigars, and he loved to eat. They told me his arm was going dead when he came to the Red Sox, but as far as I was concerned he was the smoothest, smartest pitcher I had ever seen, just beautiful style.

Actually, all the stars on the Red Sox team that year were players Mr. Yawkey had bought from someplace else—Joe Cronin from Washington, where he had been the player-manager, Doc Cramer, from the A's, Joe Vosmik from the Browns, Ben Chapman from the Senators. I thought they were all wonderful, all the guys, and to them I was probably as cocky a kid as they'd ever seen.

Moe Berg was a catcher for the club then. He was a Phi Beta Kappa from Princeton. He could speak about six languages, including Japanese. I got up in batting practice one day without my hat, bushy hair sticking out all over the place, and Moe Berg says, "What's the matter, Kid, don't they make hats where you come from?"

And I said, real fresh, "If that's all it takes to make the big leagues, *here*," and I whipped my cap out of my back pocket and jammed it on my head.

Well, that's bravado, pure and simple. A kid away from home really for the first time in his life, feeling alone, a little scared, seeking attention. Somebody wrote that Bobby Doerr pointed Foxx out to me that first day and said, "Wait'll you see Foxx hit."

And I was supposed to have said, "Wait'll Foxx sees *me* hit." I never said it, but I suppose it wouldn't have been unlike me.

They didn't have an idea in the world of keeping me that year. In March the team was going to play in Tampa, and I said to Cronin, "Am I on the list, Joe?"

He said "Why don't you look at the damn board like everybody else and *see* if you're on the list."

I said "OK, sport, if that's the way you want it." "Sport" was what I called everybody. I *know* that must have irritated him, and I have to believe he thought it was time to put me in my place.

My place, according to the list, was Daytona Beach, where the Red Sox' Minneapolis farm team was training. That night Johnny Orlando took me to the bus. I said to myself, Gee, what's in store for me now? But I was more subdued than I was upset. "Tell 'em I'll be back," I told Johnny. I'd been taking a pretty good riding from the regular Red Sox outfielders, Doc Cramer, Joe Vosmik and Ben Chapman, every one a .300 hitter. I said, "Tell them I'll be back, and tell them I'm going to wind up making more money in this frigging game than all three of them put together." Then Johnny loaned me five bucks to see me through to Daytona Beach.

I wish now that I had had a more businesslike attitude in those early years. I mean hitting was so important to me, consumed so much of my desire, was so much more exciting to me, that I tended to let other things go. I remember Bill Sweeney, the Portland manager, came up to me one day after I'd turned away from running out a ground ball. He said, "Boy, as good as you can be, if you don't run them out I'm personally going to kick you right in the ass."

I would like to think I learned from remarks like that, but I know that I was a long time realizing that the game of baseball, this game of my childhood, was to be my livelihood, my business, the greatest thing that would ever happen to me. It takes some guys longer to find things out.

I had gotten into some rotten habits, usually a matter of being so mad I'd do *anything* to show my disgust. I would have to say I was an indifferent fielder in those years. I did some dumb things. We were playing sandlot ball one day at Mission Bay, I was probably fifteen, and I'm in the outfield daydreaming, looking out over the bay, when all of a sudden some brant took off. I'd seen very few brant, and boy, there they were, a flock of them, and I was just flabbergasted. I was looking up, thinking how pretty they were, and *how*, somebody hit a ball. I looked around and couldn't find it and I'm just about satisfied that it has gone to another field when I hear it clunk down behind me.

By the time I got to Minneapolis I had these lapses of concentration pretty much built in. Playing the field was too much like being a spectator to suit me. If I wasn't slapping my butt and yelling, "Hi-ho, Silver!" chasing a fly ball, I was sitting down between batters or talking to some fan and the crack of the bat would catch me looking the wrong way. I had that happen with Stan Spence in center field one day. I never saw the ball, just heard Stan Spence's footsteps, and he almost knocked me down making a hell of a play on a ball that should have been mine.

I know I got to little Donie Bush—a little tiger, a lovable little tiger—when he was managing Minneapolis. Donie had played sixteen years of shortstop in the big leagues, he had managed the White Sox, the Senators and a couple other clubs, and the Red Sox sent him their top young players to work with. Evidently I extended him a little bit. He was supposed to have said, "It's Williams or me, one has to go," and Mike Kelly, the club owner, said if that was ever the case it would have to be him. I remember one day I went out without my glasses in right field, and somebody hit one into the sun and I lost it. Two runs scored and Bush came running out there yelling, "Where's your glasses? Where the hell are your glasses?"

"I forgot 'em, Skip."

"Well go in there and get them!" He was livid, and it was like me in those days to say, "What's he so excited about? Why does he take everything so seriously?"

I hit a double one day and I was prancing off second base waving my arms, trying to look like a base runner, and Donie Bush started yelling to me from the coaching box, "Aw right, Kid, be careful . . . don't go too far, be alert, watch that pitcher . . . look out for that pickoff." He's going on like that: "Not too far now . . . you're the winning run."

Finally I yelled, "Take it easy, Skip. I got here by myself, I'll get home by myself."

One afternoon I let two balls go through (ground balls gave me an especially hard time), and I struck out twice, and I was so damn mad after the second strike-out that when I got to the bench I kept right on going into the clubhouse, just disgusted and thinking it was my last at-bat anyway. I was half undressed when the bat boy came running in yelling for me to get back out there. We had started a big rally. The score was 6–4, two men on, two out, and I was due up. I was still fumbling with my buttons when I got out there, and wouldn't you know it? I hit the first pitch out of the park and we won, 7–6. It was that kind of year.

Donie Bush got so he could get to me with a little psychology. When I was having my troubles and packed my trunk one time and told him I was going home he didn't blow up at all, he just said, "OK, Ted, I'll line up the transportation and when you've had a nice visit you can come back." I went right to my room and unpacked that trunk.

The thing is, I was such a long time getting myself straightened out. A sharp liaison between the parent club and the minor league team would have picked this thing up right away and somebody at the top would have said, "Listen, this kid is *going* somewhere. He's knocking the damn fences down. He's leading the league in everything. Let's not worry about his hitting, let's work on his fielding."

In Minneapolis I played right field, an easy one because the field was shallow—278 feet to the fence—and I never had to go back any distance. I had a good arm, and nobody ever went from first to third on me. I never really had to throw much or field much. I always had good hands. I seldom dropped a fly ball. As the years went by I made up for a lack of speed by playing good position, watching the pitcher, knowing the batter. Regardless of what they said in Boston, where my reputation preceded me and they never let an error go unpublicized, in my heart I feel I played hitters as good as anybody.

Knowing I was no speed demon, I developed an instinct for situations that come up, by being alert to what was going on and having it register instinctively. For example, if I see the pitcher throwing this guy fast outside, working the outside corner, I can pretty much conclude the guy's not going to pull the ball, or if the count is 2 and 2 and I see the batter shortening up, bending over to punch the ball, it registers and I'm going to move in on him. These things I got. A lot of guys never do.

A remember years later playing in Yankee Stadium and Yogi Berra was batting. Berra was a hell of a hitter, a good solid hitter, but throw him a strike and he might do anything with it. I forget who was pitching, but he was tough and he got a strike on Berra. I started shading more toward the line in left field, even though Berra was a left-handed pull hitter. He swings and it's another strike, and now I

49

really shade him, and sure enough he hits a long fly down the left field line. I got over there pretty fast for me, and caught it on the line, and as I turned I could see Berra was still running all out with his head down, thinking for sure it was a big hit. I was the first man up the next inning and Berra was behind the plate for the Yankees and he said to me, "How the hell can you play me over there? I don't hit the ball over there." Well, he *hit* it over there, and I got the ball, so I must have played him right.

That July I got sick with one of those viruses I always seemed to get and I was laid up in my hotel. We had a young kid named Gene Stephens who was up with the Red Sox, and he could run like a deer. If I had had that boy's speed I know my lifetime average would have been twenty points higher. Stephens was being groomed to take my place when I retired, but he never got to be quite as good as he could have been. Anyway, I was up in my room listening to Curt Gowdy broadcasting the game and with two strikes and two men on Berra sliced another little fly down the left-field line.

Well, the way Curt described it Stephens made the catch of the year. He came out of nowhere and made a great play, and the crowd was cheering so loud you could hardly hear Gowdy. But all I could think was that I would have made the same play without it being nearly so sensational, because I wouldn't have been playing Berra where Stephens played him. If I had, of course, I wouldn't have come close.

The point is, there are ways to overcome handicaps, and one of them is proper thinking, and I know that is something I could have developed earlier, that I *should* have been developing in Minneapolis. But I was hitting .366, and driving in 142 runs and hitting 43 home runs, having a great time. I was doing so well I got away with things that undoubtedly hurt me going into the big leagues.

50

I have so many good memories of that year with Minneapolis, and one of them was getting the chance to know Rogers Hornsby. I thought Hornsby was great. He wasn't a very diplomatic guy. If he had a dislike about anything, he came out with it. He wasn't big for criticism, I don't mean that, but he didn't mind laying a blast now and again. I remember that year DiMaggio was with the Yankees and holding out on his contract. He wanted $27,000, and Hornsby said, "Who does he think he is? He's only had two good seasons." I mean, even if the owner of the club said something he disagreed with, Hornsby would say, "What the hell do you know about it?" He was all the time getting into wringers for what he said.

I liked Hornsby because he talked to me, a kid of nineteen, and boy I picked his brains for everything I could. We'd talk hitting, and I'd ask personal questions I had no business asking. "How much money did you lose at the track? How much did you bet?" The commissioner had been on his neck for gambling and he had said, "It's nobody's business what I do with my money. If I want to gamble, I gamble." He told me he won $78,000 one day at the track.

Every day I'd stay out after practice with Hornsby and maybe one or two others who wanted extra hitting. Hornsby was like any of the really great players I have known—he just couldn't get enough of it. He was pushing fifty then, I guess, but we'd have hitting contests and he'd be right in there, hitting one line drive after another—*psshewww, pssheww, pssheww.* He loved it. I never saw much of him after that, but I sure remembered him years later when Cobb and some of the others were getting on me for not hitting to left field. Hornsby never criticized me.

I think any player will tell you that in the minor leagues you get a lot closer to the fans, that the fans take more of a family interest. There's fewer of them, to begin with, and you're younger and less reserved, so you talk to them more, even while you're on the field. I was always jawing with somebody in that little park in Minneapolis. Not only the fans, but the guy in the scoreboard, which was right behind me in right field. He'd keep me posted on the scores, how the Yankees or the Cardinals were doing, who was hitting the home runs. Just having a good time. That year I met what amounted to the first girl I ever got interested in, and dated her that summer, and was so self-conscious I never even put my arm around her, never kissed her. I don't remember how I met her now, probably at the park.

For a young ballplayer there's never any shortage of available girls around a ball park. A lot of them move in pretty hard, and after a while a ballplayer learns to move pretty good himself. For me there was a long carry-over of that early fear that, boy, you mess around with a woman and you mess yourself up. I remember my first year with the Red Sox, we were in Detroit and this girl called up to the room. I was there laying on the bed listening to the radio. She said, "I saw you play today. I sure enjoyed watching you."

"Oh, you did? Well, uh, what do you want?"

"I just thought we could get together."

"Well, uh, OK. OK. Why don't I meet you in front of the theater? We'll go to the movies." She turned out to be five or six years older than me, but it worked out all right. Sometimes it doesn't. Sometimes they get carried away. Eddie Waitkus got shot by a girl in Chicago.

We opened the season that year in Indianapolis, a brand-new park, and I went hitless my first sixteen times at bat. It didn't get me down, though, and when we got to Minneapolis I hit a home run the first game. Everything began to settle into place. There was a lot of talent in the American Association that year. Toledo had two young pitchers the

Tigers had sent down for seasoning, Al Benton and Dizzy Trout, and they could throw like hell. I remember the first time I hit against Benton. A *big* guy, 6 foot 4, 215 pounds, broad shoulders. He looked like he was right on top of you, like he was forty feet from the plate instead of sixty. Intimidating. Good curve, sinker, fast ball. It was a night game in Toledo, lousy lights, and he struck me out the first three times up. I thought, Boy, if they've sent *him* down, if *this* guy can't make it, they must have some hell-acious pitching in Detroit.

And Dizzy Trout. I used to love to watch Trout pitch. Another big guy. Raw speed. Live fastball. And a colorful guy, with a big red handkerchief he'd whip out of his back pocket and use like a towel, all around his neck and across his face and arms. He'd jam that handkerchief back into his pocket and then he'd blow a pitch right past you. I hit a home run off Trout my first time up. A real screamer, out where only a couple guys had ever hit one, over the dugout in right center field. Someone said Bill Terry had hit one out there.

I looked at Trout as I went around and he had that hand-kerchief out and he was looking at me, just staring. The next time up he put one right behind my ear, really low-bridged me. Knocked me flat. Trout could be a mean son of a gun. If he decided to knock you down, you could bet your butt you were going down.

We finished fourth to Kansas City, which was a disappointment, and I got beaned by Zuber and almost ruined myself busting up that water cooler in Minneapolis, but it was still a satisfying year. I hit well, really up to standard for the first time in professional ball, and I was catching on to a few things. Something happened that August that made a big impression on me.

It was real hot in Minneapolis, hotter than anything I had

been used to on the West Coast. I was on base all the time, an average of two and a half times a game, just swinging and sweating all the time, and as thin as I was I began to get tired. One muggy hot night in Columbus I happened to pick up one of Stan Spence's bats. Geez, I thought, what a toothpick. Lightest bat in the rack. It had a bigger barrel than mine, but lighter by two ounces at least. There were imprints all over it where the ball had been hit, which showed it was lousy wood. Real pumpkin wood. But it felt good in my hands. It made me feel strong again.

I asked Stan if I could use it and the first time up, bases loaded, a little left-hander pitching, I got behind two strikes. I choked up on the bat, thinking that I would just try to meet the ball, telling myself, Damnit, I'm not going to strike out now, I'm going to get some wood on it. The pitch was low and away, just on the corner of the plate. *Unnh.* I give this bat a little flip and, gee, the ball flew over the center-field fence. Not the longest poke in the world, only 410 feet and just barely in the stands, but long enough. That really woke me up. From then on, I always used lighter bats, usually thirty-three or thirty-four ounces, never more than thirty-four, sometimes as light as thirty-one. In the earlier part of the year I'd go for the heavier ones, with better wood. You're stronger then, the pitchers are still working to get their stuff down, to get their control.

I always worked with my bats, boning them down, putting a shine on them, forcing the fibers together. Not just the handle, the whole bat. I treated them like babies. Weight tolerance got to be a big thing with me. The weight can change. Early in the season it's cold and damp and the bats lying around on the ground pick up moisture and get heavier. I used to take them down to the post office to have them weighed. Eventually, with the Red Sox, we got a little set of scales put in the locker room. I'll never forget Mr. Hillerich of Hillerich and Bradsby, the Louisville Slugger Company, put six bats on a bed in Boston. One was a half ounce heavier than the others. He had me close my eyes and pick out the heavier bat. I picked it out twice in a row.

Three on that Minnesota team made it with the Red Sox the next year: Stan Spence, Jim Tabor and myself. I was late getting to Sarasota again in the spring. I caught a bad cold driving down and had to hole up three days in New Orleans. Mr. Cassie was with me. He took his vacation and helped me drive down, and he nursed me through. It was the same virus that hounded me the rest of my playing days, usually in cold or damp weather. To this day when I ride in an open boat early in the morning when the dew is heavy, or in the cool of the evening, I hold a pillow in front of my chest for warmth.

Late or not, I was going to be the regular right fielder, there was no doubt about that, because they had traded Ben Chapman to Cleveland. Chapman had hit .340 the year before, which would tell you how they regarded me, except that it was also true that Chapman didn't get along with Joe Cronin, the manager. I think they had had a fist fight in the dugout.

That spring I was a nuisance to everybody, asking questions about hitting, asking Foxx and Cronin and Cramer and Vosmik about this pitcher or that one, the Yankee pitchers, the Detroit pitchers. I'd want to know how to hit Harder, how to hit Newsom. Tell me about Lyons, about Gomez. Tell me about Bridges. I quizzed every player on the team, and they all had something to say, and the weight of the evidence pretty much proved out.

The one guy they all said I would hit good was Bobo Newsom. I could always handle fastball pitchers and Newsom had this big freewheeling fastball. But he confused you with his delivery: all arms and legs. He struck me out three times in a row. Nine pitches, all high fastballs. Gee, a dark day in St. Louis, and he's flailing away out there, arms windmilling, and *whoom*, here it comes. I swung and missed and swung and missed and swung and missed. I thought I was absolutely going blind. The guy I was *supposed* to hit I didn't hit at all. He finally threw me a curve, a lousy one, and I hit a ball that won the game.

Cronin was great because he always encouraged that kind of talk. And gee, right from the start I hit well. I remember Herb Pennock was pitching batting practice for us. He had been a great pitcher, pinpoint control, and I loved to have him throw to me. He was probably forty-five then, and he'd keep everything inside, so you wouldn't be slamming one back at him. He always made you pull. Every now and then, though, he'd slip and get one over the plate and he'd holler like hell, "Don't hit it!" He didn't want to lose any teeth at that late date.

I was still pretty erratic in the field, all right, out there practicing my hitting form with my glove on, occasionally letting a ball go through. One time Cronin yelled out to me from his position at shortstop, "Hey, kid, how about practicing a little less of this"—he made a swinging motion—"and a little more of this"—and he fielded an imaginary ball. It's certainly reasonable to assume that at 6 foot 4, 175 pounds, a skinny bean, I looked more lackadaisical in the field than I was. A little guy with shorter limbs, making the same moves, is going to look like he's doing it quicker, like he's really hustling.

It's just as true that being more nonchalant about it than I should have was going to hurt me even when I was in the right. I remember in Cleveland one night, the ninth inning of a tough game. Cronin had jerked me out of a previous game for loafing, and he had been on my ass about my fielding, and boy here comes a line drive right at me. I got it in the glove, and dropped it. It just plopped right down in front of me. There were two outs and two men on, and instead of being out of the inning we now had the bases loaded. We finally got through it, but as soon as we did Cronin came running out there, mad as a hornet. I thought he was going to pop me he was so mad. "So help me, Joe, I tried for that ball," I said. If I didn't convince him it was because I didn't *look* like I'd tried for it.

We broke camp and went north with the Cincinnati Reds. In those days the two teams traveled a special train together, playing exhibitions en route. You'd have the whole train to yourselves, four sleeping cars, two dining cars, two baggage cars, maybe another car for the press. Traveling like that, you might play each other eighteen times as you worked your way north—Dothan, Alabama; Mobile; Greenville, South Carolina; Columbia. It was great for us, traveling with the Reds, because they had a fine pitching staff that year: Walters and Derringer and Thompson and Johnny Vander Meer. Great hitting practice.

We made our first stop in Atlanta. It was April Fools' Day. We got out to the old park there, and Johnny Orlando pointed to right field. It was a funny setup—three parallel fences, one right behind the other, like a prison compound. Johnny says, "I saw the Babe hit one out over the last one, right there."

I said, "Oh, yeah?" Boy, I was going to do that too.

But five times up and I didn't do it, and about the eighth inning I struck out with two men on, and could hardly stand it. I went out to right field seething. The Cincinnati batter hit a little fly down the line that curved foul and I ran over, got it and dropped it, then booted it trying to pick it up. I was so mad when I finally grabbed it I threw it the hell out of the park over the last fence. The ball hit a Sears

57

store across the street. Cronin pulled me out right away, and he didn't have to say a word because I was ashamed the moment I did it. The next day I hit one over that last fence, and I gave Johnny a hard look when I came in.

We opened the season in New York, and darn if it doesn't rain for two days. We paced the Commodore Hotel, waiting for it to break. My fingernails were down to nothing. Finally we get out to Yankee Stadium on the third day, and through a friend of my mother's it was arranged for me to meet a couple of the New York writers, particularly Joe Williams, my namesake, the big columnist. She thought they would help loosen me up a little.

Well, I didn't even like the sound of Joe Williams' voice. He talked like he was real New York, looking down his nose at me, a real big shot. And I am sure that I didn't impress him either, a skinny young rookie. Years later he was great for writing Ted Williams-should-be-traded stories, full of needles about my not being good for the Red Sox, but the thing that gave me a laugh was that whenever he had one of these pipe dreams he'd trade me for DiMaggio and *two other guys*, or Newhouser and *two other guys*, or Feller and *two other guys*, never even up. He must have thought more of me than he realized.

I will never forget that day sitting on the bench watching the Yankees take batting practice. I'm all eyes and ears. Lou Gehrig was still on the club, the only time I ever saw him play. He was already sick then, and nobody knew it. He looked tired just walking up the steps after the game. But there they were, Frank Crosetti and Charlie Keller and DiMaggio and Tommy Henrich and Bill Dickey. A *hell* of a lineup. And Joe Gordon. I'm watching them, studying them all, and I remember so distinctly—this was one of those ten days—I said to myself, I *know* I can hit as good as these guys. Just a young kid's reaction, seeing the greats, building up his confidence.

Red Ruffing was the Yankee pitcher. I watched him warm up, a big guy, I mean *big*, but a real easy-going style, like he didn't give a damn. When he came in with it, though, the ball whistled. I got up the first time and fouled one off, then he threw me a little curve and I fouled that off too, then he struck me out on a high fastball. The second time up the same thing: curve, curve, high fastball, strike three.

Well, here's this smart-talking kid rookie from California striking out his first two times up, and burning. I got to the bench and plopped down, and out of the corner of my eye I see ole Jack Wilson, one of our pitchers, coming to me. We'd been needling each other all spring, and I'd been telling him how I was going to wear Ruffing out, and Jack's *really* got the old needle out now. He says, "Whata ya think of this league now, Bush?"

By this time I'm boiling. I said, "Screw you. That is *one* guy"—pointing to Ruffing—"I *know* I am going to hit, and if he puts it in the same place again I'm riding it out of here."

Well it just so happened the next time up Ruffing got it high again, and I hit one to right center just a foot from going into the bleachers. I'd gotten under it a little bit or it would have gone out. When I got to second base, there was Gordon. We had played against each other on the coast in 1937, and he came over smiling. "You nervous?"

I said, "Boy, am I. Nervous as hell."

It turned out to be a wonderful first year for me. We got to Boston and I checked into the Canterbury Hotel because I was told it was one of the cheaper hotels near the ball park, but they put me right next to the railroad tracks and every time a train went by the building shook. So I moved to the Shelton into a six- or seven-dollar-a-day room, and I was there until they closed the place in 1954. My first series in Fenway Park, the first time I'd ever seen it, actually, I hit a double, a home run and a triple in a game with the Athletics, and the first two hits were off a guy named Cotton Pippen. Pippen was the same pitcher who struck me out my first time up as a professional, back in San Diego when I pinched-hit and just stood there too scared to swing while he poured three straight down the middle.

I was only hitting .280 in July, and I didn't make the All-Star team, the only one I wasn't picked for, but I was leading the league in runs batted in, hitting fourth behind Cramer, Vosmik and Foxx. Foxx was getting toward the end of his career then, but he had switched to a lighter bat, maybe thirty-five or thirty-six ounces, and he was hanging in, getting a lot of blunk hits and every now and then really crashing one. I remember on a road trip that year Jimmy hit four balls like I had never seen hit before. The first one was a real ripper in Chicago, over the left-field bleachers, and in Cleveland I was on second base and Mel Harder was pitching when Foxx hit one over the 435-foot sign, at least 480 feet in the air. Then in Detroit right after that he hit the longest ball I had ever seen—way up into the bleachers in left center. Just hard to believe.

I truly admired Foxx. He was older, of course, and he and I were a generation apart, but he was such a good-natured guy, a big farm boy from Maryland. He never bad-mouthed anybody. Always a giggle, and a "Yeah, sure, sure." He never made any bones about his love for Scotch. He used to say he could drink fifteen of those little bottles of Scotch, those miniatures, and not be affected. Of course, nobody can do that and stay healthy, and it got to Jimmy later on.

I followed Foxx in the order, and Cronin batted right behind me, then Jim Tabor and Bobby Doerr. A pretty rugged lineup, a *hell* of a lineup. They couldn't pitch around me, which gave me a perfect opportunity to drive in runs. I led the league with 143 RBI's, the first rookie to do it, and even with the bad start I wound up hitting .327. I struck out ninety-seven times that first year, going for more bad pitches than I should have, out of eagerness I guess, but I also walked a hundred times, because even then something Rogers Hornsby had told me in Florida the year before was fast becoming a cardinal rule for me: *Get a good ball to hit.* From then on I averaged less than fifty strike-outs a season, twenty-five of which would be on called strikes I just couldn't bring myself to go for.

We had a pitcher on our staff that year named Jim Bagby, a big winner for the club in 1938. Jim had a harelip, but that didn't stop him from sounding off, and he was always having fun with somebody. The visitors' dugout was on the first-base side in Detroit, and in our first game there, the first time I got up, Bagby started needling Hank Greenberg, who was playing in fairly close at first. There was one man who really got down to business in this game, Hank Greenberg. I mean he knew where his nickels were coming from. He was *all* business. Joe DiMaggio was like that.

So Bagby's yelling at him, "Well, Hank, you had better get back. You don't know this guy, you . . . better . . . get . . . back." Greenberg wasn't paying any attention. Bagby yelled at him four or five times and Greenberg paid absolutely no attention. Finally, and I can still hear Bagby loud and clear, "All right, Hank, if you want to look like me and talk like me, stand right where you are!"

That same day I hit the first ball ever to go out of Briggs Stadium after it was remodeled in 1937. The first time up I hit one against the facing of the upper deck for a home run.

On that one the count went to three balls, no strikes, and Rudy York, the catcher for Detroit, said, "You're not hitting, are you, Kid?"

And I said, "I sure as hell am." Out it goes and when I got to first base Greenberg was still looking where the ball had gone. I reached second and Charley Gehringer, who hadn't said a word to anybody in twenty years, was still saying nothing. Frank Croucher at short just looked and Billy Rogell, playing third base, didn't say anything either, but I could see him watching me. I got home and York said, "You weren't kidding, were you, Kid?"

The next time up there were two men on, and this is the one I hit out of Briggs Stadium. I got to first base and Greenberg was still looking, and Gehringer still hadn't said anything in twenty years, and Croucher at short was scraping the ground. I got to Rogell at third and he said, "What the hell *you* been eating?"

I can't imagine anyone having a better, happier first year in the big leagues. I used to send Rod Luscomb diagrams showing how the parks were laid out and where I had hit my home runs, and telling him how happy I was. I hit a home run in every park, completing the list in Yankee Stadium on the last day. Every day was Christmas. I got a chance to fish for tuna for the first time that year. We had time for things like that between series. The longer I played the fewer off-days there were, and eventually I had to give up fishing during the season, but I went out on a charter with Jimmy Foxx and Frank Hayes and Bob Johnson, off Brielle, New Jersey, and there were big tuna all around us, breaking water. Johnny Orlando, the clubhouse boy, started out with us but got seasick and we had to put him ashore on some island. He said he'd never go again. Poor old Bob Johnson was grinding up slush and chum all day, but the rest of us got eighteen or nineteen school tuna apiece, about thirty-five to forty pounds, one of the greatest days of fishing I ever had. I enjoyed being with those guys so much, a kid in the company of great players.

At the park it was even better. Babe Ruth declared me "rookie of the year." They didn't have an official rookie-of-the-year award then, so that was good enough for me. Later the Boston writers made the same designation. The fans in right field were yelling with me and for me all the time, really crowding in there to see what I would do next, and that year nobody tipped or waved his hat more than I did. I mean, right off my head, by the button. Nothing put on, nothing acted, just spontaneous. The next year things began to change and I never did it again.

I didn't go home that winter. Home was never a happy place for me, and I had met a girl in Minnesota.

I had gone to the little town of Princeton to hunt mallards. I'd only shot a couple mallards in my life before that, but there in western Minnesota I saw them by the thousands, more mallards, I thought, than in the whole state of California. I must have shot a hundred mallards my first trip. I fished Lake Mille Lacs, a real good spot for walleyes. And in Princeton I met Doris Soule. She was a cute little girl with dark hair, sort of the Dorothy Lamour type. Her mother and father were divorced—her father was a hunting guide up there—and her mother worked in the bank, and we hit it off fine.

So I didn't go back to San Diego. I took a five-dollar room at the King Cole Hotel in downtown Minneapolis. There was a heated swimming pool there, and I learned how to ice skate at the rink in the park. A lot of things I did by myself. I went to the movies a lot. San Diego seemed a million miles away. I spent the winter there, unaware of the big things that were to come—a .400 season, a world war, a pennant—and unaware, I suppose, that my troubles were just beginning.

part two

Circumstances make a career—a man being at the right place at the right time with the right material. Circumstances can make a .400 hitter. Some years, for example, might be a little better than others for pitching, almost imperceptibly better. Then the pitching might go down and the hitting creep up.

In 1941 I hit .406 for the Boston Red Sox. No one had hit .400 in the major leagues for eleven years before that, not since Bill Terry, and no one has hit .400 again, and I suppose you can find students of the game who say it will *never* happen again. But there were times when it could have happened. I could have done it myself in 1957. I came within five hits of .400 that year. What's five hits? I was thirty-nine years old, aging and aching. There had to be among a season's collection of groundballs at least five leg hits for a younger Ted Williams.

Certainly 1957 appeared to be a year for the batter. Stan Musial hit .351, and he was thirty-six years old. Mickey

Mantle hit .365 that year, the best year of his life, and maybe that was *his* .400 season. Nobody has hit .365 in either league since then. Last year Carl Yastrzemski won the American League batting championship with an average of .301. I was pleased for Carl, but it was a dubious honor: the lowest average ever to win a big league batting championship. Nobody else in the league hit .300. It was definitely not a hitters' year.

In 1941 there were a lot of big name pitchers in the American League—Lefty Gomez, Red Ruffing, Dutch Leonard, Tommy Bridges, Bob Feller, Ted Lyons, Johnny Allen, Bobo Newsom—and they might have been at their best, but who is to say?

Lyons was tough and got tougher the more you faced him, because he'd learn about you by playing those little pitcher-batter thinking games, and he'd usually outthink you. I know as a rookie when the guys were telling me about the pitchers they would come to Lyons and they'd say, "Well, he's not real fast, but he's *sneaky* fast," and "His curve is hittable, but he gets it in good spots," and "You've got to watch his change up," and "He's got a knuckleball," and "The one thing you *can't* do, you can't guess with the son of a gun." That first year I hit Lyons pretty good, but the second year he struck me out twice on fastballs in situations where I thought he would not dare throw a fastball, and he knew I was thinking he wouldn't, so he threw it anyway. Put a little extra on it. Out I went, still looking for a curve. Lyons was a smart pitcher.

But in 1941 Lyons was forty years old and you'd have to think he was over the hump. So was Harder, and Schoolboy Rowe had hurt his arm, and maybe Red Ruffing and Lefty Gomez were not at their best. Bob Feller was at the top of his game, though, and Johnny Allen, and we were seeing Trout and Benton and Virgil Trucks. Hal

Newhouser didn't get going good until later. He was wild at first, and a fiery guy. You would hit one off him and it was like you had taken his blood. He'd give you that rotten stare. He didn't think anybody was supposed to hit Newhouser. He became a beautiful pitcher, nice effortless style, fine fastball, pretty to watch. Newhouser had everything. Cronin always said he would have won in any era.

There was some great batting done that year. Joe DiMaggio hit safely in fifty-six straight games. A guy you probably never heard of, Cecil Travis, had a hell of a year—.359—and never had another like it. It was one of those years. I think, surely, to hit .400 you have to be an outstanding hitter having everything go just right, and in my case the hitter was a guy who lived to hit, who worked at it so hard he matured at the bat at a time when he was near his peak physically. The peaks met.

It was a simple formula. Choose any of the noted hitters, and none of them hit any more balls, swung a bat in practice any more times than Theodore Samuel Williams. Now, you can be a great athlete, and you can go to sleep on the bench when you should be watching the pitcher. Watch him warm up and you might pick up a clue; maybe he'll give away a pitch, or throw one he hasn't used before. You might see if he's as fast as usual, or how his curve is breaking. Pick your nose, scratch your ass and it all goes by, and you won't know enough about hitting until you're twenty-eight or twenty-nine years old, and then it'll probably be too late.

Nobody has it all. A guy's got good looks, he might weigh only 120 pounds. Or he's got a brilliant mind, and bad breath. I don't know what limitations there have been that have made it impossible for other guys to hit .400. Certainly the pitching today is not that good, not since expansion and the depreciation of the minor leagues, for the simple reason there are fewer pitchers pitching and more pitchers in the big leagues, twenty or so starting pitchers who would be in the minor leagues were it not for the expansion teams. So, overall, pitching can't be as good. The development of the slider hurt the hitter, of course. Joe DiMaggio always said he had trouble with the slider in his last years.

But Willie Mays could hit .400, with his speed. Or Hank Aaron. I always envied guys like Mays and Mantle who might get thirty or thirty-five infield hits a year without any sweat while I was puffing for my ten. Mantle got forty-eight leg hits the year he hit .365. That kind of speed does things for you: It forces the opposition to play you a little shorter at third base, a little shorter at first. They've got to be faster making a play, they've got to *worry* about being faster. Lou Brock is a hell of a base runner, but he's half again as effective because he gets the pitcher and the catcher and the rest of the infield all on edge worrying about him stealing a base.

With the infield shortened up, the hitting angles from home plate become wider. The infielder hasn't the time to cover as much territory on a hard-hit ball. It's by him before he can react. So speed is a big factor. And bat control. Roberto Clemente could hit .400 because he has such good bat control. He has sense with the bat. He protects the plate with two strikes. I used to think Al Kaline could hit .400, or Mantle. But Mantle missed the ball too much. Too many strike-outs. He was forever going for the long ball, even with two strikes. Not quite enough finesse. And it is too late for Kaline or Mays now.

What I see lacking today is the devotion necessary to produce a .400 hitter, and even with all the circumstances in the world going for you, in order to do the toughest thing there is to do in sport—hit a baseball properly—a man has got to devote every ounce of his concentration to it. Today that's a hard thing to do. Today ballplayers have a thousand distractions. They're always on the run.

In the old days we didn't fly, we rode the train. We might be ten, twelve hours on a train, and much of the talk was hitting. We didn't have television, we didn't have a lot of money to play around with. We lived in an atmosphere of baseball. We talked it, we experimented, we swapped bats. I was forever trying a new stance, trying to hit like Greenberg or Foxx or somebody, and then going back to my old way. I recommend that to kids. Experiment. Try what you see that looks good on somebody else.

A trip to the plate was an adventure for me, one that I could reflect on and store up information. I honestly believe I can recall everything there was to know about my first 300 home runs—who the pitcher was, the count, the pitch itself, where the ball landed. I didn't have to keep a written book on pitchers—I *lived* a book on pitchers. I was a guy who practiced until the blisters bled, and then practiced some more. When I was a kid I carried my bat to class with me. I'd run a buddy's newspaper route if I could get him to shag flies for me. When I played for the San Diego Padres I *paid* kids to shag flies on my days off.

Rod Luscomb used to say that in seven years on the playground I never broke a bat hitting a ball incorrectly, that all my bats had the bruises in the same spot, like they were hammered there by a careful carpenter, right on the thick of the hitting surface. That might be an exaggeration, but I believe it is true that when you put in as much time as I did you get results. Certainly from boyhood I was prepared for that kind of dedication, often to the exclusion of all else, and often to the point that the sheer agony of the concentration had side effects that hurt me, even on the verge of that .400 season.

I signed to play in 1940 for $10,000, more than double what I had made my first year. It was to begin a climb that would reach $100,000 by 1950. But I sure didn't know that in 1940. I was a twenty-year-old kid, worried about everything. I remember driving Doc Cramer, our center fielder, down to Kenmore Square one day that year, and Doc said, "You know who the best hitter in the league is right now?" We had been comparing the hitters around. "*You* are. You're the best."

But 1940 was a tough year for me. I was maturing, to be sure, but I was suffering too. Certainly l was not getting the balls to hit I got in 1939. Jimmy Foxx and Joe Cronin were at an age when they were beginning to fade, and pitchers were pitching around me a little. I wasn't hitting as many home runs in Fenway Park. I had hit fourteen there the year before, a record, and in order to install a bullpen they had moved in the right-field fence to a more accommodating distance (still not a bargain at 380 feet). They anticipated a lot more home runs, and the crowds were getting bigger, coming out to see the fresh kid.

I had been moved to left field because it was easier to play—right field in Boston is a bitch, the sun field, and few play it well. Jackie Jensen was the best I saw at it. Left field at Fenway Park is shallow, only 315 feet from home plate to the big high wall everybody makes fun of. You don't have to go back much for a ball hit to left, and to left center it's only 370 feet, where a lot of parks might go to 430. It's not a sun field, and in time anybody can learn to play the wall. When you catch onto the caroms you can hold line drives to singles.

Left field is also where the scoreboard is and I got to be buddies with the operator, Bill Daley. He'd give me the word on what was going on around the league, all the scores and everything. When DiMaggio was on his fifty-six-game hitting streak Bill would keep track. He'd tell me, "Joe just got a double," and I'd pass it on to Dom DiMaggio in center field. Anyway, left field would have been fine with me, except for one thing: It put me a little closer to the fans, and they were beginning to get to me that year. I started reacting, mostly out of my own frustration. I'd say things: "Boston's a lousy town." "The salary I get is peanuts," even though as a kid I never dreamed I'd be making so much money. Then the writers started in on me.

In 1940 my uncle was a fireman in Westchester, outside New York City. Uncle John Smith. A great guy. As a kid in San Diego I used to hang around the neighborhood fire station, playing pinochle with the firemen, sometimes getting to ride the trucks. It was always an attractive place for me. The first year I bought a new car, a big green Buick, I took it to the station and parked it out back and put a shine on it that must have been an inch thick, and the firemen would ask me about the great players I had seen and about my home runs. So it was natural for me to be attracted to my uncle's fire station in Mount Vernon, and I went down to see him whenever I could.

By then I was already going my own way. I have never cultivated "important" people, perhaps because I did not feel comfortable in a necktie crowd. My friends were the guys who delivered the magazines, the highway cop, the guy who took care of my car and wanted a ticket now and then, the clubhouse boy, the guy who ran the theater. I was a movie hound. I'd clip the movie schedule out of the paper and maybe see two or three a day.

I used to go down to an old theater in the old part of Boston to see cowboy movies, and I'd get in those wooden seats, kind of leaning back with my feet over the front seat like kids do, and one day I felt a tap on my shoulder. "Where the hell you think you are, home?" I looked up, and this guy says, "Take your feet down." He was the manager. Later when I was coming out he stopped me. "Aren't you Ted Williams?" We wound up going for a milk shake. His name was Johnny Buckley, and he has been one of my dearest friends ever since.

There was a place in Foxboro, outside of Boston, the Lafayette House, where I'd go with a friend of mine to eat because it was quiet and away from things and they'd give me extra cuts of meat. We were coming back from there one night, going a little fast down this hill, and suddenly we've got a patrol car on us. The patrolman was a corporal with the Massachusetts State Police. He gave us a little lecture and told us to watch it, but he didn't give us a ticket.

A few days later I was going out there by myself and the same car stopped me. This time he said it was just a social call. He said he had recognized the car—big shiny Buick with California license plates—and recognized me from playing ball. We got to talking and I got to thinking what a lonely job he had, so I invited him to have dinner with me. The patrolman's name was John Blake, and it wasn't long before we were fishing together and he was taking me to the police range to shoot. Friends for life. Same story.

It wasn't really a matter of being a lone wolf. But I didn't smoke. I couldn't stand the smell of tobacco. In those days I didn't drink. I liked to hunt and fish. I liked to walk. I liked a certain type of movie. I didn't want to see *Gone with the Wind;* I wanted to see John Wayne. And I wanted to do it now, bang, get it over with, and be home early. I've always criticized myself for the times I've let other guys dictate what happened to me. Like going someplace I didn't want to go, or eating late. Eating is a real sore spot with me. I don't want to hear "Let's wait awhile," because all of a sudden it's nine o'clock, and when I eat late I can't sleep well and I don't feel well the next day. I don't believe there was ever a ballplayer who ate in his room as often as Ted Williams. I'd ten times rather sit home and watch a good TV program than go out to some phony-baloney cocktail party and listen to a lot of bull. I think a lot of people are like that but are afraid to admit it.

I didn't have a great deal in common with most of my teammates. I mean, I liked them all. I can't think of one I didn't like. My roommate was Broadway Charley Wagner and he was a great guy, but a different type of guy. He didn't like to fish. He liked to eat later. He liked to dress up and make a little entrance someplace. They used to say I dressed like I was going to spend the day at the stadium, and that's about right. I still think neckties are designed to get in your soup.

Charley Wagner was my roommate for a long time and we always got along. He was a pitcher. I knocked him out of bed one morning swinging a bat. I hit the bedpost and the bed collapsed, and the way Charley tells it he looked up at me, half asleep, thinking I was the avenging angel or something, and he heard me say, "Boy, what power!" Being my roommate could be a nuisance in a lot of ways, the habits I had, so when I came back from Korea in 1953 they let me room alone. That way I could cut off the phone calls and put up the No Disturb sign and not be bothered.

I liked every one of my teammates, but I just didn't socialize with them. The only one I was real close to then and for a long time was Bobby Doerr. Bobby liked the same things I did. He liked the movies, he liked milk shakes. We talked hunting and fishing by the hour. And we'd walk— we'd walk and he'd talk about Oregon, and I'd talk about shooting ducks, and we'd talk hitting. I got to know his mother and father. His little father was one of the dearest guys. He was retired from the telephone company and I remember he got Bobby to invest in telephone stock, and after that some real good timberland in Oregon. I always envied Bobby the father he had, a father who was close to him, telling him what to do, encouraging him, helping him with his finances.

So now it's 1940 and I'm having my troubles at the park and visiting my uncle at the fire station, seeing the firemen hang around with their shirts off, getting sunburned, playing checkers, some of them playing cards. My uncle's telling me about this $150-a-month pension he's going to get, and I'm thinking, Boy, here I am, hitting .340 and having to take all this crap from the fans and writers. Then one day in Cleveland I'd had a bad day at bat and Harry Grayson, the writer from NEA, was at my locker and I was telling him about my uncle, and then I said, "Nuts to this baseball. I'd sooner be a fireman."

Well, Grayson took that and blew it all out of proportion. It was all over the papers, and that weekend we went into Chicago. The White Sox were managed by Jimmy Dykes, and with him the biggest bunch of jockeys ever on one ball team. Dykes and Mule Haas and Edgar Smith and Ted Lyons. Doc Cramer and Lyons were always squashing eggs on one another. Cramer was a great agitator himself—all the time making midnight calls to somebody or loading up a suitcase with rocks—and he'd squash an egg on Lyons and Lyons would say, "All right, you bastard, you'd better start dancing the next time you get up there," and sure enough he'd aim one at Cramer's knees and Cramer would have to skip rope.

Then Lyons would come in our dugout and he'd say, "Hi, Doc"—*yaaak*, an egg on Cramer's head. Lyons was a strong son of a gun, too. When he grabbed you, you stayed grabbed.

They were an agitating bunch of guys, the White Sox, and when I come out on the field, geez, they're blowing sirens and ringing bells, and two of them have these Texaco fire hats that Ed Wynn used to wear, and then here comes the game and I go out in left field and there's the *real* fire chief with a real white helmet on and sitting with him are eight guys with big red helmets, real helmets.

Then we go to New York and Lefty Gomez and Red Ruffing are ringing cow bells when I get up to the plate, raising all kinds of hell, so I get out of the box and I say to Bill Summers, the umpire, "Those guys can't do that, damn it, not while I'm hitting." Summers warns them, but they keep banging and a-booming, and finally he goes over there and kicks them out of the game. Gomez was supposed to have said that he'd just as soon go fishing anyway.

You say, Well, that *was* funny, and sure it was. But I'm still a kid, high strung and prone to tantrums, and more and more I'm feeling like the persecuted. Next was the incident over the pigeons. There used to be a lot of big pigeons in Fenway Park, and every now and then the groundskeeper would flock shoot them, put out a bundle of grain and kill them in bunches. They were a nuisance. I was a nut for guns, and he let me go out one day with my twenty gauge and I suppose I killed thirty or forty pigeons. Then Mr. Yawkey came out, too, and he's an excellent shot. Together we knocked off seventy or eighty pigeons. We had a hell of a time. Bang, boom, bang.

This was on an off day, a Monday. Tuesday night we're having batting practice in Washington and one of the writers comes up to me and says, "The Humane Society has made a complaint about you." Yeah? What happened? "They found out you were shooting pigeons." He didn't say anything about Mr. *Yawkey* shooting pigeons, old Teddy Ballgame is the S.O.B. they're after. I used to take my .22 out and take target practice on the 400-foot sign, too, but that was put to rest when I knocked out a few lights in the scoreboard. It turned out that a little writer in Boston named Hy Hurwitz, a guy I always had trouble with, had phoned the Humane Society. So I apologized and promised I wouldn't shoot any more pigeons.

Funny, sure, but not all my difficulties were funny to me, and I didn't know how to handle them. Joe Cronin did. Cronin was a big good-looking Irishman who could just swoon you. He married the owner's daughter in Washington, and he was everybody's favorite. He could suave those writers to death. If it were me, if I'd been the general manager, I'd have nipped it right now.

I'd have called the writer in and said, "Look, this kid is going to be a hell of a player. But he's twenty years old. How can you write such a lousy article about him? Give him a break. We're getting on his ass. You don't have to put every little mistake in the paper so that every son of a bitch in Boston knows about it. You're not only hurting him, you're hurting the club." You know, set the writer straight. *I* couldn't, though, and I sure wasn't getting any help from the front office.

I never had problems like that in San Diego or Minneapolis, and I got along fine with guys like Red Smith and Arthur Daley in New York. Isn't that funny? Well, my way of handling it was to get nasty right back. If there were eight or ten reporters around my locker, I'd spot a guy who'd written a bad article about me and I'd say, "Why should you even come around me, that crap-house stuff you've been writing." So that would embarrass *him*, and he'd get mad, and then off we'd go.

Take Dave Egan. They called him The Colonel, the big columnist for the Boston *Daily Record*. He could write some elegant things, beautiful things, make you think Ted Williams was responsible for the entire American League.

Then, boy, he could tear me down, write rotten stuff. And the other columnists followed his lead.

Like I said, I didn't go home the winter of 1939. It had always been a struggle at home, the tension, my father and mother never really together, my brother always in some kind of scrape. While I was trying to help my mother, she was giving everything to my brother, and I was mad at that. I tried to give my mother everything she wanted, but I could never give her all I *really* wanted to give her, because she would have given it to my brother. If it was a refrigerator or a washing machine, he'd hock it. My mother never had a vacation in her life. Never. She didn't want to spend the money. Or she'd go and buy old clothes or old furniture or something that someone was peddling, and it would pile up out back.

I remember when Eddie Collins, the Boston general manager, came to the house those few times before I had a chance to make it presentable. There were holes in the chairs white mice had made years before. One Christmas we had had a new rug in our house. We also got a little second-hand Lionel train that year, and the transformers on it got hot and the tar melted on the rug. The rug with the spot on it was still there. I mean, it was never a happy place for me, and in 1939 my mother and father separated and there was more grief, so I just stayed away. And do you know what Harold Kaese wrote the first time I did something to displease him? "Well, what do you expect from a guy who won't even go see his mother in the off season."

Before this, I was willing to believe a writer was my friend until he proved otherwise. Now my guard's up all the time, always watching for critical stuff. If I saw something, I'd read it twenty times, and I'd burn without knowing how to fight it. How could I fight it? Part of it, of course, was that I'd slipped a little bit in 1940. My batting average was actually higher, up to .344, and I led the league in runs scored, but everybody was expecting me to hit home runs and I only hit twenty-three, and only seven of those were in Fenway Park. I was moody a lot. I'd go in spells. Jimmy Foxx was always in my corner, but he called me a "spoiled boy" that year, and I guess I acted like one. If I got mad and didn't run out a ground ball, Cronin would chew me out, which was right, and I'd be sorry and full of remorse, so the next couple times I'd sprint like mad to first base even when I was a sure out. That was also the year I got booed for making an error and then for striking out, and the unfairness of it hit me. I vowed that day I'd never tip my hat again.

I guess the only real fun I had that season was when Cronin let me pitch a couple innings in Detroit. The Tigers were on their way to the pennant, they had Greenberg and York and Gehringer and Higgins, a hell of a lineup, and they were beating our brains out, about 11–1 in the seventh inning. I was always saying what a loss it was to baseball, my not following up on my pitching career, and when we got so far behind and Cronin said "Who the hell we got to pitch?" I heard myself saying, "Me. I'll pitch."

"You want to pitch?"

"Sure."

"OK. Pitch."

I pitched the last two innings. My greatest claim to fame was striking out Rudy York with two men on. I gave him a real good sidearm curve, it broke about a foot, right over the plate, and he took it. I guess he didn't know what to expect, whether I would throw it over the backstop or what. To this day York claims I quick-pitched him. I didn't, but he always says, "You quick-pitched me."

The Tigers scored one run in the two innings, my two-inning big league pitching career.

Then here comes 1941 and everything is fun again. I mentioned circumstances. The biggest thing going for me to hit .400 was Fenway Park in Boston, and before you question the logic of that, let me explain. First it had a good, green background. Mr. Yawkey kept all the signs out, everything was green. There were no shadows. And then there was that short, high fence in left field. You say, But Williams was a pull hitter to *right* field. That's correct. But it gave me a different kind of advantage. Even though I didn't hit out that way, I always said to myself, If you swing a little late it won't be the worst thing in the world, because there's that short fence, the defense isn't there, and slices or balls hit late can *still* go out.

So I didn't worry about hitting late, and what did that do for me? It allowed me to develop the most valuable luxury a hitter can have: the ability to wait on the ball.

By waiting, you get fooled less by the pitch. By waiting, and being quick with the bat, you can protect the plate with two strikes. You can follow the ball better. I never complained when I was late on a pitch, but it burned my butt to be early, to be in front of the ball, because that meant I wasn't waiting. Sure, sometimes you wait too long and the ball is past you. But that usually means you are going to get the same pitch the next time, and nothing pleased me more than to get a second crack at a pitcher who thought he had put one past me. I couldn't *wait* to get up again.

Hal Newhouser knocked me down with a pitch one time, then struck me out on three fastballs. Detroit's pitchers were all like that—Trucks, Trout, Benton, Newhouser. They loved to challenge you, brush you back a little, then pitch to your strength. When I came back to the bench I growled at somebody, "Five bucks says if he throws that same pitch to me again I'm going to ride it out of here." Newhouser did, and I did.

I remember Bill Dickey of the Yankees was giving me a lot of conversation that year. When he was catching, he'd try to get you distracted. He'd say, "How much you weigh now, Kid?" and, *whup*, there goes a strike. And then I'd take a real close pitch, a ball, and he'd say, "How big does that ball look to you, anyway?" Then I'd take another one *real* close and he'd say, "Just how the hell big *does* that ball look to you?"

Well, Cramer was on second one day and he gave me the closed fist. Curve ball coming. He'd picked up Dickey's sign. So I'm looking for a curve. Bump Hadley's pitching for the Yankees and he rears back and gives me a fastball and it's almost past when I give it one of those late little quick swings. Line drive, right center field, home run. The next day I read in the paper where Dickey said, "Williams hit the ball right out of my glove," which was perfect because it meant that I had waited.

Now, the second thing that worked in my favor that year was an injury. I had chipped a bone in my ankle sliding into second base about the second week of spring training and for the first two weeks of the season I did nothing but pinch-hit. The early season was never my time of year anyway. It's cold in Boston, you have a lot of chilling, adverse hitting winds. I never hit as well in cold weather as I did in dead of the summer. Never. And, *and*, we had gotten Joe Dobson from Cleveland in a trade.

Dobson wasn't pitching regularly for us, so every day we'd go out and he'd throw me batting practice. We'd make games out of it—"OK, Joe, ninth inning at Detroit, bases loaded, two out," and so forth. I got the most batting practice of my life, and the best, because Dobson had a hell of a curve and a good overhand fastball, and he always bore down. Every day that his arm would hold out, and the blisters on my hands would hold out, we'd go out there like it was all-out war, one-on-one.

Well, for me it was great fun, and I was about as sharp as I could ever be. My hands were good and callused. First I'd get the blisters, then the calluses would start growing, real big, hard ugly calluses. I'd bet if you checked today you'd find most hitters don't develop calluses like they used to. They wear golf gloves, and they don't hit that much. So I began to pinch-hit, and almost everything I touched was a line drive. When I finally got back into the lineup, the weather had turned warm, and I mean I got off to a flying start.

I remember going to New York early that year, and why they didn't pull the shift on me that day I'll never know. Mario Russo was pitching, a left-hander with a sidearm fastball that sank. He was good in the Stadium because right-handers couldn't get the ball in the air off him. First time I'm up, boom, a base hit between first and second base. Next time up, boom, another hit between first and second. I got four straight hits between first and second base. Gordon was tightening up on me all the time, shading over toward first, but he never quite got over far enough.

The .400 thing got bigger as the season went on because a lot of guys had hit .400 for two months and then tailed. And, truthfully, it got bigger to me with the years. I had to think then that I wasn't going to be the last to do it, or that I might even do it again myself. Late in the season, when it looked like I might make it, I went on Harry Von Zell's program—he had one of those radio talk shows then—and Harry asked me if I was going to break Hugh Duffy's record. Duffy had hit .438 for the Reds back before the turn of the century, the highest average of all time. I said I hoped not, because I liked Hugh Duffy too much.

Duffy was a coach for the Red Sox when I first came up. A little squib of a guy. Looked like he weighed about a hundred pounds. Duffy used to tell me, "Son, you've got form and power. But the form is most important. With it you get the power. Don't monkey with your form." I remember in spring training I'd rip one back through the box, practically dehorn the pitcher, take his whiskers right off, and Duffy would squeal, "Thata boy, Ted, thata boy." He really liked that one.

Everybody was interested as we got into September. I'd go into Detroit where Harry Heilmann was broadcasting the games, and Harry would take me aside and say, "Now, forget about that short fence, just hit the ball where you want it, hit your pitch, *get those base hits*. You can hit .400. You can do it." Heilmann had hit .403 for the Tigers in 1921, and he was the opposing announcer, but he was for me. Just about everybody was for me. The fans in Yankee Stadium gave Lefty Gomez a hell of a boo in September when he walked me with the bases loaded after I had gotten three straight hits.

The only guy who tried to put me down was Al Simmons. He came over to me in the dugout tunnel one day near the end. He was coaching for Philadelphia at the time. He had hit .390 one year for the A's, and he was another real big guy, but a different animal from Heilmann. Simmons had a kind of swaggering way about him. The kind of guy who when somebody else was in the batting cage, would say, "Buy him a lunch, he's going to be in there all day." Simmons wouldn't win any popularity contests.

I'm sitting there on the bench and Simmons says, "How much do you want to bet you don't hit .400?" Just like that.

I said, "Nuts to you, Simmons, I'm not going to bet I'll hit .400. I wouldn't bet a nickel on it."

It came to the last day of the season, and by now I was down to .39955, which, according to the way they do it, rounds out to an even .400. We had a doubleheader left at Philadelphia. I'd slumped as the weather got cooler, from a high of .436 in June, down to .402 in late August, then up again to .413 in September. In the last ten days of the season my average dropped almost a point a day. Now it was barely .400. The night before the game Cronin offered to take me out of the lineup to preserve the .400. They used to do that. Foxx lost a batting championship to Buddy Myer one year when he sat out the last game and Myer got two hits.

I told Cronin I didn't want that. If I couldn't hit .400 all the way I didn't deserve it. It sure as hell meant something to me then, and Johnny Orlando, the clubhouse boy, always a guy who was there when I needed him, must have walked ten miles with me the night before, talking it over and just walking around. Johnny really didn't like to walk as much as I did, so I'd wait outside while he ducked into a bar for a quick one to keep his strength up. The way he tells it, he made two stops for Scotch and I made two stops for ice cream walking the streets of Philadelphia.

It had been such a happy, exciting season to come to this. In Detroit that July I had hit what remains to this day the most thrilling hit of my life. I was in my second All-Star game. The year before I'd hit a couple of little groundballs in St. Louis, nothing to be proud of, and we'd lost to the National League, 4–0. This time I had a double that drove in a run in the fourth inning, but Arky Vaughan of the Pirates had hit two home runs for the National League and he looked like the hero of the day. We went into the ninth inning trailing 5 to 3. There were five men scheduled to bat in front of me, and when Frankie Hayes popped out I had to think I wasn't going to get another chance. Then Kenny Keltner of Cleveland beat out an infield hit, Joe Gordon singled and Cecil Travis walked to fill the bases. Joe Di-Maggio was up. The excitement in Briggs Stadium was terrific. The game probably should have been over on the next play. Joe grounded hard to the infield, a double-play ball, but Travis distracted Billy Herman as he slid into second and Herman's throw to first was wide. Keltner scored and it was 5–4, with two outs and runners on first and third.

Claude Passeau was pitching for the National League. Passeau was always tough. He helped pitch the Cubs to the pennant in 1945. He had a fast tailing ball that he'd jam a left-hand hitter with, right into your fists, and if you weren't quick he'd get it past you. He threw it a little flat, not overhand, so it wasn't quite as good as some of the sliders you see today, but he was a competitor and I knew he wasn't going to walk me if he could help it, because in the eighth inning he had struck me out. I was late on that one, and as I came up in the ninth I said to myself, Damn it, you've got to be quicker, you've got to get more in front of this guy. *You've got to be quicker.*

He worked the count to 2 and 1, then he came in with that sliding fastball around my belt and I swung. No cut-down protection swing, an all-out home run swing, probably with my eyes shut. My first thought was that I was late again. Any time you hit a ball late chances are it'll pop into the air, because you're swinging slightly up (the ideal swing is not a level swing, it's a slight upswing, despite all the advice you hear) and if you're behind you hit under it. I had pulled it to right field, no doubt about that, but I was afraid I hadn't got enough of the bat on the ball. But gee, it just kept going, up, up, way up into the right-field stands in Detroit.

Well, it was the kind of thing a kid dreams about and imagines himself doing when he's playing those little playground games we used to play in San Diego. Halfway down to first, seeing that ball going out, I stopped running and started leaping and jumping and clapping my hands, and I was just so happy I laughed out loud. I've never been so happy, and I've never seen so many happy guys. They carried me off the field, DiMaggio and Bob Feller, who had pitched early in the game and was already in street clothes, and Eddie Collins leaped out of the box seats and was there to greet me. I've got a picture of Del Baker, the Detroit manager, kissing me on the forehead. Somebody said, "Did you kiss the Kid?" and Del Baker said, "You damn right I did." Everybody was shaking my hand, clapping my back and mussing my hair, and Eddie Collins was in there and Tom Yawkey and Herb Pennock and I don't know who all. Somebody said later that Artie Fletcher, the Yankee coach, shook my hand twelve times. It was a wonderful, wonderful day for me.

Now it was the last day of that 1941 season, and it turned up cold and miserable in Philadelphia. It had rained on Saturday and the game had been rescheduled as part of a Sunday doubleheader. They still had 10,000 people in Shibe Park, I suppose a lot of them just curious to see if The Kid really could hit .400. I have to say I felt good despite the cold. And I know just about everybody in the park was for me. As I came to bat for the first time that day, the Philadelphia catcher, Frankie Hayes, said, "Ted, Mr. Mack told us if we let up on you he'll run us out of baseball. I wish you all the luck in the world, but we're not giving you a damn thing."

Bill McGowan was the plate umpire, and I'll never forget it. Just as I stepped in, he called time and slowly walked around the plate, bent over and began dusting it off. Without looking up, he said, "To hit .400 a batter has got to be loose. He has got to be loose."

I guess I couldn't have been much looser. First time up I singled off Dick Fowler, a liner between first and second. Then I hit a home run, then I hit two more singles off Porter Vaughan, a left-hander who was new to me, and in the second game I hit one off the loudspeaker horn in right field for a double. For the day I wound up six for eight. I don't remember celebrating that night, but I probably went out and had a chocolate milk shake. During the winter Connie Mack had to replace the horn.

While I'm having a nice memory of Bill McGowan, I might explain what has always been thought of as my unnatural serenity around umpires. Writers I blew up at and the fans I hollered at never seemed to understand it. The umpires, baseball's traditional bullseyes, Ted Williams *never* hollered at. To begin with, I never doubted the sincerity or the integrity of an umpire. Some were better than others, some controlled the game better, some would get to stammering around and let the game get out of hand, but all of them are a dedicated bunch of guys, gung-ho, a special breed that make umpiring a life's calling. The mistakes they made were *always* honest mistakes as far as I'm concerned—heat-of-the-battle, spur-of-the-moment things. The things I reacted to were opinionated, thought-out, written-out lies.

It's probably true that umpires liked me, just as they liked the Musials and the DiMaggios and the Greenbergs—for the simple reason we never showed them up. We didn't yell at them or make a fuss and get the crowd on them, which can really happen in the home park. Why not? Because you can't really do anything about a bad call, number one. And number two, I never thought they were that wrong. Jocko Conlan called me out on a bad pitch in the 1947 All-Star game at Wrigley Field in Chicago, a low pitch by Ewell Blackwell. Blackwell was a gangly guy, six foot six, and he was tough to follow, and there was a crowd of white shirts in the background and Jocko just missed the pitch, that's all. I'm sure he knew it as soon as he called it. All I said was, "Damn it, Jocko, that's no strike," put my bat on my shoulder and walked off. It must have been fifteen years later. We were in Arizona, in spring training, and Jocko was working our game. Ordinarily we didn't see much of him because he was a National League umpire, and we were talking before the game. Jocko said, "You know, Ted, the worst strike I ever called was the one against you in that All-Star game in 1947." He said, "But you didn't complain. I always chalked you up for that one. The fact is, I didn't see the ball."

I would say that most big league umpires are capable of calling a ball within an inch of where it is. I felt that as a hitter I could see it within a half inch. I know I could. A lot of times I'd take a third strike and McGowan or Ed Runge or somebody would ask me, "Did you think that was a strike?" And I'd always tell him the truth. "Yeah, but I was fooled by the pitch." Or I might say, "I just couldn't unload." I never lied to them.

On the other hand, if I had a point to make, I made it. Bill Summers was a great umpire. He was like Cal Hubbard. He took complete charge of the game. One day he called me out twice on low pitches. All I said at the time was, "Hell, Bill, those aren't strikes." But the next day we were in the dugout before the game and I stood up against the wall, flat, so my knees wouldn't protrude, and I said, "Bill, touch where you think my knees are." He said, "OK, they're right here . . . uh," and he hit my leg four inches below the knee.

Well, I got to be so finicky about the strike zone the pitchers were always yelling, "Yah, yah, Williams gets four strikes," which is what they said about Cobb, Ruth, Gehrig, Foxx and about every other good hitter. It wasn't true, but I'll tell you what happened one time. Bob Lemon was pitching for Cleveland, about 1951. I have to rate Lemon as one of the very best pitchers I ever faced. His ball was always moving, hard, sinking, fast-breaking. You could never really *uhmmmph* with Lemon.

This year, however, he was having a bit of a tough time getting started. He was probably 8 and 8 or something. And on the day I'm talking about he got the count 2 and 2 on me, and gee, he zings one right down the middle. Fooled me. I damn near threw the bat away, when, ". . . *ball three!*" And I just held on to it. Lemon was absolutely flabbergasted. He looked, and he could hardly stand it. He jammed his glove in his pocket, pulled down his hat and came on in to home plate and started chewing the umpire. Jim Hegan, the catcher, was chewing him out too. "For crying out loud, where do you think that pitch was?" "Yah, yah, you're blind, for Chrissake. What are you helping *him* for"—pointing to me—"he don't need any help, the bastard's hitting .370. *I'm* the one that needs the help." By now I can't help laughing, and Lemon turns on me and says, "What the hell are you laughing at, Williams? The ball was right there. You should have creamed it." Finally he stormed back to the mound and uncorked a hell of a pitch and struck me out.

They used to write a lot of bull about my eyesight, how I could umpire standing sideways better than the umpire could standing behind the plate. How I could read license numbers on cars before another guy could see the license, and could see ducks coming in and tell what they were and how many before anybody else could even see them. Or how I could read the label on a phonograph record while it was going around the turntable. All this exaggeration was supposed to explain my taking close pitches.

What made it worse was that when I took my physical with the Navy in 1942 they announced my eyesight as 20–10, and the intern said, "This guy's got terrific eyesight." He gave the writers something to elaborate on. When they wrote about my hitting they'd bring up this "superhuman" eyesight, and dig up stories about how as a kid I used to hold one hand over one eye to exercise the other. This was supposed to prove I had become a good hitter by developing this terrific eyesight.

Well, at this late date they probably won't believe the truth. When I was a kid somebody gave us some hazelnuts for Christmas. You couldn't open the damn things because they were so hard—big, tough nuts, like lumps of steel—and inside they were gritty and you'd have to dig to get the little pieces of meat out. It wasn't worth the trouble. My brother Danny and I took the nuts into the back yard and started throwing them around, hitting them with a broomstick. Darn if he doesn't hit one right back at me and into my right eye. I knew it did some damage, because a lot of times after that when we'd get up early to make a game trip to Long Beach or someplace I could barely see out of the eye. Usually it cleared up in a couple hours, but at times it would bother me all day.

As a teenager in school I was always checking it, holding a hand over the other eye to see if the bad one was going to be OK that day. I never had any work done on it or anything, never had it checked, never wore glasses, but a lot of times during my professional career I couldn't see well.

To this day when I overexert and get tired I have a hell of a time reading or seeing anything critical.

Sure, I think I had good eyesight, maybe exceptional eyesight, but not *superhuman* eyesight. A lot of people have 20–10 vision. The reason I saw things was that I was so intense. I saw ducks coming in because I was *intent* on seeing them, I was looking all the time, I was alert for them. And I trained myself from a sandlotter to know that strike zone so I wouldn't be swinging at bad pitches. If as a batter I made a good umpire, it was discipline, not super eyesight.

I'll tell you one more story about umpires, because it was one of the funniest things that ever happened to me. When I tell it, it always seems like a drawn-out presentation, but I read *The Old Man and the Sea* and that was sure drawn out, so I don't feel bad about telling it.

We were playing the White Sox about 1946 and as I said they were a real rhubarb team, what with Dykes, who I love, a real fiery guy, a great agitator—you could hear that foghorn voice all over the park—and Mule Haas and Edgar Smith and Lyons. Dykes would give you a blast and then he'd say, "*You hear me?*" and you could hear him for five blocks. He lost his voice later on, just wore it out, and I'd go up to him and lean real close and whisper, "I can't hear you, Jimmy."

Joe Haynes was pitching that day, and he was always tough for me. His ball was sailing all the time, sailing in, right under your chin, but that was calculated, because Haynes had pinpoint control. You had to be alert with Haynes. He was always trying to hit you in the elbow.

Anyway, in the first inning I hit a double for two runs. Now remember, Haynes can put the ball right where he wants it. Red Jones is the umpire. Next time I get up, *wheesshh*, right behind my ear, down I go. This is 1946 now, and everybody is back from the service, gung-ho, big crowds, bigger salaries, everything is tight, and the league has issued warnings about beanball contests, because there'd been a lot of them. The next pitch comes in and, *zoop*, down I go again.

Red Jones was the kind of umpire who took control of a game. He goes right out to Haynes and Haynes comes in. They're standing there yelling and out comes Dykes and there's a big rhubarb, but Red Jones warns 'em: Throw one more like that and out you go. So on the next pitch I hit one right by Haynes's ear, base hit to center field.

Now it's my third time up, Haynes still pitching. Standing in the box, I'm facing the White Sox dugout, over there. Except this time Haynes is trying to hit the outside corner, and it's just outside, and from over there it looks like it's right down the middle. Jones says "Ball one!"

Nobody kicked except the White Sox bench, and they raised hell. "You S.O.B.! Give him everything he wants, yah, yah." Next pitch, out there again, ball two. "You homing no good blind bastard!"

Jones stops the game right there and goes over to the bench, with Dykes and all of them yelling at him. He says, "You guys keep it up and I'm clearing the bench. Just keep it up." And cripes, here comes another one a hair outside, misses again. "Ball three." Boy, you never heard such screaming and yelling, and Red Jones goes right over and orders the bench cleared. Everybody out but the nine on the field.

We're standing at home plate, and the condemned have got to pass by to get to the tunnel through the Red Sox dugout. It was the only route to the clubhouse. The first guy gets to Jones and he says, "You homer, you get away from home and you're horsemeat," and off he went. Next guy says, "For crying out loud, you give the guy everything in the world and he's hitting .360. Don't give the *pitcher* a break." And off he went. And Dykes chewed him out, and Haas chewed him out and so on down the line.

After about twelve guys had passed, along comes Wally Moses. Now, Wally Moses was a nice quiet little guy, never raised his voice at anybody. He was traded to our club afterward and everybody liked Wally. When he got to Jones, he stopped and said very seriously, "Red, I've been in the big leagues eleven years. This is my eleventh year in the big leagues. I've never been thrown out of a game in my life. Honest to Pete, I never said a *word* to you on the bench. I was way over in the corner. I never said a word."

And old Red Jones, I'll never forget him. He said, "Wally, I want to tell you. It's like this. It's just like a raid on a whorehouse. The good go with the bad."

Joe DiMaggio won the Most Valuable Player award in 1941, despite my .406, but I sure wouldn't knock that. Di-Maggio was a great player, and he hit in those fifty-six straight games and the Yankees won the pennant. The Red Sox were second. The next year, 1942, I felt I should have been given a little more consideration because I won the triple crown—.356 average, 137 RBI's, 36 home runs—but Joe Gordon got it. Gordon had his greatest year and the Yankees won the pennant again. And we were second again. The voting tends to go to the team that wins, which is right. But I have to think the reason I didn't get more consideration was because of the trouble I had with the draft.

War was imminent. I had gone to my draft board right after the season, about November of '41, and told them everything about me, how much money I had in the bank, how much I sent my mother every month, *every*thing. I was put in III-A, which meant I had a dependent. I went on up to Minnesota to fish and see my girl, up where they had had that terrible blizzard, when scores of duck hunters were marooned on the lakes and froze to death.

On December 7, I'd just come back that morning from hunting ducks to this little hotel in Princeton, Minnesota, and was eating breakfast in the kitchen when it came over the radio that the Japanese had bombed Pearl Harbor. Frankly, none of this war talk had meant a damn to me up to then. I had read where some admiral had said if the Japanese got too frisky we could take them in six months, so I'd pretty much dismissed them as a threat. Hitler had been giving Europe fits, and things were looking bad all over, but it hadn't sunk in on me yet. All I was interested in was playing ball, hitting the baseball, being able to hunt, making some money.

I look back now, reading about World War II, and I say to myself, Gee, those Germans were sure raising hell, but at the time I was so wrapped up in my own problems I just couldn't get too concerned.

In January I got a notice I could be called at any time. I had been reclassified as I-A. A friend of mine suggested I go see the adviser to the governor's Selective Service Appeal Agent, an attorney, because I was the sole support of my mother. She worked for the Salvation Army, but she didn't get anything, and she and my father were divorced. So I told this man my story, as honestly as I could—I've never been a liar, never could lie very well—and he said, "You're right, you should still be three-A."

He took it to the Appeals Board, but they voted me down. This really got the attorney mad, and he said he was going to go to the Presidential Board, to General Hershey. Well, I had nobody to advise me, no father, no mother there to tell me anything, no real personal big league friends to go to and say, "Tell me what to do," so I just let him take charge, and about ten days later I got word I was back in III-A—I was deferred by the Presidential Board. I thought, Well, this is the top of the heap, I'm going to be all right.

In the meantime, I got my 1942 contract, and boy, I remember I put it in my wardrobe trunk. $30,000. The end of the rainbow. But now some awful things are being written about me, mean things about my draft situation. The Japs are really running wild, and patriotism has invaded the pressbox. Bill Corum takes out after me, and Paul Gallico.

They're writing, "Williams ought to get in the service. He doesn't have to hide behind anybody. He can get in." And "Ted Williams isn't going to spring training, is he?" And yow, yow, yow. There are a million ballplayers in III-A—Gordon played baseball that year, DiMaggio played, Musial played—but Ted Williams is the guy having trouble with the draft board. I remember I had a contract to endorse Quaker Oats, a $4,000 contract. I used to eat them all the time. But they canceled out on me because of all this unfair stuff and I haven't eaten a Quaker Oat since.

Well, Joe Cronin writes and tells me I ought to go see Mickey Cochrane at the Great Lakes Naval Training Center. Cochrane, the great old Tiger catcher, had joined up and was running their athletic program, and by now it's quite obvious we aren't going to win the war in six months. Cochrane had a new car, a Lincoln Continental with push-button doors, and he drove me around the Great Lakes center. There were 10,000 guys there, and Cochrane's all decked out in his Navy uniform, buttons shining like mad, and he gave me the big pitch. I met a few of the guys, and I'm weakening. I'm about to enlist right now.

Then he says, "Gee, it's going to be awful tough to play

ball. You try to play ball this summer, they'll boo you out of every park in the big leagues."

Boy, I saw fire. I said to myself, I don't give a damn who they boo or what they do. I've heard plenty of boos. I'm going to play ball if I can.

Then Mr. Yawkey got into the act. He said he didn't think it would be smart for me to come to spring training. That was the *first* mistake the Red Sox made with me. I made up my mind that I was going to go anyway. All I could think about was that big contract, and the very fact I was entitled to be III-A, and now for the first time in my life I would be able to get my mother out of hock a little bit and fix up that house. My mother and father had divorced by this time and I was bitter about that. Divorce was the last thing I would have considered. Now, looking back, I can see how it was the best for both of them, but then it just tore me up.

Well, it turned out a lot better than I thought it would. Will Harridge, the president of the American League, called me and told me to keep my chin up, that I wouldn't have been deferred in the first place if I wasn't in the right. I heard a few remarks in the spring, not from other players, from some smart-alec fans, and I got a letter one day that was nothing but a blank piece of yellow paper, and that burned me up, but by the time the season started it was mostly over. I let a couple of the wolves in left field get under my skin one day and sulked around the base paths enough for Cronin to fine me $250. I said I was going to take ten pounds of raw hamburger out there to throw to them, but that was just talk. Near the end of the season I signed up for naval aviation, which took the heat off completely. In November I got called, and five of us, Johnny Sain and Buddy Gremp of the Braves, Joe Coleman of the

Athletics, Johnny Pesky and myself, went to Amherst College for preliminary ground school—navigation, aerodynamics, math, aeronautics, all basic stuff. I wasn't exactly overconfident about getting through, not having gone beyond Herbert Hoover High, but I had no trouble fitting in and I made up my mind I was going to give it my best.

It was cold at Amherst, there was snow on the ground. I came up with a hernia one day when we were all trying to see how many chin-ups and push-ups we could do and how fast we could swim. That meant two months in the sack at Chelsea Naval Hospital before rejoining the group at preflight training at Chapel Hill, North Carolina. I'll never forget getting off the train at Chapel Hill, just at dusk, and marching up in front of the administration building with the other recruits. The cadets already there were hanging out the windows watching us, and as we passed, one guy hollered, "OK, Williams, we know you're there, and *you're going to be sor-ry.*"

I never was sorry. All of it was absolutely different from anything I'd ever been through, and even the hairiest times were interesting. I damn near killed myself in Amherst. Two of us were flying Cubs and I didn't see some power lines across a river—we were flying upriver—and I just barely cleared at the last second.

We went on to Kokomo, Indiana, for basic flight training, and the day we got there it looked like a flying circus. The air was black with planes. We'd been told, "Always stay 1,000 feet away from any other airplane and 1,000 feet above the terrain, and make nice easy 45-degree turns." But here we see about 150 planes in the air, all flying around each other, maybe 200 feet apart. There is a big round mat that everybody's landing on. It looked like flies on a garbage can.

I said to Johnny Pesky, "What the hell's going on?"

My dad held me for my first picture. He was only an occasional pipe smoker, something I never tried. My mother cut my hair in the style of the day—the Buster Brown—and I hated it. Evidently my brother Danny didn't go for it either, by the look on his face *(below, right)*. My mother's uniform and lifetime work was Salvation Army.

San Diego was a ballplayer's town, year-round, and by the time I was a pitcher at Herbert Hoover High (*above, opposite*) I was hooked. I signed my first professional contract with the San Diego Padres at age 17 (*above*) and discovered the joys of paychecks and train rides. On our first trip north, I was the kid of the group, the guy with the lapels flapping (*far left, opposite*). George Myatt, at the top of the train steps, is still in baseball, but the others are dead or gone to other things. Jimmy Kerr, standing below Myatt, is a fireman now in Baltimore. I used to think I wanted to be a fireman.

The greats of the game were a thrill to be around for a kid who wanted to be one himself. In the spring of 1940, the Boston-Yankee lineups at Sarasota, Fla., included *(above)* Joe DiMaggio, Jimmy Foxx, T. Williams and Bill Dickey, a pretty fair bunch of hitters. I weighed 178 pounds when I met Babe Ruth *(below, left)*. My manager in Boston then was Joe Cronin. We could sit and talk hitting *(below, right)* for hours.

In 1941, Hugh Duffy (*left, above*) gave me a target: his all-time-record .438 batting average. Duffy was then a coach for the Red Sox. I didn't really threaten his record, but I hit .406, and had my biggest single thrill in baseball: the home run that won the All-Star game (*below*). Joe Gordon of the Yankees has my hand as I cross home plate. Joe DiMaggio (No. 5) scored ahead of me. No. 30 is Merv Shea, a Detroit coach.

No kid ballplayer ever had as much attention from the fans as I did in Boston those first few years. As temperamental as I was, they made me their darling.

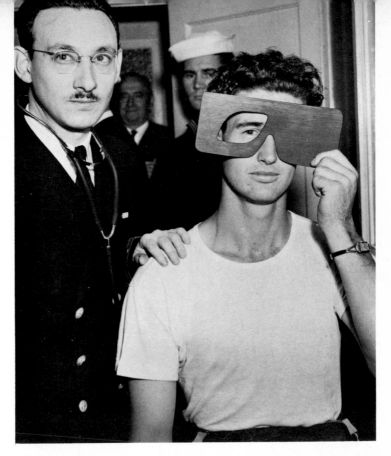

The Navy doctor who checked my eyes in 1942 *(above)* said I had 20-10 vision. From then on the writers always gave my eyes more credit than they deserved for the hitting I did. In May of 1942, I was sworn in *(below)* as a Naval Aviation cadet.

Ballplayers trying to become pilots at Amherst, Mass., in 1942 included, from left, Joe Coleman, Johnny Sain, me, Johnny Pesky and Buddy Gremp.

Lou Boudreau (*above, right*) was a great player and a clever manager. I liked him despite the "Boudreau Shift" he devised against me in 1946, my first year back from the service and the year the Red Sox (*below*) won the pennant. We had an outstanding lineup: (*from left*) Wally Moses, Johnny Pesky, T. Williams, Bobby Doerr, Rudy York, Joe Cronin, Dom DiMaggio, Pinky Higgins, Hal Wagner, Mickey Harris, Dave (Boo) Ferriss.

The Boudreau Shift *(below)* and others like it, with the defense loaded to the right, frustrated me to the point that I even bunted *(above)* for a hit during the 1946 World Series with St. Louis. The Cardinal catcher is Joe Garagiola.

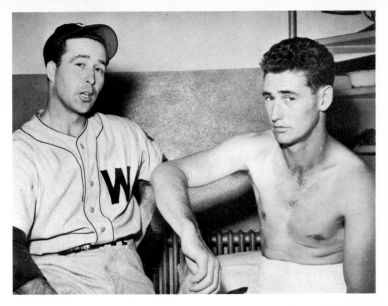

I went into the Series in the grip of a slump that was not relieved any by being hit in the elbow with a pitch from Mickey Haefner *(left, above)* in a pre-Series exhibition game. Whirlpool treatment *(below)* helped get the elbow down to size, but I never felt swishy at the plate. I was awful.

Back home in San Diego (*above*) in 1946, and giving a bat the once-over. (*Below*) I tried not to miss too many chances to set the writers straight, but they weren't all bad. Arthur Sampson, on my left here, was a dear friend.

After a game, win or lose, there were always a lot of questions *(above)* from writers doing their job, and from some doing more. I used to hang around long after the other players had gone, weighing my bats *(below)*, checking my equipment, not wanting to leave.

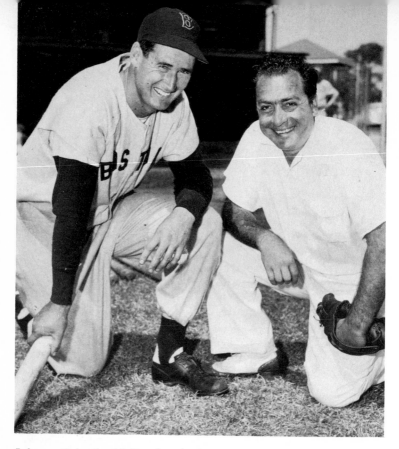

Johnny Orlando (*right, above*), the Red Sox equipment manager, nicknamed me "The Kid" my first year up. We have been close ever since. The manager who stood out most in my experience was Joe McCarthy (*below*), who once said he would play for nothing if he could hit like me.

I told Eddie Collins *(left, above)* he was the man who "came West to bring me East" when he signed me for the Red Sox, "and I hope you don't regret it." I loved Eddie Collins. Neckties I did not love. I considered them a detriment to comfort. In 1950, I broke my elbow in the All-Star game and was hospitalized *(below)*. It was my biggest disappointment. I never hit as well again.

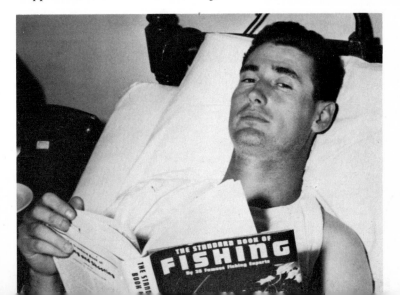

I thought when I hung up my uniform *(above)* to go to Korea in 1952 that I was through as a baseball player, but I had a lot to live for—foremost being my daughter, Bobby Jo.

They were all coming in at the end of their flying period. They'd gone out separately but they were coming in together. Awful.

Flying came easy for me. But poor Pesky. He was a great little athlete. A boxer, wrestler, basketball player, he could run like hell and he was a tiger on the obstacle courses. But he couldn't swim a stroke, he'd go right down, and he flew an airplane like he had stone arms. One time at Amherst, on a real windy day, we were flying Cubs. If you hold a Cub too tight, the wind blows you off the runway. You have to crab, or you have to slip.

Poor John lines up the runway, comes in and, *whoosh*, the wind blows him away. Around he goes. He tries again and the wind takes him again. He made eight approaches that day. It looked like they were going to have to shoot him down.

They finally got Pesky out of there. In an airplane he was a menace to himself and everybody else, but he was certainly officer material so they moved him into O.C.S. and he actually got his rank before I did. I suppose everybody runs into a problem or two learning to fly. My first time in a variable-pitch prop, a Navy SNV, I came close to putting plane, instructor and myself in the ditch. The operating theory of the variable prop is simple enough: At low pitch (less angle to your prop blade), you don't bite as much air but you can get more revolutions per minute. At takeoff, that's what you want, more horsepower on your engine. To get going you want to do more work faster.

Now, once you're in the air, your engine need not work so hard, you want to save fuel, so you put the prop in high pitch, which gives you a bigger bite of the air. You get fewer r.p.m.'s, but you're maintaining speed and your engine doesn't have to work as hard—good performance with less fuel consumption. For some reason, this point eluded me. I thought, Low pitch, low r.p.m.'s; high pitch for take-off. Exactly opposite to what was right.

I was at the chocks for my first check-down flight in the SNV, still without that point clear in my mind, and without realizing what could happen. I was at the chocks and I put my prop in low pitch, which was right, and my flaps down, full rich mixture, and so forth, and I started down the mat for the takeoff. Suddenly the thought struck me: You've still got to do something with that prop, and I jammed it back into high pitch. While I was at it, I cranked the flaps up, which was wrong too. We would never have made it off the mat. We'd have gone right into the boon-docks, no doubt about it. But the instructor was in the back seat and he broke his watch scrambling to get the flaps down and the prop back in low pitch.

He didn't say anything, but when I got to 1,000 feet I sensed something had been wrong. At 1,000 feet, you are supposed to switch your gas tanks from reserve to left or right main, bring up your flaps and put your props from low to high pitch. When I started checking out, I knew I'd made a mistake of some kind, but I went on through the period and when we got back the instructor said, "Well, you did pretty good, but do you realize what you did on takeoff?" I still wasn't sure, so he told me. "I'll have to give you a down." A down was an unacceptable flight. It was my first down, and the only one I ever got.

We had put in a hundred hours of flight time at Kokomo when we moved on to advanced training at Pensacola, Flor-ida, and gee, I was in great shape. Maybe the best shape of my life. I weighed 178 pounds. I felt I could run like a deer. I know I ran the half mile better than sixty cadets one day. We had a baseball team at Pensacola, Ben Chap-man was there and he played, and Bob Kennedy and some others, but I didn't have my heart in it at all and I played lousy. By this time I was more interested in flying, it was going to be my job for the duration, and I was also enjoying the pleasures of Florida's fishing for the first time.

Things had slowed down at Pensacola. There were more cadets than there were planes and the program dragged. With time to spare I started fishing around. I had read an article in *Field and Stream*, by Ray Pete Holland, that said a ten-pound Florida snook tied tail-to-tail with a twenty-pound muskie would drag the muskie all over the lake. I'd fished for muskie in Minnesota and I thought, Boy, I sure want to catch one of those snook. A buddy and I saved our gas ration stamps and went down to Everglades City to fish the canals there, and on my second or third cast I got hold of a fifteen-pound snook. It took off like nothing I had ever had on fresh-water equipment. It was everything Pete Ray Holland said it was.

The two of us went wild catching snook. Late the second afternoon we stopped by a fish house on the Tamiami Trail and told the guy we had caught a mess of snook, and he said, "Bring 'em on in, I'll buy 'em off you."

"How much do you pay?"

"Eleven cents a pound."

We weighed out 110 pounds, which is quite a haul of snook. It was the first and only time I ever sold a fish. I made up my mind right there that after the war I was going to come down a week early before spring training just to fish the Florida waters. As it turned out, a week wasn't enough. I stretched it to two weeks, then a month, and before I knew it I was a Florida resident.

I became an instructor at Pensacola, flying Navy SNJ's. They gave me the choice and I took it because it would mean extra flight training and I figured I would need all I could get if we were going into combat. In May, the day I was made a second lieutenant, Doris Soule and I got mar-

115

ried at the base in Pensacola. Doris had moved to Boston after that first year and took a job in a beauty parlor and had stuck with me all during my troubles with the draft board. We would have been married before, but when I signed for naval aviation one of the rules was "No married students." Right after that I got my orders to go to Jacksonville for operational training—combat training.

At Jacksonville I set the student gunnery record, which seemed pretty important to me then because our instructor had flown in the Pacific, had shot down a Japanese Zero, and he said if he could have shot better he would have bagged eight or ten. "Hell," he said, "I just couldn't shoot."

We were flying hard, now, and the orders soon came through for the Pacific. I was in San Francisco waiting for a boat when the war ended. If you had your orders, though, they were carried through—if you were scheduled to go to Siberia, you went to Siberia. They just didn't put a stop to things. I was in Honolulu when they finally froze me.

Pesky was already there, playing ball, and a young kid pitcher everybody was talking about named Bob Lemon. Since we were stuck there anyway, we all got on ball teams, and I remember I met Dick Wakefield in Honolulu. He had set the league on fire for Detroit in 1943 and 1944, and they'd finally called him up in 1945. If you ever met Dick Wakefield, you met a wonderful guy. One night at dinner we got to needling each other about what we were going to do in the 1946 season, and I was getting to him pretty good.

I said, "Gee, Dick, they tell me you're a banjo hitter. They say you hit a lot of cheap home runs." One word led to another and before the night was over we had made five separate bets for 1946, each one a thousand bucks: who will lead in home runs, RBI's, salary, and so forth.

You know that's going to make the papers, the first word

116

from Teddy Ballgame since 1942, and sure enough, Happy Chandler, the commissioner, sends us each a personal telegram, canceling the bet. He had to do it, of course. I always thought Chandler was an excellent commissioner, a lot better than people gave him credit for. He was closer to the players, more intimate than any commissioner in my experience.

If you know anything about me, you know that 1946 was the only year I played in a World Series, and that it ended in a frustration that grew, like the importance of the .400 season, to a terrible dimension as the years passed. Who was to know at that time I would not get another chance? The first World Series Ty Cobb played in he batted .200, but he got two more chances. The first World Series Stan Musial played in he batted .222, but he got three more chances. Babe Ruth hit .118 in the 1922 Series, but he played in six others. This was it for me.

Until 1946 we had made a business of finishing directly behind the Yankees. My first year, 1939, we were fifteen games behind as they won the pennant. The next year they finished third, but we were fourth. In 1941 we were second again, and they were seventeen games ahead of us. In 1942, my last season before the service, we won 93 games, but the Yankees won 103. No excuses. They were flat out better than we were.

But in 1946 we had a wonderful team. Everybody was back from the service—Pesky, Bobby Doerr, Dom DiMaggio, Mike Higgins. We had traded for Rudy York of the Tigers, and we picked up Wally Moses from the White Sox. The pitching was great—Tex Hughson, Boo Ferriss, Mickey Harris, Joe Dobson—and we got off to such a fantastic start that after two months we practically had the pennant clinched. I remember I was wearing out Cleveland pitchers that year, and in the first game of a doubleheader with the Indians in June I hit three home runs, the first with the bases loaded when we were behind 5–0, the second with two on to tie the game, the third in the last of the ninth to win it, 11–10.

Lou Boudreau, managing and playing shortstop for Cleveland, had a home run and four doubles in that game, his greatest day, and I suppose the futility of it must have hit him, because in the second game he came up with his shift. Boudreau had it figured: "I can't stop this guy from hitting home runs, but practically all his base hits are going to the right side of the diamond. Probably 85 to 90 per cent. I can sure cut into his doubles and singles." He had nothing to lose. Cleveland was in sixth place.

When I came up for the second time in the second game, the Indians started moving around, swinging to the right. The third baseman, Kenny Keltner, moved behind the bag at second; the shortstop, Boudreau, moved to the right of second base; the center fielder, Pat Seerey, moved into the right fielder's position; the right fielder moved to the line; the second baseman moved closer to first and back on the grass in short right; the first baseman moved to the line behind first. The only man remaining to cover the entire area left of second base was the left fielder, George Case, and he was about thirty feet behind the skin of the infield.

Gee, I had to laugh when I saw it. What the hell's going on? This was my second time up in the second game. I had doubled to clear the bases in the first inning, giving me eleven runs batted in for the day. (You can't use a shift that radical with men on base.) In effect, they are now telling me, "Go ahead, hit to left field, have yourself a single. We'll sacrifice singles to take away your doubles and home runs any day." They're tickled to death if I go to left because the only thing they're really afraid of is the long ball.

But even the Cleveland pitchers hadn't caught on to what

the shift could do, because they still pitched me extra care-ful, nothing inside that I could pull into the teeth of that stacked defense. Against the shift that day I walked twice and grounded to second base. You could hardly say it hurt me right off. As the season went on, the Cleveland pitchers were still being coy. I hit nine home runs and batted .400 against the Indians that year.

There is no doubt, however, that the shift hurt me later on. By the next year everybody had one kind of shift or another. We played an exhibition game in Dallas and my first time up the entire Dallas team, everybody but the pitcher and catcher, went out and sat in the right-field bleachers as a joke. None of the legitimate shifts went that far, of course, but some were more radical than others, and by then it was beginning to upset me. The shift was taking away base hits, I knew that, but the sad part was that on those occasions when I *had* to go for the long ball, say in the eighth or ninth inning, and really put the wood to it without getting it quite high enough to go out of the park, boom, they stopped me. You have to get good pitches to hit home runs, and I wasn't getting them very often. Some teams didn't even go into the shift until the late innings. On June 2, 1947, I was batting only .277. Al Simmons, still predicting doom for me, came out and said, "Well, that's the end of Williams—he can't hit to left field." And others were saying, "Williams can't beat the shift."

If you get down to tight mathematics, knowing I was a pull hitter, knowing I averaged 85 per cent of my hits to the right of center field, knowing I was counted on in Bos-ton for the big hit, the home run, and often couldn't afford to settle for the easy punch single to left, you have to think it took points off my lifetime average of .344. But how much? I won the league batting championship four times against the shift after that, and I missed it by two-tenths of a percentage point another time and once I lost it for not being up enough times officially. Under present rules, with bases on balls, I would have had that other championship.

But the story you read was: "Williams is too proud, he's too stubborn. Williams isn't trying to beat it." The hell I wasn't. I was just having a hard time hitting to left field. Every spring after that I'd experiment, shifting my feet, trying to drop balls into left field, blunking them into short center, seeing what could be done. But I was having a hard time. Ty Cobb, who used to give me a blast every now and then for not swinging at close pitches (pitches near the strike zone but not in it), wrote me a two-page letter outlining how *he* would beat the shift.

At the 1947 World Series in New York I met Cobb outside the stadium restaurant, and we went around behind the telephone booths to talk. He said, "Boy, Ted, if they ever pulled that drastic shift on me—" and he laughed and kind of shuddered, seeing with his mind's eye the immortal Ty Cobb ripping line drives into those wide-open spaces in left field. Well, Cobb was a great athlete, in my estimate the greatest of all time, but he was an entirely different breed of cat. He was a push hitter. He choked up on the bat, two inches from the bottom, his hands four inches apart. He stood close to the plate, his hands forward. At bat he had the exact posture of the punch hitter that he was. When he talked hitting, he talked Greek to me.

He used to say your stride depended on where the ball was pitched, and I *know* you can't do that—stride where the ball is—because you don't have time. On the average you've got less than two-thirds of a second from the time the ball leaves the pitcher's hand, and if you don't know what it is, where it's breaking, until the last twenty feet, you've got less than a quarter of a second. You *have* to anticipate, and you sure can't wait to make your stride then, because your lead foot has to be planted solid for your swing to be right.

Cobb was up high with his stance, slashing at the ball, pushing at it; I was down, with a longer stroke. The arc of my swing was much greater than Cobb's. I was anything but a push hitter. In those days I really pulled the ball because I was strong and at the top of my game. Mickey Vernon used to say he hated to play first base when I was hitting, because I hit the ball so hard.

But I listened to Cobb because I was ready to listen to anybody who might help me beat that shift. Paul Waner tried to help me, and from him I got the germ of the answer. "Gee, it's easy," he said the following spring. "Just move away from the plate and chop down on the ball."

It was easy all right, but it wasn't chopping down on the ball that made the difference. It was moving away from the plate. My normal stance was so close that, since they were pitching me tight to *force* me to pull into all that congestion in right field, I could do little else. All I had to do was stand a bit farther away from the plate, so that I would have room and time to *push* the ball a little more. Waner said swing *down* on the ball, but as long as I was snug up to the plate like that I couldn't swing down on those inside pitches. I know this. I beat that damn shift a lot more than people realize. There's no doubt, though, that it was a smart move on Boudreau's part, if mainly a psychological one. If it were necessary I'd have a shift for Frank Robinson right now, or Harmon Killebrew. Certainly Killebrew.

Well, a real funny thing happened. We went into this slump in 1946, after getting off so fast, and we were having a hell of a time clinching the pennant. At one point we lost six in a row, and though we had led the second-place Tigers by as much as sixteen games in September, we couldn't seem to finish them off. The Red Sox traveling secretary, Tom Dowd, kept a supply of champagne on the train for two weeks, waiting for the celebration. We stopped hitting, we stopped winning.

And then Tex Hughson shut out the Indians on Friday, September 13, in Cleveland, and against the shift I sliced a ball over Pat Seerey's head in left center field. The ball rolled all the way to the wall, and I made it all the way around, sliding into the plate like a rookie, the only inside-the-park home run I ever hit. Someone said, "Is that the easiest homer you ever got?" And I said, "Hell no, it was the hardest. I had to run." We won, 1-0. We had our pennant. On a home run to left field.

We had such a big lead it was just a matter of time, anyway. And the truth is I didn't know we'd been carrying around that champagne, I wasn't much to keep up with the gossip. I was always in the shower, out, bang, gone when the game was over. I was all excited then about tying flies for my fall fishing. I had a good friend in Cleveland, Bill Whyte, who was teaching me how to tie flies. Every night after the game I'd go up to Bill's little bitty shop over the firehouse, a block from the hotel, and we'd tie flies. I couldn't wait to get there, so I never knew about the party. Well, Dave Egan, The Colonel, didn't hesitate to set me straight in the eyes of the world: "Ted Williams," he wrote, "is not a team man, he is utterly lacking in anything that even bears remote resemblance to team spirit." I have to think Jim Thorpe would have slugged him.

Now comes the series with the Cardinals, and for me it was ill-fated from the start. They were all gassed up after a tight race. They even had to play the Dodgers in a play-off to break a tie. We had won the pennant by twelve games, and for the last month we just fiddled around. It had been the kind of season that positively breeds overconfidence. We never lost the lead after the second day. At one point we won fifteen games in a row. As a team, as an *entire team,* we hit over .300. The first game of the year, my first since before the war, I hit a 400-foot home run in Washington and was off to such a great start that everybody was convinced I would win the triple crown. Halfway through the season I was hitting .365, I had 27 home runs, 91 runs batted in. I was at peace with the world. I was even ghostwriting a daily column for the Boston *Globe.* Fancy that.

The All-Star game that year was played at Fenway Park, full house, big cheering crowd, and nothing happened to disturb our confidence. The American League beat the National League, 12–0. Bob Feller, Hal Newhouser and Jack Kramer shut them out on three hits. We got fourteen. Claude Passeau walked me in the first inning—I'm sure we were both thinking about that All-Star game in 1941—and in the fourth I hit a home run off Kirby Higbe, then singled in a run in the fifth, singled again in the seventh, and finally hit a three-run home run off Rip Sewell in the eighth.

Everybody got a charge out of the last one because Sewell threw me his blooper pitch. His "eephus ball," they called it. How he controlled it is anybody's guess, because it came to the plate like a pop fly. It had a twenty-foot-high arc. I remember watching him warm up, standing in the dugout with Bill Dickey, and saying to Dickey, "Gee, I don't think you could ever generate enough power to hit that pitch out of the park." Nobody ever had. Dickey said the way to do it was to advance a step or two as it came toward you. Kind of run at it. That's about what I did, and I hit it into the bullpen in right field.

I probably hit .250 the last month. I tailed off so badly I lost my lead in everything: Mickey Vernon won the batting championship; Hank Greenberg, having his last great season, finished strong to win in home runs and runs batted in. I did lead the league in runs scored and slugging and bases on balls, and when the season was over I was voted the Most Valuable Player for the first time, which surprised hell out of me because I didn't think I would ever get it.

But everything seemed to sour that last month. Elmer Valo made some tremendous catches of balls I hit to right field in Philadelphia and Boston. On the last one he leaped onto the wall at Fenway Park, one-handed the ball, and hurt his back so badly coming down he had to be carried off the field. That seemed to put the cap on my frustration and the next time up I got booed for half-swinging at a pitch and then not running out the little grounder I hit. When I caught the ball that ended the game I threw it *and* my glove high in the air. A childish stunt, but I was disgusted.

It wasn't only me. The whole team lost its zip, one of those miserable, endless things. When you get off to the kind of start we did, you're not expected to have slumps.

So with the Cardinals in the playoff and time on our hands the American League decided to have a practice game to sharpen us up, the Red Sox against a group of league all-stars. We played the game in Boston. It was thirty degrees. There were about 2,000 people in the stands, in overcoats. The weather was awful. Little Mickey Haefner, a left-hander from Washington, was pitching and in the first inning he threw me a little sidearm curve ball. I saw it coming, and I kind of held up waiting for it to break. It hit me right on the tip of my right elbow. Shoosh, the elbow went up like a balloon. It turned blue. The World Series was to begin three days later, but I couldn't take batting practice for two days.

While we were on the train to St. Louis before the first game, Egan came up with another big scoop. I was going to be traded for Hal Newhouser of Detroit when the Series was over. There was never any foundation to the story whatsoever, but there it was in the papers, and how do you think *that* made me feel. I have always said I could hit well in Detroit, that if there was one park in baseball I thought I would have had a chance to break Ruth's record in it was Tiger Stadium, because I saw the ball so well there, but what a time to start a crazy rumor like that.

Then a week later Egan had me going to the Yankees for DiMaggio. There apparently was a germ of truth to that report, but of course it never materialized. I know New York was one town I did *not* want to play in. I didn't like Yankee Stadium. A bad background in center field when the crowd is big, and all that smoke hanging in there. It's not a conventional park. As an outfielder, you had to get used to it. I remember when Gehrig hit the first ball ever hit to me in Yankee Stadium, my rookie year. He didn't really rip it, just a mediocre line drive, and I staggered around and staggered around and finally caught it right where I had started. I always felt jacked up in Yankee Stadium because of the crowds, but I never wanted to play there.

Well, we got to St. Louis, big favorites to win the Series, and I took my first batting practice and the elbow didn't feel too bad. I can't use that as an excuse and I won't, but I remember wishing we'd never had that lousy game in Massachusetts. The Cardinals had a fine pitching staff: Howie Pollet, Red Munger, Murray Dickson, Alpha Brazle, and a lean-faced little left-hander named Harry Brecheen. We had seen a couple of them in the spring, but none had been in the All-Star game and they were still new to us. Pollet, another left-hander, had won twenty-one games. Nice to look at, good control, moved the ball around like Warren Spahn. He started the series against Tex Hughson, who had won twenty.

Eddie Dyer was the Cardinal manager and he had been quoted before the game as saying he planned no changes for me, but when I got up to lead off the second inning the Cardinals started moving around. They were going into a shift, all right, but they were waiting until the last second to show it, I suppose to give me a little psychological jolt. I can't say I was surprised. By this time shifts were nothing new to me.

Dyer's shift was a little different from Boudreau's. He let Marty Marion stay at shortstop and moved his third baseman, Whitey Kurowski, around behind second and just shaded everybody else to the right. In other words, he left *two* men, the left fielder and the shortstop, on the left side of second base instead of just one. Sometimes it was Kurowski instead of Marion, depending on the situation with men on base.

Pollet and the rest of the Cardinal pitchers crowded me the whole Series, trying to force me to pull. The first time up I hit a shot to right field and as soon as I hit it I thought, Boy, that's out. It hit the screen a foot foul. Then I grounded out. The next time up I walked, then singled, then walked again, and finally fouled out. One hit for the day, and I remember so well thinking, Gee, only one hit. I'll have to do better tomorrow.

We won the first game, 3–2, in the tenth inning on Rudy York's home run. York turned out to be our big bat of the Series. He did an awful lot for our club that year. He had more information about more pitchers in the league than anybody. He was all the time stealing signs. He could see a pitcher come down and do something to change his pitch and pick it up right away. York was a big, good natured, easy-going Indian, but a powerful guy. I wouldn't have wanted him to get mad at me.

The next day we faced Brecheen. On the surface he had

had only a so-so year—won fifteen, lost fifteen—but that son of a gun knew how to pitch. They called him the "Cat." He could really tantalize right-hand batters, give you a little here, a little there, and damn if he didn't wind up beating us three times. He shut me out that day, and the rest of the team too. It was 3–0, and the Series tied 1–1 as we went back to Boston.

I won't bother to recap all the details, sad as they were. I got only five hits for the Series, all singles, one of them a bunt. The shift might have taken away another two or three. I know I wasn't going to have anything given to me, because everything I hit went to right field except that lousy little bunt. I drove in one run, in the fifth game, and scored two. Seven times I got up as the lead-off man in an inning. I walked five times.

None of it is very impressive, and as the Series wore on I was as frustrated over it as the headline writers. I remember a big headline in one of the Boston papers after the third game: "WILLIAMS BUNTS." Not the score, not the result of the damn game, just "WILLIAMS BUNTS."

The Series was tied, 3–3, into the seventh game. I was up in my room at the Chase Hotel the night before the game, a hot night in St. Louis, just lying there in the bed with the lights out and the window open. I wanted so badly to do well, and I had done so poorly, and now there was one game left. Grantland Rice and another writer came to the door and just came right on into the room. I always felt Grantland Rice was one of the fairest writers I ever knew. He wrote the facts. I don't remember him ever giving anybody the blast.

Well, he was there to boost my morale, that's all. He insisted we go out to dinner, so I took them to a little place I knew in South St. Louis and I remember telling Grantland how I'd give anything if we could win tomorrow, that I didn't care if I didn't get a hit, just so we won that game. Tom Yawkey had spent a lot of money. He had waited a long time. So had Boston. The Red Sox hadn't won a world championship since 1918.

It just wasn't going to happen. I hit two fly balls that last game that Terry Moore and Harry Walker made fine catches on. Both of them were 400 feet or more, and one in particular I thought might have gone. Walker had to run a long way, but it was too high. Both of them were a little too high. I got up for the last time with the score tied, 3–3, in the eighth, and the lead run on third. Brecheen had come in to pitch, relieving Dickson. I hit a foul ball that split Joe Garagiola's finger and they had to hold up the game to get Del Rice in to catch, then popped out to Red Schoendienst. In the bottom of the inning Enos Slaughter scored all the way from first on Walker's double. Johnny Pesky took the relay and held the ball. Nobody yelled to him, not Doerr or Higgins or anybody, so you can't blame Pesky. And Slaughter just kept on running. By the time the ball got to the plate Slaughter was there, and the Cardinals had won, 4–3.

So much of that Series, with its great disappointment, is lost to my memory now. I know I was certainly jacked up for it. I remember I had seen my first World Series game in 1939, New York vs. Cincinnati, and how much it affected me. We'd played the Reds that spring coming north, I'd hit their best pitchers pretty good, and that day in 1939 I said to myself, Boy I could hit in this Series. I got so emotionally involved just watching it that I vomited after the game.

I do think it is hard to hit in a World Series. For anybody. It is usually played in cooler weather, for one thing. You play half the games in a strange park, and usually against pitchers you never saw before. I never got going, I never really felt swishy at the plate. Orlando Cepeda had a

Series like that a couple of years ago. He hit .150. I've always felt Rogers Hornsby was the greatest hitter for average *and* power in the history of baseball, but in his only two World Series he hit .228 and .240. Just cold, that's all.

Well, it was over and I was just so disgusted, so unhappy, and I couldn't believe we'd lost. I was shell-shocked. I was so disappointed in myself. Just sick inside. I gave my Series check to Johnny Orlando, the clubhouse boy who had always been there to give me consolation when I was down. When I got back to the hotel to pack I felt in one of my coat pockets and there were twelve blocks of seats I had forgotten to give away. Gee, what next? I remember I went over to the train that night. I had been reading these stories about getting traded, and now we'd lost, and I went into my little compartment on the train, and I didn't come out until about ten thirty. When I got in there and closed the door I just broke down and started crying, and I looked up and there was a whole crowd of people watching me through the window.

part three

The Red Sox made three big mistakes with me during an otherwise neat-and-clean relationship, First, when they tried to keep me from going to spring training in 1942 during my battle with the draft board; second, when I was asked to manage the club in 1955 even though I still had plenty of playing days left, was not prepared to manage, was not qualified or trained and I *knew* that the change could lead only to heartache, because attendance was bad and the team was bad. The first guy who gets it in a situation like that is the manager, and you can be certain the Boston press would have made it perfectly clear who *that* was.

The third mistake was when Tom Yawkey tried to get me to retire in 1959 after the only really bad year of my career. I held on for another season, which is fortunate because it came down to one of the most thrilling moments of my life. If in the end I didn't make it as the greatest hitter who ever lived—that long-ago boyhood dream—I kind of enjoy thinking I might have become in those last years the greatest *old* hitter who ever lived. It gives you something to think about when you're waiting for the fish to bite.

Certainly there was never any threat of my going out peaceably, because even with my own maturity the years from World War II were loaded with troubles—things that happened that will mark me forever, I suppose, as a maverick guy, a guy who could not reach an armistice with his environment. They made for some lively headlines: gestures at the fans, spitting in all directions, a flying bat that hit the lady on the head, getting shot down in Korea, unloading a few words on the Marine Corps and the damn politicians, a couple of well-publicized divorces, feuds with other players—feuds, for crying out loud, that never happened.

I said I would not want to relive any of it, but that's not quite true. I wouldn't mind another crack at 1946 through 1950, just before I hurt my elbow. They were such big years for baseball, and for me. I was stronger than when I first came up, I was smarter, I was more businesslike, I was charged up more sensibly than I ever was before. We were in the pennant race every year. They had to be the most important years for me, even with all the bitterness that kept building.

We won the pennant in 1946, but missed winning the World Series, a big disappointment. The talk around baseball that winter, though, was of the new Mexican League and its millionaire founder, Jorge Pasquel, who was shoving money at American ballplayers in stacks to get them to defect. American major league management called it "raiding," Pasquel called it the third major league.

Before anybody realized how far he would go he had

signed Mickey Owen of the Dodgers, Max Lanier of the Cardinals and Sal Maglie of the Giants to fancy contracts. They were all top-flight ballplayers. Lanier was probably a better pitcher than Brecheen or Pollet. He would have made the Cardinal staff unbeatable that year. The word got around that Pasquel was going to really open up his wallet for Musial, DiMaggio and Williams.

In Cuba he sent word that he wanted to see me. We were down there with the Senators for an exhibition series. I remember we played in a nice little park in Havana where the outfield sloped up, the main part of the field was down in a gully, and early in the game I came running down the slope to catch a fly ball and dropped it. In Latin America they don't boo you for a bad play, they whistle, and I heard those whistles for the first time. It was a new thrill. I had been blasted by experts in every imaginable way. This was art in a new form.

After the game I went up to Pasquel's hotel room, more out of curiosity than anything else. I was actually a little scared. There were already stories that players who jumped to the Mexican League would be banned for life. That eventually happened, but Lanier, Owen and Maglie beat the rap. There were also stories that the guys who already jumped weren't finding the end of the rainbow.

I knew the moment I got in Pasquel's room I wasn't interested. The room was filled with smoke, his friends were puffing on those big Havana cigars, and there was Pasquel. He had diamonds all over him, diamonds on this finger and that finger, a big diamond stickpin. I mean, every one of them three- or four-carat diamonds, *big* diamonds. He absolutely glittered. And I'll never forget, when he talked he sprayed you. Nothing intentional, but he kind of spit his words out, and he sprayed you.

He spoke good English, and I could see where he could

make a fellow starry-eyed. He offered me $300,000—a three-year contract at $100,000 a year. I was making $40,-000 with the Red Sox. I had some questions about how you would get your money in and out. I'd begun to hear things. (Getting their money proved to be a big problem for the guys who jumped. Mickey Owen told some hair-raising stories.) The thing is, it all seemed phony to me. I was on the verge of big money anyway, and the only team I wanted to play for was the Red Sox, so it was easy for me to say no.

Mr. Yawkey was certainly never frugal around me. He gave me a $10,000 bonus that year for not playing some exhibition games. I told him I had agreed to play ten at $1,000 a game. "Gee, Ted, I wish you wouldn't do that, you could get hurt," he said. I told him I needed the money, that it was only ten games. He said, "Forget the money, I'll give you $10,000 not to play."

I signed for $70,000 in 1947, but what I wanted more than money was to redeem myself for that awful World Series. It was a long winter. I had been humiliated. I remember how jacked up I was that spring, determined to do better, to learn more about hitting to left field away from that shift, talking for hours to Paul Waner about it. Waner was out of baseball then, but he lived there in Sarasota.

The season started and Boudreau really had the shift going now. The same Cleveland pitchers I wore out for a .400 average in 1946 I hit about .200 against in 1947. They all pitched me low inside, tough-breaking sliders, low inside, *making* me pull. The infielders they had moved over into short right field were getting groundballs and throwing me out. Groundballs that should have been hits. Gerry Coleman of the Yankees bobbled a couple out there one day and everybody got excited because they were scored as hits instead of errors, but hell, he was fielding them in the *out*field. But I was adapting more than they realized. In May I was hitting .220. At the end of the year I led the league in everything and won the triple crown—.343 average, 32 home runs, 114 runs batted in. In the All-Star game I got a double and a single off Harry Brecheen, and that pleased me a little bit too, because he had murdered me in the Series.

But in 1947 our pitching went sour. Boo Ferris, Tex Hughson and Mickey Harris hurt their arms. They were all done. Three pitchers who had won sixty-two games in 1946 won only twenty-nine in 1947. The whole club seemed to wilt. Johnny Pesky had one of those years. He gained thirty pounds during the winter. He had a great year in 1946, but that winter he stayed around Boston, he was married then, and he just ballooned. As a club we went down, down, and finished third behind the Yankees and Detroit.

Now, I happen to believe the Most Valuable Player award is something that should be above personalities, and therefore something you either accept graciously or lose graciously. I never made any bones about it one way or the other. I was happy when I won it, but never flabbergasted when I lost. In 1941, when I hit .406, Joe DiMaggio was named the Most Valuable Player and I didn't feel robbed or cheated, because DiMaggio had that fifty-six-game hitting streak and he was a great player on a great team that won the pennant. Funny it should work out that way, but it was pointed out to me later that over that same fifty-six-game period, Joe hit .408 and I hit .412. Nevertheless, I believe there isn't a record in the books that will be tougher to break than Joe's fifty-six-game hitting streak. It may be the greatest batting achievement of all. In 1942, when I won the triple crown, we *still* didn't win the pennant, the Yankees did, and Joe Gordon had probably the greatest year

135

of his life. As I said, I thought I might have been given more consideration that year, but I was certainly not bitter over Gordon's selection.

Now, 1947 comes along and DiMaggio wins again, this time by one point. He hit .315 to my .343, 20 home runs to my 32, drove in 97 runs to my 114. But the Yankees won the pennant, which is always a factor, so on the surface the vote was OK with me. But then it came out that one Boston writer didn't even put me in the top ten on his ballot. A tenth-place vote would have given me two points and the Most Valuable Player award.

The writer's name was Mel Webb. He was, as far as I am concerned, a grouchy old guy, a real grump, and we didn't get along. We'd had a big argument early in the year over something he had written, and I'd said, "That's a lot of crap you're writing about me," and oh, he got offended as hell. I didn't realize until much later that he hadn't even put me on his ballot. The commissioner should have gotten in on that, and I don't know what the Red Sox did but they should have gotten in on it too. The Most Valuable Player award shouldn't depend on being buddy-buddy with a sports writer.

I think without question that Boston had the worst bunch of writers who ever came down the pike in baseball, with the Cleveland bunch a close second. Certainly there were a few Boston writers I confided in, writers like Burt Whitman, a wonderful man, and Ed Rummill of the *Christian Science Monitor*, and later on Arthur Sampson. Sampson was with the *Herald*, which was always a more conservative newspaper and didn't go for printing a lot of garbage. The busiest dispenser of that was Dave Egan—The Colonel.

Austen Lake of the *American* was always trying to psychoanalyze me, and I came pretty close to hitting Hy Hurwitz one day in the clubhouse. I thought Bill Cunningham was a swell head. He had been a football player. He was out of school twenty-five years but he was still an All-American. He spoke well, he could play the piano, and he walked around with a fancy cane. He was actually a pretty good writer, he had talent, but you've never seen such a swell-headed Irishman. And so perceptive. The first time he saw me, my first year up, he wrote, "I don't like the way [Williams] stands at the plate. He bends his front knee inward, he moves his feet just before he takes a swing . . . I don't think this kid will ever hit half a Singer midget's weight in a bathing suit."

Egan always claimed I poisoned the climate between the writers and the other Boston players, and I wouldn't mind taking some of the credit for that. I remember way back when I used to sit on the bench with Doc Cramer, and one of them who had been giving me a hard time would sit down nearby and I'd yell, "Hey, Doc, something smells, did you notice?" I know our players and others, even *umpires* would come to me and say, "Boy, you're really right about those Boston writers."

I think certainly any professional sport has to have press coverage, has to have color written about the teams, has to have its adversity written up, but you can do all that without being unfair, without picking on somebody, without making a damn mountain out of a molehill, without putting somebody on the spot. In Boston they weren't content to do it that way. After a while I didn't cooperate because I didn't want to.

Sure, I was more agreeable and accessible to the writers in New York and Detroit and other places. Grantland Rice, Frank Graham, Arthur Daley, Red Smith—I thought they were great. Red Smith is a hell of a guy, a nice humble guy. I thought Joe Williams was a balloon head, and Bill Corum, and I didn't particularly go for Dan Daniels, because I thought he was too pro-Yankee, but the others I enjoyed being with and cooperating with. Why wouldn't I? They'd come in and ask a sensible question and I'd give them a straight answer, honestly, without politicking, without covering up, without being coy, just out with what I had to say. Dumb questions I didn't answer, because they showed me the guy didn't have enough interest to do some research, so I wouldn't let him waste my time.

But the Boston writers would come around pumping, pumping, always after something controversial, always listening at the keyhole, always out to put somebody on the spot. I imagine part of it was they were as frustrated as we were, frustrated over our being a team that was always near the best in the league without *being* the best, and still supposed to win pennants when we really weren't quite capable of it. Whatever the reason, it did not justify the abuse.

I really felt the front office should have done a lot more to cushion us from those things. I couldn't politic like some of them could. I'd see a manager or somebody with his arm around a guy I knew he hated and I'd cringe, but that's the accepted way to handle press relations. The smart way. I was never that smart. I used to kid Joe Cronin, "Gee, Joe, you're the greatest politician I ever saw," the way he'd handle those guys—*smooth*. Rogers Hornsby could never do that, neither could Ty Cobb, and this could be their fault, too, because they should have been in baseball longer than they were. They were deadly honest no-compromise guys, and they wouldn't take anything off anybody.

Since I was of that same cut, the front office should have at least kept the writers away from me, or me from them. Eventually we got a rule put in where they weren't allowed in the locker room after the game, and I was one of the instigators. Joe McCarthy was the manager then and he went right along with it. He liked the idea, too. But we only barred them for fifteen minutes. I'd like to have made it an *hour* and fifteen minutes. I became a clockwatcher in those days, the only time in my life. If I caught somebody trying to cheat, trying to get in before the deadline, I'd let out a roar. "Not yet, you chowderheads, not yet." I had a sign put up by my locker—"No Writers." That's silly, of course, but you can't imagine how bitter I was.

You talk about poisoning the climate. Who do you suppose is administering the poison when you pick up a paper and read, "Williams feuding with Vern Stephens," or "Williams and Dom DiMaggio play side by side but they don't say much to one another," knowing there is no truth to either story? I have to think, too, that the Boston press poisoned the climate between me and the Boston fans, because fans always pick up the cues from what they read. You know Teddy Ballgame's ears are going to pick up every word that comes out of those stands. There was a guy named McLaughlin who got to be a real pain. Johnny Orlando, the clubhouse boy, knew him. A little curly-haired guy. He was there every day in left field waiting for me. He'd say, "Yah, yah, ya look like a Coca-Cola bottle, ya big stiff." He'd say, "Did you read the *Colonel* last night?" Egan had ripped me again. He'd say, "Where were you last night, anyway?" He knew where I was—I was in bed by nine o'clock. But he'd give me that treatment, just aggravate the daylights out of me.

Then I noticed one season I hadn't heard his voice for a while, and I asked Orlando, "Where's McLaughlin?" and Orlando said, "Oh, he's in jail. They got him locked up. He's a Mafia guy, you know." Well, McLaughlin wasn't heard from again for about a year, and one day I'm out there and I hear this voice. "Yah, yah, ya look like a damn Coca-Cola bottle." When I came in I said to John, "McLaughlin's out."

The women never bothered me. I don't know if they felt sorry for me or what, they just never bothered me. The women I liked. Kids pretty much do what their parents do, but I always felt they were for me. They always waited for me after the games. I'd be as late as two hours coming out sometimes, hanging around to drink a couple beers or to get my ankle taped, to get a little whirlpool, maybe to take extra batting practice or bone my bat or weigh it, maybe to tell Johnny Orlando what was wrong with my uniform. I always wanted my uniform to fit exactly right because I didn't want any distractions at the plate—sleeves too tight, pants too baggy, hat too small. Nothing to throw me off. I even hit with the label of the bat down so I couldn't see it and get distracted.

Anyway, I'd hang back in the clubhouse, maybe just to sit and read my mail, anything to delay me, and still they waited. When I came out they were always there, but I kept them under control: "All right, all right, Bush, let's have a single file here, and the first one who touches me goes to the end of the line," like that, and I'd sign until I ran out of time. I always tried to sign them all, but it could be a pain because you might sign 150 and just *have* to leave and miss the other 50, and the ones you miss think you're a meathead. You can't please everybody.

I said I have done things I was ashamed of. I'll never forget one time I'd agreed to go to some youth function, a fathers-and-sons night. I was real keyed up, and I had this bad day at the park. They were all booing me, and I was mad, and afterward these two guys were waiting for me to take me to this fathers-and-sons thing. I got in the car and I started cussing the fans—"Those goddamn chicken-livered sons of . . . Those dirty . . ." and then I turned my attention on the town. "Boston is the worst . . ." And I'm going on, and then when I got to the place I find out the two guys I'm with are ministers. Gee, I never felt so bad in my life.

Well, you balance things out and you'd think, Here's a guy who scores pretty low in conduct around a ball park. But look at it another way. I am quite sure that anybody who knows me knows I never criticized my teammates, never overstepped the manager, never criticized a manager, never was critical around umpires. I was never a politicker. I didn't break training rules or stay out late or get into trouble with the law. I never once went into the front office except when I was called. I felt that was Mr. Yawkey's private sanctuary, something he should be able to have, where a ballplayer can't just barge in.

I think too you will find the ballplayers liked me, and I know there are guys like Carl Yastrzemski and Bill Skowron and Rocky Colavito and Al Kaline and Harvey Kuenn who have been generous with their praise for the times I have worked with them on their hitting. I didn't get into fights with my teammates—though the writers were always trying to stir up a feud with somebody, Junior Stephens or Jimmy Piersall or somebody—nor, for that matter, with the opposition.

I'll tell you, though, I *almost* got into one. I called Vernon Kennedy a string of names one time after he threw at me. I was twenty-one or twenty-two at the time. Kennedy was pitching for the Browns and I thought he tried to bean me, and when I was running to first base I called him all these names. Afterward I found out he was a street fighter of the first rank, that he could lick his weight in wildcats. But he didn't pick up the challenge. He never heard me.

Come to think of it, I did come pretty close to a fight with Jim Tabor when he was with the Red Sox in 1941. It was the year I hit .406, a happy, hectic year for me, and it so happened it was the same year Lefty Grove won his

141

three hundredth game. The Red Sox had a big party the night Grove won it. They took a picture to give to Grove, a picture of him and all the players, all except me.

So help me, I didn't know they were going to have the party. Same thing in 1946, the night we clinched the pennant and I was off tying flies when they popped the champagne, except this time—in 1941—I was a young kid completely wrapped up in himself. I didn't associate with too many of the players and I flat out missed the party. Somebody there asked, "Where's Williams?" and Jim Tabor was supposed to have answered, "Williams ain't here. He's too damn good for the rest of us."

Tabor was from Alabama, a strong-built guy, about six foot two, with a trim waist. A lot stronger than I was. We were rookies together in 1939. We had played together at Minneapolis when he was fresh off the Alabama campus, a big baseball and basketball star. I liked him, actually. A sort of tough, rough-hewn guy. I remember we both got new Buicks that first year and when I came back to Boston the next season mine looked newer than when I bought it. The polish on it was thicker than the metal. But gee, you should have seen Tabor's car. He'd bought a convertible and the top was ripped, there were dents in the fenders, the finish was dull and dirty, it looked like he had driven it through an air raid.

Two or three days later, Jack Wilson came to me and said, "Did you hear what Tabor said at the party?" and gave me the story. Old Jack liked to agitate. Right away it began to well up inside me. Tabor sat three or four stalls down from my locker and every time I looked at him I got madder. I'm sure he'd forgotten it, he wasn't paying any attention. The third or fourth day, I was in the trainer's room after the game getting my ankle untaped. I had to get it taped every day because of the injury that spring.

Tabor came in and was standing there and when I saw him I saw red. "You dirty bastard . . . You goddamn . . ."

He was startled. He said, "Don't you call me that."

And I repeated it. "You dirty . . ."

He had a bottle of beer in his hand, and I thought, Boy this is it. Tabor was a pretty fiery guy himself. But he didn't make a move, and they kind of separated us, held him off, and it's a funny thing, he never got gay with me after that. He could see how mad I was, and nothing ever came of it. The closest I ever came to a rip with a player.

That didn't mean the Boston writers weren't hoping, though. I remember when Billy Hitchcock was with our club. A hell of a guy, but a rough, tough ex-football player who not only liked to knock you out of the play at second base but liked to give you something to remember him by, too, like an elbow on the side of the head, *uumph*—"Uh, excuse me." You know, deliberate but not quite obvious. To the players it was always obvious and it was the kind of thing that could get both teams fired up and on the field, and was sure to get somebody thrown out of the game.

We were in Boston late in the spring, playing what was then an annual exhibition game with the Braves at Braves Field. The Red Sox had the first-base dugout. Earl Torgeson was playing first for the Braves, and Torgeson was a pretty quick-tempered guy too. Sure enough, here comes Hitchcock sliding back to first on a play and he just can't help himself. *Ummph, whack.* He gives it to Torgeson.

Right away they're at it, directly in front of us, and I happened to be the first one out of the dugout and out there. I leaped right on Torgeson's back, grabbed his arms and down he went, and I'm trying to hold him there, yelling to him, "Cut it out, damn it, cut it out," trying to keep him from moving and the fight from getting out of hand. Everybody was out of both dugouts now, and they finally got Hitchcock settled down and everybody relaxed. No damage. Typical baseball players' fight. So what do you think the writers did? They went to Torgeson afterward and asked him, "Did Williams hit you while you were down?"

I admit I reacted to the fans, to what I thought was prejudiced and unfair abuse. There were always a few who paid their way in for no better reason than to let me have it. They eventually had to put special police in the left-field stands because some of the comments were so foul. They used to write how bad *my* mouth was. I was in kindergarten compared to some of those guys. They threw things, too, and after a while the club took to roping off that portion of the bleachers closest to the field, giving us a demilitarized zone.

My response ordinarily was to just sass them back. I remember when I first started in Boston there was a guy behind third base who gave me a hard time. I tried to hit *him* with a foul ball. Jack Wilson, who I could handle pretty well, was pitching for the Athletics then, so I aimed three or four fouls in this spot behind third, but never got close enough. I finally missed and blooped one and it fell inside the foul line behind third for what should have been a double. I was so surprised I barely made it to first. Cronin fined me $250.

I have no excuse for the way I acted later, for the things I did at certain sensational moments when I couldn't stand it any more and just *reacted*. Blew up. I am sorry for them, and ashamed, and I would probably do them again if the conditions were the same. That's the way I am. I never acted. I think a lot of athletes are actors, who kind of like to play the role, giving you all those faces and charging around. But I never, never, never acted. Nothing I ever did was premeditated. Always spontaneous, boom, get it off my chest. I've always been a fierce swearer. That can be embarrassing too, like the time in the car with the two ministers, but I swear to blow off steam. Even now when things are going rotten, when I'm mad about something and I wake up in the night, I'll just let off a *stream* of abuse at whatever the problem is.

The chronology of the incidents blurs in my memory, perhaps because of my shame and hurt. The record says that I made "gestures" to the fans first in May of 1950, after I had dropped a pop fly in the first game of a doubleheader with Detroit, then fumbled a grounder in the second. This was a frustrating year for us, anyway, and we were losing to the Tigers, 13–0, in the sixth inning when Aaron Robinson popped one into short left. I dropped the fly, they began to boo, and when I came in I gave them the donkey ears, which hardly seemed adequate.

After that I hit a grand-slam home run, a futile gesture in the face of a 13–0 score, so they booed me some more, except louder. I'd have been better off striking out. In the second game we were leading, 2–0, when Vic Wertz hit a squiber to left field and I came in hard to get the ball. It took two good bounces and I anticipated a third, but it skidded and hit my arm and went through, and I didn't know where it was. It rolled to the wall and by the time I got it two runs were in and instead of leading we were tied. This time they really let me have it, and when I got to the dugout the kind of gestures I made were a heck of a lot more to the point than donkey ears. They were not the kind you see in polite company. I was sorry immediately. I was called in to see Mr. Yawkey and he said, "You've got to promise me you'll never do this again." I said I wouldn't and we issued a formal apology that made eight-column headlines in the Boston *Globe*: "Williams Apologizes." Newspapers never print their retractions that big.

In 1956 I was in a stew over something—I *stayed* in a stew in those days, the boos had been coming pretty regularly—and in July when I hit my four hundredth home run off Kansas City's Tom Gordon I happened onto a new method of expressing myself. I spat toward the pressbox as I crossed home plate. A sort of "Here's to you, boys," type of thing. Then a couple of days later, standing at home plate, I turned and did it again. I could have picked a better time. It was Joe Cronin Night, they were celebrating Joe's admission into the Hall of Fame. The Commissioner, Ford Frick, was there and all kinds of dignitaries. By now it was getting to be expected of me, what the writers were calling these "great expectorations."

And then in early August came the capper.

We were playing the Yankees, 0–0 in the ninth inning, a full house at Fenway Park—36,530 fans, the biggest crowd since World War II. Mickey Mantle hit a high pop fly behind shortstop, and I came running in hard, running hard all the way and yelling, "*Mine, mine, mine.*" All the shortstop had to say was "Take it, take it," but he didn't and I braced myself for the collision. When you're hollering hard and running, the baseball sort of *jumps* at you. This one did. I got it in my glove and it popped out.

I was furious, because I'd dropped the ball, and because I felt I didn't get any help from the shortstop, and because the fans were booing like hell. Certainly it was my fault, but when I heard those boos I was steaming. Mantle wound up on second base, but he didn't score, because right after that I made a running over-the-shoulder catch of a drive by Yogi Berra to end the inning. Now they were cheering, and *that* made me madder still because I hate front-runners, people who are with you when you're up and against you when you're down.

Well, if I'd had a knife I probably would have stuck it

in somebody. This was after I'd gotten back from Korea and I was pretty much to the point where I was low on everything and everybody. There was a clown behind the dugout earlier that year who had hit me with a hot dog, and I would have gone into the stands after him, but the players held me back. So I showered him with a few worthwhile curses, and you should have heard the people around there, real shocked, you know: "Oh, there's women in the crowd! There's women in the crowd!" like all I had to do all day was smile and wave my hat when guys threw their garbage at me.

So I came running in after the catch of Berra's ball and I spat toward right field and spat toward left field. Then, after I got inside the dugout, I leaped back out and spat again. And boy, that *really* got them going. In our half of the eleventh, the Yankees brought in Tommy Byrne to relieve Don Larsen with the bases loaded. Byrne was a left-hander, and a pretty good one. I stood pretty close to the plate, watching him warm up, and he practically dusted me off just warming up.

But after he got two strikes he got cute and on a 3–2 pitch he walked me. Walked in the winning run. Even *that* made me mad. I didn't want any walk, I wanted to hit the damn ball. I threw my bat in the air, and almost didn't go to first base. Del Baker, our first-base coach, had to remind me. I was just disgusted with the whole thing.

Mr. Yawkey was in New York at the time, and he heard Mel Allen's account of the game on radio. Evidently I'd been spraying it around pretty good that year, because that broke the camel's back. Mr. Yawkey fined me $5,000, a fine equaled only by one given Babe Ruth in the history of baseball punishment. I apologized. I said I was especially sorry about the $5,000 it was going to cost me. Actually, Mr. Yawkey never did take it out of my pay. He kept me hanging for a while, then he said, "Aw, Ted, we don't want your money." If Babe Ruth paid his fine, his record is safe.

The next day the papers were writing that I ought to quit baseball. I think they felt they finally had me on the ropes. They really poured it to me. It was awful. I have to admit it got to me. I was sick with worry, I was beginning to wonder about myself, how deep I'd gotten into things, wondering if it was worth it. This was one of the times an old stockbroker friend of mine, Owen Wood, would come to me at my hotel room and say, "Now, just relax, Ted, everything's going to be all right." Owen knew about adversity, he had lost his shirt in the market a couple times, but I wasn't so sure things were going to be all right.

That night we were playing Baltimore. It was family night in Boston, another big crowd, and everybody was in for the kill. All the TV people and the writers, even the ones from New York and Detroit, were there saying, probably hoping, "They'll nail Williams to the cross tonight," meaning the fans. Well, the greatest reception I ever got was that night when I came to home plate. Without question, the greatest reception I ever got.

I said to myself right then and there, Boy, these fans are for me. They're showing those lousy writers, and they're showing me. From that day on I was convinced. I knew I had played for the greatest fans in baseball. I pretty near had to laugh at anything they wrote after that, because I knew it wouldn't mean much to those fans. And it just so happened that I hit the home run that won the game in the ninth inning. When I crossed home plate I made a big display of clapping my hand over my mouth.

That was the end of the spitting. I let loose one in Kansas City one night, but that was an afterthought. I didn't run out a groundball to first and they booed me and I spit. It was headlines in Boston, and four lines down in the story in the Kansas City paper. The Kansas City guy knew his journalism. Will Harridge, the American League president, probably thinking he had to do *some*thing, fined me $250.

That September I accidentally flipped a bat into the stands and hit Joe Cronin's housekeeper in the head. The bat had too much stickum on it and I was so mad over striking out I tried to throw it away hard, but it stuck to my hands and flipped up into the air. It was an accident, certainly unintentional, and the lady was just a queen about it. I felt awful.

The fans booed like hell. There was a picture taken then of me kind of half dancing, kicking one foot up in the air, with my hands over my head and my eyes shut in a big grimace. This was called "Williams throwing a tantrum." What it really was, I saw that bat going into the stands and geez, I flinched.

The little lady's name was Gladys Heffernan. She was sixty years old. She was Cronin's housekeeper, but I had never met her. When I got to the first aid room the blood was running down her head and I about died. She just smiled and said, "Don't worry, Ted, I know you didn't mean to do it." That Christmas I sent her a $500 diamond watch. I wouldn't mention it except that she deserved it. A real little queen.

I am sure of one thing: I would never spit at those fans again. I've heard players talk about the *fans* of Detroit, or the *fans* of Cleveland, but the Boston fans were the best, and I think you could say that I had them right in my palm. What I hadn't realized before was that they enjoyed being intimate with me, with the kind of ball park we had, them right on top of you, and a press that made it possible for them to really be exposed to a player. Too many cases prove the point. For example, the day I went to Korea and they all joined hands in the park and sang farewell to me. The day I came back. The ovations I always got. The crowds that would wait around after the games. That night and the night of my last game. The huge signs they used to unfold in the stands: "Ted Williams, Greatest American Since George Washington." I was, in the final analysis, the darling of the fans of Boston. From the earliest days I was their guy, because I was exuberant, I was natural, I was different. I am sorry I was late finding out, but I'm glad I *did* find it out.

I have to laugh. I was in the outfield one day, standing there during a game, and this one guy leaps out of the stands and comes running over to me. I think he'd been encouraged by a couple beers. He said, "Ted, I just wanted to tell ya, the fish are biting at Cape Cod Canal." They had a picture in the paper the next day showing him holding up his hand to me, and the caption said, "Fan tries to sock Williams." Another guy came up to me in the on-deck circle, shook my hand and gave me a big bear-hug. I've got a picture of it, the brim of my hat jammed against his shoulder. The police carted them both away.

Just a spring or two ago, in Ocala, one of the Red Sox minor league players said to me, "You know, my dad used to be out there in left field when you played, and he used to boo the hell out of you."

I said, "Yeah?"

"Yeah. He used to go out there and have a few beers, and he'd really have fun giving you the old razzberry. But you know," he said, "my old man liked you."

I had to smile. "You tell the old rascal I'd like to have a talk with *him*," I said.

And the kid said, "Well, he's dead now."

The thing that writers like Egan and Bill Cunningham and Austen Lake and Huck Finnigan kept harping on until the day they died, and probably the bitterest pill of all for me because it was so unfair, was that, as Egan wrote, in the

"10 most important games of his life, Williams hit .232." In capsule: the .200 in the World Series, seven games; one for four against Cleveland in the playoff for the pennant in 1948, and one for two and zero for two against the Yankees in 1949 when we lost a one-game lead with two games to play. In those last two I walked twice each game. That was against Vic Raschi and Allie Reynolds, two pretty fair country pitchers. I put one right up against the damn fence the last day, but it was caught.

Well, if you have a mind to you could take any man's record apart. You could say this hitter hit his home runs in a bandbox, or this All-American quarterback had unusually good receivers. You could say there weren't any hitters in the American League in 1968 and that's why Denny McClain won thirty-one games. Cassius Clay didn't fight anybody. Glenn Cunningham didn't run very good times. He didn't have to run against Jim Ryun. You could criticize anybody.

I think that Joe Louis was the greatest heavyweight fighter who ever lived. I loved his style, his punch, his aggressiveness, he fought everybody, he fought more often than anybody, he knocked out more guys. To me nobody will be a greater heavyweight than Joe Louis. But what did they say? They said, "He couldn't take a punch." He got knocked down a few times, sometimes by guys you never heard of. What they *didn't* say was that he was moving in all the time, not bobbing and weaving and flashing or running around, but coming in, stalking you, stalking you. Some guy tags him coming in like that, and down he goes. That's supposed to make the point.

It's the same—you can take any ten games you want out of a guy's career and pick his record apart if that's how you want to judge him. But if you're fair, you've got to say in the end, The guy played *twenty-two years*. And there were a lot of games where he *did* come through. They don't talk about the time the Yankees came into Boston in 1948, one game back, and I beat Tommy Byrne the first day with a two-run home run and knocked them out of the race.

They don't talk about going six for eight when we won our last three—two against the Yankees—to force the play-off with Cleveland. They don't talk about the eleven-game winning streak we went on in the last three weeks of 1949 to take the lead, and I won four of the games with home runs off Hal Newhouser, Steve Gromek, Allie Reynolds and Eddie Lopat.

I led the league four times in RBI's in those years when we were in the pennant race. I led six times in runs scored. I think if you'll check you'll find that no batter who ever played this game had a better on-base percentage than Ted Williams. To space all that out so that, as the Egans would say, I helped only my own average would have been a damn miracle of self-service.

Egan was great for this. One day in Detroit, I think it was 1955, we were behind, 4–3, tying and winning runs on base, two away, and I struck out. Before the score was up Egan had fired off the most vicious thing you've ever read. I got the paper in the mail the next morning in Detroit (I always kept up with my critics). "Typical Williams, never hits 'em when we need 'em, yow, yow, yow." You would have thought I was the first man who ever struck out with the bases loaded.

The next day, the very next day, we're losing again, 3–0, and it's the ninth inning and damn if we don't get three men on again, two away, and I'm up. All I could think of was Egan. It seemed he was always inspiring me with something like that. The Tigers brought in a left-hander, Al Aber. He had a sidearm, kind of crossfire delivery, tough for a left-handed hitter. Well, I got him to 2–0, and I hit a home run to win the game. That didn't put an end to Egan for good, of course, because he could always be illogical, but the reason I bring it up is that *nobody* can do it all the time.

Then they would say I took too many bases on balls, and they'd quote somebody like Ty Cobb. "Williams sees more of the ball than any man alive, but he demands a perfect pitch. He takes too many bases on balls." I have two arguments for that. The best years I had for driving in runs were the years I had Joe Cronin hitting behind me, my first year, and when I had Vern Stephens hitting behind me. A pitcher would think twice before he would walk me, boy, to pitch to Cronin or Vern Stephens.

It makes a tremendous difference. In 1957, when I batted .388 and hit 38 home runs, I only drove in 98 runs. We were a team of banjo hitters; the two guys in front of me didn't average .220. The guys behind me weren't much better. I batted third in the lineup, which meant there was at least one time every game I could not possibly lead off, and even then I led off ninety-nine times, darn near a fourth of my total times at bat. Compare that with my first year when I hit 60 points lower—.327—but batted in 143 runs, hitting behind Cramer, Vosmik and Foxx, with Cronin behind me. I had opportunities unlimited.

I had other good hitters behind me some years, like Rudy York, Bobby Doerr and Vic Wertz, but the pitchers worked around me even with them, and in other years when the Red Sox lineup wasn't exactly murderers' row they often just flat out walked me. They gave me a league record in 1957 with thirty-three intentional walks. Paul Richards was quoted as saying that the one exception he knew of to the rule against putting the winning run on base was Ted Williams. Bob Feller said he would never pitch to me in a close game if there was a base open. *Any* base. It's pretty obvious with that kind of respect I wouldn't be getting much to swing at in a close game.

All right, so Cobb and Joe DiMaggio and a couple of others said I took too many close pitches, "begging walks," that I should have gone for the close pitch when we were behind and needed runs. Al Simmons used to say I was "helping the enemy." My argument is, to be a good hitter you've got to get a good ball to hit. It's the first rule in the book. Now, if I'm a real dangerous hitter and they're pitching me cute, a little outside, a little low, a hair inside, I'm not going to get that ball I can really hit, I'll have to bite at stuff that is out of my happy zone. Out there I'm *not* a .344 hitter, I might only be a .250 hitter.

My argument is, if the guy behind me is a .300 hitter and, having walked me, they *have* to pitch to him, they'll probably *have* to get in his happy zone, his .300 zone. A good hitter, I believe, can hit a ball that is over the plate three times better than a great hitter can hit a questionable ball that is not in the strike zone.

Fortunately, of course, pitchers still make enough slips, or get in situations where they can't walk you, and a guy like me winds up averaging .344. But the greatest hitter in the world can't hit bad balls well. My first couple years with the Red Sox I went for bad pitches. Not often, but enough to learn a lesson. I was too anxious. I made outs I should not have made. You've *got* to get a good ball. You hit a ball in that happy zone, something happens. In that tough zone, once in a while it happens. In that *real* tough zone, it seldom happens. When you start going for the pitch an inch off, the next time that pitcher will throw it *two* inches off, then three, and before you know it you're hitting .250.

I never gave them that luxury. As a result, I walked 100

times or more almost every full season I played professional baseball. I walked 100 times in San Diego, 140 times in Minnesota, 120 times my first year with the Red Sox. I averaged 130 walks a year my first five seasons in Boston. I led the American League in bases on balls eight times, six in a row (a record), and I don't know anybody they pitched tougher to than Ted Williams. I never had a manager ask me to swing at close pitches, or even hint at it. And isn't it funny? I begged so many walks I wound up second to Gehrig in all-time bases-loaded home runs, in the top five in total home runs, in the top three (behind Ruth and Gehrig) in runs batted in per time at bat.

I can't say it was so irritating when Cobb and DiMaggio criticized me for taking close pitches. As far as I was concerned nobody in the history of the game hit any more balls in practice, pleasure or dead earnest than I did, so I felt I was a qualified judge and that my logic was unassailable. Neither do I pretend, however, that I walked to first base on 3-2 pitches without ever saying to myself, Damn, I wish I'd swung at that first strike. For some reason I didn't swing. Either I was looking for something else or the pitch fooled me. Things happen fast at that plate, and I always told myself that if you get fooled by a pitch with less than two strikes, let the pitch go by, *take* it.

They used to write that I didn't have take signs from my managers, that I was always on my own up there. That's not true, but when the score was tied or it was late in the game, they sure didn't give me any take signs. By the same token I can't ever recall swinging at a bad ball on a 3-0 or 3-1 count. Maybe on a 3-2 count. There was a time against Bob Lemon, runners on first and second in Cleveland, two outs. On a 2-2 pitch he threw wild and the runners advanced. Now it was 3-2 and Boudreau went out and told Lemon not to give me anything to hit with first base open. So Lemon uncorks one about six inches outside, and low, and *unnnh*, I swung at it. Struck out. With Lemon you could have trouble keeping your rules.

I have always said I took the first pitch 95 per cent of the time. I'm talking about the first pitch in a game. That way I could refresh my memory on the pitcher's speed and delivery, see what he's got going, give myself a little time to get settled, to get the tempo. I know if you could hold a $10,000 home run contest for Ruth and Mantle and DiMaggio and Greenberg and Foxx and all the great hitters, giving each one six swings, every one of them would take a couple pitches before they swung. What about that other 5 per cent? Well, sometimes the first pitch is so tempting, such a big balloon coming in, that I took a cut to keep the pitcher honest. Bob Lemon didn't throw balloons, of course, and one day I hit a home run off him on the first pitch. Somebody said, "What the hell are you doing swinging at that?" I said, "There is one guy"—pointing at Lemon —"I don't want to get ahead of me."

In 1949, with Stephens hitting behind me, I wound up with more official times at bat than any time in my career. Stephens was at the top of his game, and I had a couple of hitters in front of me who were always on base, Dom DiMaggio and Johnny Pesky. We had a great thing going. In 1949 both Stephens and I drove in 159 runs. Nobody has driven in that many runs in either league since.

I remember being bothered because the writers had been writing about this "feud" with Stephens. If Stephens was ever mad at me, or feuding with me, I never knew it. I always thought he was a great guy, a personable guy. He was the fashion plate of the club, a sharp dresser, and everybody liked him. There was never any coolness between us. Just for spite, we decided to never shake hands in public view. Any applause we had for each other was confined to the dugout.

Anyway, during the last game of the season I was on second and Vern hit a blue-darter into left field, a base hit. Ordinarily I would have scored, but the ball was hit so hard right at the fielder I had to hold at third. That bothered me because I felt some people might think I should have gone home and Stephens should have led for the season in RBI's. But he'd do that, Stephens, hit those vicious line drives. He was a *strong* little guy. Nobody booed.

The other thing they *always* harped on was that I wasn't a "team" man. This had to hurt me. Certainly it had hurt Jim Thorpe. But you can say anything you want about the game of baseball, it's an *individual* game first, and it's impossible for me to help you field the ball, or for me to hit the ball for you. The greatest thing I can do for the team is make damn sure I'm doing my best. The best thing I can do for you, a teammate, is give encouragement. I can't do your job for you.

I have to admit that in my heart I always wanted to be the best, the best at the playground, the best in high school, the best on the team, the best in the league, no matter what it was. I think anybody competitive should feel that way, and I also think it's natural to be a little jealous of somebody who has beaten you out. I never thought I was jealous to the point of being cool to anybody or disliking anybody. I just never went for a lot of handshaking on the field and phony back-clapping. I still don't like it, because I think most of it is put on for the fans. But what you read was that Stephens and I didn't speak, or that I didn't like George Kell when he came to our club in 1951 because he once beat me out of the batting championship.

Take Dom DiMaggio. The wolves in left field were always yelling how he was playing his position *and* mine. "You oughta give him half your salary, ya big bum," that sort of thing. I could have been a little miffed at that, but the fact was Dom and I got along good. He was quiet, but he was great to play with because he'd talk under a fly ball, holler good to let you know what was happening. And he *was* a great outfielder, he could get better position on the ball to left center, so I made it a point to concede to him. I never wanted to give him the feeling we might collide, because I was forty pounds heavier. We never had any problems at all, but the thing you read was, "Williams and Dom DiMaggio play side by side but don't say too much to one another."

Another was Jimmy Piersall, who played center field later on. I always felt a little sorry for Jimmy, the problems he'd had, the nervous breakdown. He was always so high strung, nervous, excitable, emotional. We would kind of give each other the needle, he seemed to like that, and whatever we said was *always* interpreted wrong. In the outfield he was all over the place, making catches. He was a hell of an outfielder. So he'd say to me, "Awwright, damn it, if I've got to play my position *and* yours, give me some room."

Actually, that was the only objection I had with Jimmy, that he tended to extend his territory a little. He'd be making tough plays on balls that would have been easier for me. But again, I always gave the center fielder priority because most times he would be coming *in* on the ball where I would be going sideways. It's an easier play for him.

They always wrote in this connection that "Williams isn't a leader." One of the most overused, most overrated phrases in athletics is "He's a leader." If you win, you're a leader. If you lose, you're not a leader. I don't know of any position in sport where the man—and what he says and the way he acts—is more important than the example he makes, the contribution he makes. I'm talking about the guys out there on the field, not managers and coaches. There is no question in my mind that in the annals of professional basketball Wilt Chamberlain is the most devastating, most dominating force ever to play the game, every statistic will show it, but when all the statistics are in, people will say, "Well, he only won one championship, and Bill Russell won ten." Russell was the great leader. But you can never make me believe that Chamberlain had the players with him that Russell had.

The Red Sox made Carl Yastrzemski the team captain three or four years ago. They asked me what I thought. "All right. Fine," I said. So they had a lousy year, finished fifth. The next year Dick Williams is the new Boston manager. He says, "We're not going to have any captains on this club. No more captains." That year Yastrzemski led the league and the Red Sox won the pennant, and now everybody starts saying what a fine leader Yastrzemski is. Would he have been a leader if the Red Sox had finished—hell, *second?* I'd have been considered a great leader if we'd won in 1948 and 1949, when we were that close to it.

I remember one year when the Yankees had won the pennant, which they always seemed to be doing, and Gil McDougald had had his greatest season. I was in Boston to sign my contract, and a press conference had been set up. I usually took those opportunities to straighten somebody out. One of the writers said, "Why don't we win more, don't we have a leader?" I said, "Well, I don't know. I think pitching is important, hitting is important, fielding is important. I think balance on a club is important. What do you mean by 'leader'?" He said, "Well, someone like the Yankees have. Someone like McDougald." Probably a damn Irish writer out of Boston.

I said, "Tell me why you think McDougald's the leader on that club."

He said, "Well, gee, the pitcher gets in trouble, McDougald goes in there and starts talking to him, settling him down. He's *important* to that club."

I said, "Yeah, you think so, eh? You know the real reason he went in there? Probably because Casey Stengel rubbed an ear lobe or picked his nose to signal for McDougald to get out to that mound and slow that son of a gun down until he could get another pitcher warmed up." That ended that.

The 1948, '49, '50 Boston teams were fine teams, but we didn't win the pennant and I feel doubly bad about that because of Joe McCarthy. He finally quit during the '50 season, I think out of his own extreme disappointment. But Boston people forget that there were three or four other good teams in those days. Cleveland and Detroit had excellent pitching. When they talk about the great pitching staffs of baseball, they have to talk about Bob Feller, Bob Lemon, Mike Garcia and Early Wynn of Cleveland, and Hal Newhouser, Virgil Trucks, Paul Trout and Art Houtteman of Detroit. When they talk today about the great Yankee teams of all time, they always mention 1947 through 1950, and we played them even over that span. They were always j-u-s-t a little better on the road. But what made those years memorable for me was Joe McCarthy.

McCarthy was hired in 1948 to manage the club. He had won eight pennants with the Yankees. A tough guy, a disciplinarian. Strict curfews, no poker playing, watch your step. Boy, the writers saw trouble ahead for me. McCarthy was *really* going to straighten out Williams. I remember reading about it and saying to myself, Gee, this is the end. This is the end for me in Boston. Years before, when I was a fresh kid talking about being traded, somebody mentioned the Yankees and I read where one of their officials said, "Oh, yeah? A pop-off like Williams wouldn't last two minutes with Joe McCarthy."

Well, the first thing they didn't realize was how much my attitude had changed from the prewar years. I was a lot more serious. I had responsibilities. I wanted to make money. I was *going* to make big money, big contracts coming up. And I know now they didn't know McCarthy. They put it to him: "What about Williams?" And straight off he said, "If I can't get along with a .400 hitter, it'll be *my* fault."

So we got down to spring training, and his rule with the Yankees had been that players wear ties in the dining room. All I had ever worn was sports shirts. I didn't want to wear a tie, I didn't want to dress up. That first night in spring training I ate in my room, and when Joe McCarthy came into the dining room, with all the writers around, he was wearing the biggest, gayest sports shirt you ever saw.

From the beginning there was an atmosphere around McCarthy's ball club that we had never known before or since. All managers are serious, all managers have rules, all managers have a way of doing things. But McCarthy was the complete manager. You could sense that something extra, that completely businesslike attitude. He was for the players, but he didn't play favorites. His pets were the lesser guys, the guys he could make examples of.

Billy Goodman was one of his pets. He tried Goodman at first base, and Billy turned out to be a hell of a first baseman, a real cat around first. He put Billy on third, he put him on second, he put him in the outfield. Goodman could play anywhere, a one-man bench. He was a skinny guy, narrow shoulders, kind of white-faced and unathletic looking, but he could hit. He was always around .300. He led the league in 1950, hitting .354, and still played five different positions. The thing was, McCarthy could make an example of Goodman because Goodman was the kind of guy who never showed you up with the writers or anybody. McCarthy didn't worry about the writers. Every other manager I've known was press-conscious. All managers bull the press, but McCarthy did it less.

Of those I played for, I thought Mike Higgins was a good enough manager, and Lou Boudreau. I was closer to Cronin. Cronin was a real ballplayer's manager and he was great to me. He could have been distant, but from the beginning he took an interest. There were so many things I loved about Joe Cronin. When he chewed me out I deserved it, and I'm sure if I told him I felt he should have protected me more—which is true—he would say, "Pro*tect* you? For crying out loud that's all I ever did was protect you."

Cronin did a great job in 1946, when he managed from the bench. I always felt it was selfish of a club to have a guy play *and* manage, as tough as it was. One thing Cronin had over McCarthy, he was always stirring up the hitters, getting them talking, dragging information out of them. He had been a great player, he could do the things he talked about. Lefty O'Doul was like that, and Hornsby, and I suppose now the young Washington players are finding out I'm like that, because when I go into a clubhouse right away everybody wants to talk hitting.

Cronin always made sure we got enough batting practice. He could appreciate the problem. I've been around more lousy outfits where the pitching coaches were all the time fretting over the pitcher's arm: "Now, Danny boy, don't overdo it. Are you sure you're all right?" Or telling him to "Keep the ball down, keep it low," instead of saying, "Look, this is batting practice, this ain't pitching practice.

Get the ball over. Throw strikes." Not them, not the damn pitching coaches. Screw the hitters.

The thing that separated McCarthy from Cronin, and McCarthy from all the rest, was his control of the players. He got more out of his players than anybody. He knew how to get his message over. Here was a disciplinarian who probably had fewer discipline problems than anybody. He was distinguished-looking, with that big lantern jaw, that slow easy gait, that air of importance. He wasn't frogging around the clubhouse being buddy-buddy, he was back in his drawing room smoking, asking the coaches questions, getting things mapped out. He was never big for conversation with the players, and except for Cronin I never had much to say to managers.

Usually McCarthy would sit down at the end of the bench away from the others. I remember he'd be sitting there, and I'd come back to the dugout after really ripping one, and he'd say in a kind of monotone, looking straight ahead, "If I could hit like you I'd play for nothing. I'd play this game for nothing."

The only time he ever got mad at me was over my own foolishness. Ballplayers horse around, and McCarthy didn't go for that, so as a team we were a far cry from the Ted Lyons–Doc Cramer eggs-on-the-head routine, but one day on the train heading for Boston Sam Mele and I got to horsing around. Sam had joined the club that year and was playing right field for us, a good guy and to this day a dear friend. We're on the train and he was coming down the aisle where I was standing and I said, "And where do you think *you're* going, Mele?"

He pointed around me, half grinning, and I said "Oh? You think so, hunh?" and we started sparring, just flicking light punches at one another, and he hit me a little punch right under the ribs. It didn't hurt at the time, but it felt kind of funny.

That night I could hardly draw a breath. The next day it was painful just to move my upper body. I would start to walk and I had to give with it. I tried to play and a ball got over my head, and it hurt just moving after it. From that little bit of horseplay I had torn some ligaments. Silly. McCarthy finally took me out of the lineup and I was out two weeks, and don't you think we got our asses chewed by McCarthy. No more horseplay. Not long after that they traded Mele to the Senators. He blamed me.

In those years I was always last to leave the park. I'd sit around after a game weighing my bats, fooling with my glove, checking out new shoes, seeing how many pounds I'd lost, checking my uniforms. I must have hated to leave. After we lost to Cleveland in the playoff for the 1948 pennant I was in there a long time, so down, feeling blue. Everybody was getting organized, getting dressed, end of the season, good-by, good-by, and I was just hanging around with my sweatshirt still on. Finally I got showered and dressed and was walking through the training room when I heard this voice behind me. "Well, we fooled 'em, didn't we?" It was McCarthy.

"What do you mean, Joe?"

"Well, they said you and I couldn't get along, but we got along pretty good, didn't we?"

I said, "Yeah, we did, Joe."

Joe McCarthy was something special. I loved Joe Mc-Carthy.

There is no doubt we had an outstanding lineup those years. Cronin was the general manager. He got Mr. Yaw-key to go on another spending spree and we had excellent pitching again. Ferris, Hughson and Harris were done, but now we had Ellis Kinder, Jack Kramer and Mel Parnell to go with Joe Dobson and you can't be much better than Kinder and Parnell were. Rudy York was gone, but Mr. Yawkey had bought Vern Stephens from the Browns. Pesky had slimmed down a little. McCarthy moved him to third base and put Stephens at shortstop. Goodman played first, Dom DiMaggio was in center, Doerr on second, Stan Spence and then Al Zarilla in right, and Birdie Tebbetts was the new catcher.

Birdie Tebbetts had caught for the Tigers. He had some good years and later, of course, he became the manager of the Cincinnati club. He must have been studying for the managership then, because he was very big on psychology. Whenever we played Detroit he used to barber me. I had been hitting Detroit real good, even with his needling, and one day he said, "We can't get you out trying to cross you up, so from now on I'm going to tell you what's coming." Darned if he didn't. "Curve ball," he said, and here's a nice big fat curve with me looking for a fastball. He crossed me up two or three times that way before I started believing him, then I crashed a couple and he cut that out.

Tebbetts had a way about him. He came as close as anybody to getting me to tip my hat. We were on the train to Boston after a series in Chicago and he and Bobby Doerr and Joe Reichler of the Associated Press—one of the accurate journalists I have known—were giving me the business, telling me how I could be Mayor of Boston if I would just once acknowledge the cheers. I said, "No, I can't, it wouldn't be me."

Birdie said, "OK, I've got a better idea. How you can really put one over on 'em. The next time you hit a home run, tip your hat and smile and look up at them, and while they're cheering and you're smiling, you yell, 'Go to hell, you S.O.B.'s!' They won't know what you're saying."

That kind of appealed to me a little bit, and I said I might just do it. But there was a rainout the next day, and by the time I hit my next home run, the day after, the mood had passed. Tebbetts said he and Doerr kind of leaned forward on the bench, watching to see what I'd do as I trotted around, and he said I was mumbling to myself, struggling to reach a decision. But there was never really any danger of me tipping my hat.

I used to tell Birdie he was a hell of a nice guy, real personable, but a dumb catcher. This was 1948 and I was trying to get him to pitch differently to Lou Boudreau. Boudreau was wearing us out. Finally he said, "All right, you're so damn smart, *you* call the pitches." We worked out a little system. If I wanted a fastball I'd put my hands on my hips, a curve ball I'd touch my cap, a change up I'd put my hands on my knees, something like that. The way Birdie tells it, Boudreau doubled to left center on my first call and I had to chase the ball, he doubled again to the same spot on my second call and I had to chase the ball again, and when Birdie looked up to get my next signal I was turned the other way, ignoring him. He came out as far as the pitcher's mound and yelled, "What's the matter, Bush, lose your nerve?" It makes a good story but the truth is that every time I signaled for a pitch Birdie ordered the opposite. I'd signal curve, he'd order a fastball. After a while I got disgusted and quit. End of a promising catching career.

The irony of those 1948–49–50 teams was that we were good enough to convince a lot of people we should have won a couple pennants, but weren't good enough to actually win them. I don't think baseball has ever been played any better than it was from 1946 to 1950, everybody fired up, a lot of good teams, excellent hitting, fine pitching, and it just wasn't so easy to win. You certainly couldn't blame Joe McCarthy. He got us right to the brink, to the very last day, two years in a row. One victory would have meant the pennant both times. I think it proves how much he got out of the club.

It's true that certain players do better for certain managers. I always thought Bobby Doerr was a little tense under McCarthy. He wasn't quite as loose as he had been with Cronin. I thought Tex Hughson could have helped us more, he had been a great pitcher until his arm was hurt and I thought he still had some left, but apparently McCarthy didn't feel that way. Hughson and Doerr hung out a lot together that year. But over all, Joe McCarthy got more out of his players than anybody.

One thing we certainly did not have those years was the kind of runaway start that had made it so easy for us in 1946. In 1948 we were eleven games behind before the end of May. In 1949 we were twelve games behind on the Fourth of July. In 1950 we were eight and a half games behind in June, when McCarthy quit. Each time we made charging gung-ho comebacks. We actually got a pretty good lead—about five games—on Cleveland with three weeks to play in 1948, then had to rally again to force the playoff.

Two terrific individual performances beat us. Lou Boudreau did everything for the Indians but drive the bus that year. He managed great, he worked with the pitchers great, he played great position at shortstop, he hit for average and he drove in runs. I've never seen clutch hitting like he did that year. Boudreau was a hell of a player, boys. One of the greatest seasons in American League history was Lou Boudreau's 1948 season.

The second and decisive performance was that of Gene Bearden. Bearden was a left-handed knuckleball pitcher who ordinarily wouldn't draw a second glance on a staff that included Bob Feller, Bob Lemon, Early Wynn and

Mike Garcia. But Bearden had one of those years. He led the league in earned-run average and he won twenty games. To force the playoff we had won our last three games, and I remember how good I felt. I got six hits in those three games, two doubles against the Yankees on the final day. We won, and Hal Newhouser beat Cleveland to tie the race. We had the impetus. We came back to Boston with what appeared to be a big advantage, playing at home. But—

Bearden pitched the playoff game. Every ball he threw was a little knuckleball or a little breaking curve. Knuckle or curve, knuckle or curve. We got four hits. I got one of them, a single. He beat us, 4–1. No contest. Bearden never had a season like it. Two years later he was out of the big leagues.

One thing Boudreau did not have that year was my number. I had learned to stand away from the plate a little and was getting some leverage on those inside pitches, and the shift wasn't nearly as effective. I hit .380 against Cleveland pitching, and was glad to be able to do it to a deserving bunch of guys. For the season I hit .369, only a handful of hits away from .400. But 1948 was Lou Boudreau's year and his were the hits people talked about. I remember one of them best, and if we were looking for something to hang our frustration on, this was it. He hit a home run down the right-field line in Fenway Park, and *every*body thought it was foul. Everybody except the umpire. I can't say it was, I wasn't standing on the line. It was a dead, foggy night, hard to see for sure. But there was the biggest rhubarb you ever saw. The home run beat us, 2–1. Take that away from him, and what? No playoff? Who knows.

I do know any time you have to go the full route, all 154 games, to reach a decision on a pennant you will have a good supply of incidents to torture yourself with. We went into Yankee Stadium for those last two games of 1949 leading the Yankees by one game. We needed to win only one of the two to win the pennant. We should have clinched it in Washington the series before, but we lost two out of three games there. Ray Scarborough beat us and we threw another away on a wild pitch. We had been an almost unbeatable team in Boston that year—won sixty-one, lost sixteen—and a patsy on the road. We won only thirty-five of our seventy-seven road games.

Against the Yankees in those final games we blew a 4–0 lead in the first game and lost, and there were two big Yankee breaks that cost us the second: Pesky got thrown out at home when he went back to third on a ball that the wind held up, Pesky thinking Cliff Mapes would catch it. Mapes got it on the first bounce and made a perfect throw. Then with the Yankees up, a man on, Gerry Coleman blooped a soft liner into right field and Al Zarilla came in like a streak and made a hell of a sprawling effort trying to catch the ball. He actually hurt his knee real bad on the play. The ball rolled through for a triple and the winning run.

These are the obvious ones. The one I remember, the one that really grinds on me to this day, was our opening game with the Yankees that year. We were in Fenway Park, Mel Parnell pitching. We had a seven-run lead in the seventh inning. McCarthy took me out of the game. He thought we had it won, everybody did, and damn if the Yankees didn't come back to win, 11–9. First game of the season. And we lose by a game on the last day. Just frustrating.

That one hit me harder than the playoff loss to Cleveland. You couldn't take anything away from Boudreau in 1948. But here the Yankees had had a million dollars' worth of luck.

I had no idea at the time, of course, but I would never

be that close to a pennant again. The whole team was heartbroken. Sick. To come that close twice in a row was an awful cross to bear. I remember sitting at my locker and seeing McCarthy come in and wondering where he had been. He had been over to congratulate the Yankees. He had perked up pretty good, but I know it hit him hard. I don't think he ever got over it completely, because when we got off to a poor start in 1950 he quit baseball for good and went home to Buffalo. He had reached the saturation point.

The five-hour train ride to Boston was the longest I've ever been on. It was like a damn funeral train. Everybody was stunned. We had come so far, had made up so much ground. The whole year had just wound up terrible. For me it had been the biggest year of my career for home runs (43) and runs batted in (159), but I missed the batting championship that last day, too, when George Kell of Detroit got two hits off Bob Lemon to beat me out by two-tenths of a point. There was a welcome-home crowd waiting at the train in Boston, but all I wanted to do was get out of there, get packing and go some place out in the sticks where I could fish. Fishing has always been a great refuge for me. I was off almost immediately for the Superior National Forest to fish for muskies, then after that I went down to Stuttgart, Arkansas, to fish and hunt duck. I was there a month. After a couple weeks or so I got a call from Fred Corcoran. He said I had been chosen the Most Valuable Player in the American League. I told him it couldn't be right. The Yankees had won the pennant, remember? Joe Page had had a great year, and Phil Rizzuto. "Yeah, but you're it," Fred said.

It was the second phone call in two years that was important enough to interrupt my fishing. In January of 1948 I was down in the Everglades going for snook when my daughter Bobby Jo was born in Boston. My wife, Doris, had gone into the hospital two weeks early. She was having dinner with friends at the Copley Plaza when she suddenly went into labor. They didn't get word to me for a day. I couldn't get a flight out right away, and by the time I got to Boston I had been tried in the newspapers and found guilty. The crime of the century. One of the papers conducted a man-on-the-street survey to see what "people" thought of Jack The Ripper. Harold Kaese wrote that "Everybody knew where Moses was when the lights went out, and everybody knows now where Ted Williams was when his baby was born—he was fishing."

Well, Bobby Jo was the most important thing in my life from the moment she was born and for a long time after that, she turned out to be the cutest little fisherman you ever saw, all blond and leggy, but I sure wasn't going to apologize for something that didn't concern anybody but Doris and me. "To hell with them," I announced when I got to Boston. "They can't run my life."

Oh, boy, now they really *were* offended. Paul Gallico beat his breast for about a thousand words. He called me a mucker and he wrote, "You are not a nice fellow, Brother Williams. I do believe baseball and the sports pages would be better off without you." He said he wouldn't pay a dime to see me play again, which was fine with me, because I wouldn't want him to get in for less than full price. Finally somebody asked Doris what she had to say about it, and her reply was perfect. "Well," she said, "Bobby Jo has Ted's eyes and my mouth . . ."

I left a few days later to get back to my fishing. There was nothing I could do in Boston, and naturally they continued on without me. It was the old story. You can make a case out of anything if you want to, or you can be fair to a guy and not make a big how-do-you-do out of a little thing. I always thought the Yankee players were protected from this sort of thing, that even their real bad actors were written up in angelic terms by the New York press. You can protect a guy and everybody will love him, or you can dig at him and everybody will think he's an S.O.B. Of course, the Yankees were winning, you get a good press when you're winning, and we were losing and there were forty-nine million newspapers in Boston, from the *Globe* to the Brookline *Something-or-Other*, all ready to jump us for it, so it's understandable.

I am sure that my love for fishing has cost me an awful lot. I am sure you could say the same about a lot of guys, guys who had ability, who could have accumulated something, who let fishing or hunting or whatever it was that captured their interest get in the way of those hours when they could have been applying themselves to moving ahead. Guys who just said, "The hell with it, all I want to do is get by and do some fishing." I know by this time I was so anxious to get to Florida to fish I could hardly stand it. Around 1950 we finally bought a home there, in Miami, the first home I ever owned. It meant something to me then, but not at much as it should have. I was not as excited about it as I should have been. I was wrapped up in my fishing, and I wanted to be there where those fish were, where I could fish all day.

I don't mean that fishing ever took away from my baseball. It never did that. I quit fishing during the season after about 1946 because I knew it could hurt me. I remember I caught a 400-pound tuna in Ipswich Bay during the season one year. It was a real hot sunny day in July and I had just taken off my shirt about half an hour before the tuna hit. I was two hours bringing it in, two and a half hours bareback under that sun, and that night I was burned until hell wouldn't have me. The next day I had to get into that wool uniform. Cotton was no good because it evaporated the sweat too fast and you could get a chill. I must have gobbed on a half inch of Noxzema so I could stand it.

That woke me up a little bit, but I still would go for bass, or to practice my fly casting, on off days. Then I began to realize it was doing something to me. I would fish for two hours with a fly rod—*blup*, reel in, *blup*, reel in, *blup*, reel in—and the next day I would feel something in my wrist. It was an altogether different motion, and a different feel—a six-ounce fly rod or even a sixteen-ounce golf club, swinging those, and then swinging a thirty-three-ounce bat. It throws you off.

I was a long time realizing, though, that baseball players are perishable merchandise and if they don't take advantage of their spare time, that if they don't start something, nobody will do it for them. After a while I got interested in the stock market. I subscribed to *The Wall Street Journal*, I started reading *Fortune*, reading *Forbes*, just fascinated as hell. I had a friend who was vice president of the State National Trust in Boston. He became invaluable to me. He was so interested. He would come out every afternoon and sit in the bleachers in left field, a big bald head you could spot, the top just as brown as anything. He got me started, then he died, and that hit me as hard as anything. I wish now I had gotten interested sooner. I was in a position where I could have had a half million dollars in the stock market. But in those days when I should have been doing it I didn't want anything to disturb the routine: Grind it out with baseball for seven months, then go to spring training in March, and the three and a half months in between for fishing and hunting.

Why fishing? All right. It's the outdoors. The beautiful surroundings. The trees. The streams. The ocean. The fresh air. It's the anticipation of a strike, the anticipation that with

173

every cast something might happen, the love of *making* a perfect cast. The love of just being there, away from the telephones, away from people. I can't think of anyone who had more fun out of life than Zane Grey. He had that big three-masted schooner and he just traveled the world, hunting and fishing. I would love to have just that type of setup someday. About a seventy-five-foot shrimp-type boat, with a nice gun room and a trophy room, and go anywhere I please.

It has always seemed a contradiction to some people, my love for a sport that would require so much patience. Old no-patience Teddy Ballgame willing to wait half the day in an open boat for one nibbly strike, and no guarantee he'll get it. Well, I don't necessarily show great patience fishing. I'm willing to wait, because I know if I do it right things will happen. Be in the right place at the right time and I know I have a hell of a chance to catch a fish. I could wait for hours and hours on a deer stand if I thought I was in a good place to get a shot. That's patience, but look how little patience I have with a crappy cast or a bad maneuver in the boat. Or no style, no talent for fishing, especially with a guy who is supposed to know what he's doing but doesn't.

I know the guys I gave downs to as a flight instructor at Pensacola weren't the eager young guys just learning, they were the hotshots who were coming through, maybe instructors from someplace else, guys who were *supposed* to know or *thought* they knew and didn't. With guys like that I had no patience. I don't have patience with somebody in the boat who frogs around. I had a professional photographer down on the Keys one time, taking some movies of me tarpon fishing. A good photographer, and I liked him. I got a tarpon on and it was running toward the boat. Gee, it looked like it might be going to leap right in the boat. I started yelling to the photographer in the other boat, "Get ready, get ready, he's going to jump right into the boat."

Doggone if he doesn't—on his first jump, right into my boat. I'm in there thrashing around with the tarpon, and I yelled to the photographer, "Did you get it?"

"No," he said, "I missed it."

I couldn't believe it. I told him to pack his things and get to shore, get his ass out of there.

But I could stay in a duck blind for a week and never raise my voice and be perfectly happy. Just sitting there thinking about the ducks, watching for them. I remember one time in 1948. A little duck lake outside of Princeton, Minnesota. There was a fellow in town named John Callus. He ran a restaurant and he was a hell of a hunter. Three ducks go up and he could crack every one of them. But he didn't like to sit on a spot, he liked to keep moving, he was like a little Indian hunter, moving around, moving around. I'd been coming back with some nice mallards and he wanted to know where I'd gotten them, so the next morning I took him with me.

We got to the lake before light. I got out my best decoys, checked the wind, set up the best possible duck blind, camouflaged clothes, big Magnum twelve, shell boxes all set, everything just right. He said, "All right, I'll set up at the other end of the lake." He went over and set up. We had scared quite a few ducks coming in, so I knew it would be just a matter of time before they'd be back. We got a shot or two when they went, but we'd do better when they came back. I settled in. It couldn't have been more than two hours when I looked up to see John gathering up everything, all his decoys and everything. He was pulling out.

Well, it wasn't twenty minutes after he left the lake when, *swooossssh*, here they come. A nice little flock, and all of them trying to get into my decoys. Thirty minutes after that I walked back into town with six nice mallards. Old John couldn't believe it.

I never felt I had to shoot a lot of game or catch a lot of fish to enjoy it. Being there is enough. I just like to be there. But I want to be in a nice boat, I want it to be rigged right, I want nice tackle. If my tackle isn't good I don't want to fish. If the gun doesn't suit me, I don't want to shoot. I have at least $5,000 worth of guns, and maybe some of them I don't shoot twice a year. But I like them. I know they're good guns. I'm happy just picking them up, a thing of beauty, of workmanship. Pride of ownership. It's a stab in my heart when I see a spot of rust on one of them.

The 1950 All-Star game was played in Comiskey Park in Chicago. I always enjoyed the All-Star games, getting a chance to see the other league's great pitchers, seeing a Koufax or a Drysdale or a Robin Roberts, finding out what I could do against them. Some of my biggest thrills were in All-Star games. I remember the kick I got the year before in old Ebbets Field in Brooklyn, when I didn't get any hits at all. I was playing with a cracked rib and I made a catch off a long drive hit by Don Newcombe with the bases loaded. One of those over-the-shoulder backhand catches. It helped save the game for the American League and in describing it the next day somebody said, "There isn't a better defensive left fielder in the league than Ted Williams." That might have come as a shock to some of my boosters in Fenway Park, but it had to be a lift for me. It showed I had made some improvement over the years.

But I always said they would never get me out of the game running into a wall. Running into walls was for guys looking for a short career. Pete Reiser comes to mind. I read where Pete Reiser whammed into a wall one day on a home run that went way up into the stands, past his reach. What's the sense? You hit the wall and maybe you don't get hurt, but you're out of position to make a play and the batter takes an extra base. If you do get hurt, he takes *two* extra bases. And if you get hurt bad, you're out for a long time and how does that help your club?

In an important game you go as hard as you can go, but you always fight that wall. I was always backing into the left-field wall in Fenway Park, that short fence, but I was used to it. The thing that worried me there was the scoreboard. I thought if I ever leaped up for a ball and came down on the scoreboard, onto those slots where the scores are put up, I could get seriously hurt. They don't pay off on your fielding. In the end it all comes down to what kind of a hitter you are. There are a lot of great fielders. The guys people remember are the hitters. The biggest name in the history of American sport was a hitter of baseballs, Babe Ruth.

In 1950 I had signed for what then was said to be the largest contract in baseball. Bob Feller had probably exceeded $100,000 in Cleveland because he had a gate-percentage deal with Bill Veeck, but this was the largest stipulated figure on a contract up to that time. By the 1950 All-Star break, I was leading the league in home runs, I had eighty runs batted in, and with the warm months ahead, months I always rolled in, I really thought I was on the verge of one of my greatest seasons. Then in the first inning at Comiskey Park Ralph Kiner sent me against the wall to catch his long fly. All I had ever said about wall-crashing was coming back to haunt me.

I knew I had hurt my elbow the moment I hit, using the elbow as a brace as I made the catch, but I had no idea how bad. Running in I was rubbing it and Casey Stengel asked me if I was all right. Casey was managing the American League, a guy I love, a great manager. He knew about those Boston writers, too. He had his leg broken in a car accident one year when he was managing the Braves and Dave Egan said it was the biggest and luckiest break Boston baseball ever had. Stengel used to say if the guys who criticized Ted Williams had a piece of the club they would sing a different tune. He was always on my side.

As the game went on, Stengel could see my arm was paining me, and he kept asking, "Are you all right? Are you sure you're all right?" And I kept nodding, OK, OK, because I wanted to play. In the eighth inning I got the single that put the American League ahead, but by now the elbow's a balloon and I'm in great pain. I went out of the game. The White Sox trainer took a look at it, but nobody thought it was serious. I remember coming out of the shower holding my arm to my side and holding it in my lap on the plane to Boston. Johnny Buckley met me at Boston Airport, and as we drove through the Sumner tunnel, going over that pebbly road, every time we hit a bump, boy, it went right through me and I let out a yelp. "Geezus, John, slow it down, will you."

The next morning I went to the clubhouse and Doc Fadden gave it one quick look and sent me right down for X rays. Pretty soon two doctors came out, they had the X rays, and I could sense something was wrong. One of them said, "You've got a pretty serious thing here. We're going to have to operate."

It hit me like a bomb. We were right in the middle of the pennant race. I was thinking about losing time. "All right," I said, "let's get it over with." That afternoon I went into the hospital, and the next morning they operated on the elbow for two hours.

Well, Doc Fadden told me later that neither doctor held out much hope for a complete recovery. I was thinking about time, and they were thinking about permanent disability, but they sure weren't telling me that. One of them wanted to take the whole tip out, the radius. That was the usual procedure. The other held out for the thirteen little chips I'd broken off the bone. He said, "Leave as much of the radius in as possible, this guy's a ballplayer, it's his only chance."

The doctor's name was Shortell and if he hadn't had his way I would have had a stiff elbow for life. Privately, even Dr. Shortell didn't give me much chance of coming all the way back. I remember going fishing with him in Maine while I was recuperating and how he seemed to be watching me and just kind of waiting.

I was back in the lineup in two months. For a while I just hung around fingering a ball, watching the games, but then they got anxious. Cronin was anxious. Steve O'Neill was anxious. O'Neill had taken McCarthy's place as manager. So I went back into the lineup and in my first game got four hits, one of them a home run, against the Browns. But the elbow wasn't strong, there was still a lot of pain. When I first took the cast off I couldn't extend it to within four inches of the other arm. After that I just went down, down, down. The last two weeks of the season were miserable for me. I wasn't doing the club any good, I wasn't doing myself any good, the fans were on me, the writers were on me. We had been hot on the heels of the Yankees, and then we tailed off badly. I was miserable.

The only manager I ever had trouble with was Steve O'Neill. I won't say he was the worst manager in the world. He'd been in baseball a long time, and he was an awfully nice guy, really, but I didn't think he knew baseball, I didn't think he had great control of the club, and he was the only manager I didn't enjoy playing for. That winter I fished the salt-water flats of the Florida Keys, fishing for bonefish off Key Largo. The fishing wasn't important, the important thing was that I poled that boat every day across those flats, building up strength in the elbow. I did special corrective exercises at night, lifting weights and squeezing things, and I poled the boat four or five miles every day, and in the spring I began to feel a little strength coming back.

Well, every year until this one I played all the spring training games, even if I didn't want to. The management always gives you that little jab—"You're a big player, the fans come out to see you play, they'll want their money back if you don't play"—so I played. But this year I'm thinking about that elbow, worried about getting it right. I didn't want to be rushing things again. So I made an announcement: I'm not going to play all the spring training games this year.

Damn if it isn't 1942 all over again. You would have thought I had spit on the flag. We were at war in Korea then, and Bob Coyne, the cartoonist for the Boston *Traveler*, draws this picture of a GI behind a rock, shells exploding all around, and off to one side the spoiled Ted Williams in his clean white baseball uniform saying, "I'm not going to play all those spring training games." It shows you how strong the feelings were that some of them had. Bob Coyne wasn't a bad guy, but he aimed low there, and I never talked to him again until a few years ago. It was just about that time I made some comment about the spirit on the club, and O'Neill hopped on that. He said, "Williams isn't bigger than baseball," whatever that meant.

So I got down to Sarasota, and I'll be a son of a gun if I didn't play the first spring training game, the second game, the third game, the fourth game. I played eight straight games. The guys on the club are laughing about it, and I'm feeling more and more like a damned idiot, so I decided I'd speak to O'Neill. I said, "Gee, Steve, my arm still bothers me. I'd like to do this thing right. I don't have to play all these games, do I?" No, no, no, we just want to see if you're going to be all right, don't worry, don't worry.

The next day I'm right back in the lineup, and the next day after *that* I'm in the lineup, and boy I'm getting madder by the hour. Finally I couldn't stand it any more and I went up to O'Neill's room at the Sarasota Terrace and knocked on the door. It was an off day and he was sleeping and I really had to bang on the door to wake him up. I said, "God damn, Steve, I just want to know why I'm playing every game there is." The only time I ever charged into a manager like that in my life. I said, "I don't have to play every game. It ain't helping me, it's hurting me. I don't understand it and I sure as hell don't like it."

He said, "Well, Ted, we just want to find out if you're going to be all right, just want to see how you're going to do," yow, yow, yow.

How I'm going to *do?* You'd think they would have known by this time what I could do. I could understand being anxious to get me back in when the pennant race was hot, but not when we're playing lousy exhibitions and I've got the time to do it right. Don't misunderstand me. Spring training is important. It's a must. Even as a young player you have to learn to pace yourself, and you're sore as you can possibly be for a while. It takes time to get the body ready to play. You've got to get your hands toughened up or you develop blisters. They've got to be callused. Your muscles in your hands have to be ready or you're so sore you can't swing a bat, sore and stiff.

I'm still strong today, but for swinging a bat, for quickness, the muscles aren't ready like they would be after spring training. You start seeing the ball, really ripping it, within two or three weeks, but you need four or five to be really sharp, maybe not at age twenty-two, but certainly at thirty-two. Spring training does that for you. You can't just tape up an injury like they do in football and go out on the field. You can't play with a heavy sty or a big blister. It's too exacting a game.

But playing all those spring games isn't important, not to a guy getting on. I would have much preferred to spend the time taking extra batting practice. It was obvious I was having problems. They should have given me the courtesy to go my own pace. Instead, they crammed it down my throat. Here I was making a trip to Lakeland—two hours over there, play four innings, two hours coming back— then to St. Petersburg, to Tampa, to Melbourne. All around the damn state.

Well, it ended up I was real unhappy about the whole thing, and he just never let up. I still played most of the exhibition games, four or five innings apiece. I don't think I got any time off, and the elbow just didn't come around. I'd pull back and a regular egg would pop up on it. I knew that season I would never be the hitter I was before. The balls never really flew off the bat they way they had. That year there was enough weakness in it for me to know I wouldn't be hitting with authority again for a long time, and with not nearly as much power.

I struggled to hit .318 for the 1951 season. I did play 148 games, which was about 60 more than I had played in 1950. I hit thirty home runs, only two more than I had hit in about half the time in 1950. I drove in 126 runs. But the team was fading that year, all the way to fifth place, and after that I never had the opportunity to drive in so many runs again. That winter O'Neill was fired and Lou Boudreau was brought in to be the new Red Sox manager. The first announcement he made was that nobody's job was safe, that all the Red Sox players were "expendable," and that that included Ted Williams.

part four

Despite my damaged elbow, and despite my previous service, and despite approaching my thirty-fourth birthday, I was called up from the inactive Reserves into the Marines in 1952 for the Korean war. I would not return until late the next season. Together, the two wars took four and a half years out of my career. Much has been made of this, and much speculation over what I could have done or would have done with those vital years. I wonder myself. I was not alone, of course. Hank Greenberg lost two years, most of a third and part of another in World War II. Bob Feller lost three years plus. Joe DiMaggio lost three.

I was singled out for sympathy because I was called up twice. In my heart I was bitter about it, but I made up my mind I wasn't going to bellyache. I kept thinking one of those gutless politicians someplace along the line would see that it wasn't right and do something. I know that winter my number had come up, that it would just be a matter of time. At spring training in Sarasota there was a big cheese man from Ohio, a baseball fan who told me he knew Senator Robert Taft. "I'm going to personally see Senator Taft about you," he said. "I know him like a best friend. I'll talk to him about it."

The way I understand it, all Taft said was "I have some reservations as to the fairness of it, whether these fellows should be going back, but I don't interfere with a thing like that." I wish I had the letter I got from him. John Kennedy, who was a Massachusetts Congressman then, told Fred Corcoran he tried to do something for me but couldn't. Evidently none of them could. I didn't say anything, but I was bitter because it wasn't fair. They haven't called up the Reserves for Vietnam yet and for the flyers that's a bigger war right now.

I think if it's an emergency everybody goes. But Korea wasn't a declared war, it wasn't an all-out war. They should have let the professionals handle it. A lot of the professionals on duty for Reserves didn't go. The war in Vietnam is another undeclared war. If I had a kid over in Vietnam I'd be screaming. The unfairness of the Selective Service is obvious when you know how the draft laws and the exemptions work. There's only one way to do it, of course, if you're going to have a draft, and that's to draft *every*body.

The doctor who gave me my physical gave the elbow a long look. I thought he was going to defer me, but after quite a little delay he said, "The arm's all right." So I went to spring training knowing I was going back into the service any day. I hadn't signed my contract yet and one afternoon Joe Cronin and I were taking a ride and he said, "You know, Ted, I'm not asking you to take a cut, but the word is that you're going in the service. Our advance sales are not very good. I'm wondering if you would stand for $90,-000 this year."

I had been raised to $100,000 just the year before.

I said, "Sure, Joe, anything you say."

It didn't matter, really, because six games after the season started I was made a captain in the Marine Corps.

My last game in Boston they declared Ted Williams Day. Dave Egan, sentimentalist to the end, wrote, "Why are we having a day for *this* guy?" I didn't want them to have any days for me, either. I didn't want to be obligated and I said so. But they had gone too far, the Mayor had proclaimed it and they went ahead. They gave me a Cadillac, five or six friends of mine, and a big memory book which 400,000 fans had signed. The Governor and the Mayor were there, and a Korean veteran in a wheelchair. Everybody held hands and they sang "Auld Lang Syne," and I have to say it moved me quite a bit. They say I tipped my hat, but I didn't. I just took it out of my back pocket and held it up in the air and pointed to the left-field stands where all my conversationalist friends were, and I said, "This is the greatest day of my life. I'll always remember it. It is a day every ballplayer looks for, and one I thought I'd never have. I never thought when I came to the Red Sox fourteen years ago that they were such a wonderful organization. They've been wonderful to me."

We were playing Detroit. Dizzy Trout pitched for the Tigers, and he pitched well. The score was tied, 3–3, in the seventh inning, two men out, Dom DiMaggio on base, my last time up. Dizzy threw me a low inside curve, a pretty good pitch, and I hit it into the right-field bullpen. We won the game, 5–3. That night I threw a party at the Hotel Kenmore. I invited bellhops, cab drivers, bartenders, bat boys, cops—guys I knew. I had to think at the time that it was my last home run in big league baseball. I was thirty-three years old. I would be thirty-five when I got back. Chances were I wouldn't play again.

I felt we should have been in Korea, just like we should

be in Vietnam, and I think the Koreans themselves have shown their appreciation, they've been pretty loyal allies. They knew we never coveted any of their territory. South Korea has made a great comeback since that war. That ought to be a message for some people. But I also felt we only half tried to win. I'll tell you one thing, though. The guys I met in the Marine Corps were the greatest gung-ho guys I ever met. I gripe, but there were guys in there with four kids, right out of the Reserves too, and I'd hear them say, "I'm not going to bitch about it, this is the right thing we're doing."

Two weeks after the 1952 season started I was on my way to Willow Grove, Pennsylvania, for an eight-week refresher course in flying. Gerry Coleman of the Yankees was called in at the same time. By this time my old Navy SNV was practically obsolete. Jets were the thing. A great friend of mine, Bill Churchman, had just come back from Korea, where he had flown the SNV, and he said, "Listen, if you can get in jets, do it. If you take an SNV into a target at 400 miles an hour, you have to go out at 400 miles an hour. You take a *jet* in, you're going 420, you release your bombs, you get the hell out of there at 500."

I could certainly see the logic in that. I kind of wanted to fly jets anyway. I got my name put on the list.

Well, one Saturday afternoon, a real pleasant, clear day at Willow Grove, I was warming the top bunk when, *swisssssssh,* a plane came over the field. Little while later, *swisssssssh.* The plane again. Finally I got down and looked out and sure enough it was an F-9 jet, zooming up the field and flying around raising hell.

About fifteen minutes later, you could hear the sirens and the fire engines, everything beating it out of the base. I jumped into my car and went after the fire engines, not knowing what had happened. I've always been a fire engine chaser. When I got where the engine stopped, they were trying to put out this fire where a plane had gone down.

It was the F-9. It had come in, exploded and was burning. There were people crowding around. A big crane was pulling out part of the tail, pulling out part of the engine, pulling out a tire, pulling out this and that, making a hole about thirty feet wide and four to five feet deep. They'd found the canopy off to one side, but they couldn't find the pilot; he'd apparently ejected.

When they neared the bottom somebody said, "Hey, it looks like the fellow got out; he must be over there someplace." Then they dragged out a shoe with a foot in it. Oh, Christ, he was mangled. The worst thing I'd ever seen. I saw two guys spin in and crash one time, but they were in one piece. This guy was *crunched*.

Despite that, I was impressed with the jets the minute I got in one. Easy to fly, easier than props because they had no torque, less noise, tricycle landing gear. Wonderful flight characteristics. Turn one over and it would just r-o-l-l, nothing to it. We rushed into ground school at Cherry Point, North Carolina. They had a baseball team there, but I wasn't going to be playing any baseball. I had the word on that.

We moved on to operational training at Roosevelt Roads, and I almost landed in a sugar-cane field there one day. It was real windy and I was too high coming in so I just chopped the throttle, a perfectly natural thing for a guy who had been used to conventional piston-type engines. But I chopped too far, and the jet started settling in, and now the wind was pushing me back. I was getting low and I knew I was going to be short of the strip, so I poured the coal to it. What I had forgotten was that the fuel regulators on these jets aren't the same as conventional engines, there's a little time lag, a protective device so you

187

don't flood it out. I was just about into that cane field when the power came and I got that little *uumph* that put me up. It would have been embarrassing.

After that we went to cold weather training school in the Sierra Mountains, living on canned stuff, spruce sprouts for beds, parachute for a tent, and I like to froze my tail off. Sure enough, down with another virus. When we got to Tokyo, everybody went out on the town except me. I stayed in bed for two days feeling lousy.

Somebody wrote one time that I had privately resigned myself to my fate, that I thought I was going to Korea to die. That's not true. The thing that always brought me to my senses about relative dangers was the F-9. When I flew it I always marveled at how good a plane it was and how much better I had it than some of those guys in the South Pacific who flew over water all the time and in equipment that wasn't as good.

I have to say this. I never felt the Marines got the kind of equipment they deserved. I remember landing at Pohang in Korea, lousy old corrugated mat, crummy quarters, a real dog box. Cold and damp and awful.

The commanding general greeted us, and we went to our different squadrons. I was with the Third Marine Wing, we had a photographic section, and two squadrons formed the one wing. Mine was the 223rd. I inherited a bed one of the guys had made—a major who was going home. It was two two-by-sixes, three feet apart, and the springs on it were the rubber inner-tubing off a jet's tires. It was all bent up, curved on either side from being squeezed together so long.

We got checked out on field procedure, landings, operating procedure, emergency procedure, and we took a couple of practice flights and made some bombing runs on an old bridge, and we went on into combat.

After about eight or ten missions, I began to get real sick.

The weather was miserable, cold, foggy, misty. My ears and nose plugged up. I was going to the infirmary every other day. Well, I was out on this one mission, far above the thirty-eighth parallel. Our target was an encampment, a large troop concentration. We were nearing the target when I lost visual reference with the fellow in front of me. I swung out to pick him up, and when I got back on target I was too low.

We were supposed to be pretty low anyway, using daisy cutters that day, anti-personnel bombs that hit and spread out. But now *I* was a target for I don't know how many thousands of gooks in that encampment, and sure as hell I got hit with small arms fire. When I pulled up out of my run, all the red lights were on in the plane and the damn thing started to shake. The stick stiffened up and was shaking. I knew I had a hydraulic leak. Fuel warning light, fire warning light, there are so many lights on a jet that when anything serious goes wrong the lights almost blind you. I was in serious trouble.

I started to call right away. I had a plane in front and one to the side, but I couldn't pick anybody up. All of a sudden this plane was right behind me. The pilot was a young sandy-haired lieutenant named Larry Hawkins, from Pine Grove, Pennsylvania. He could see I was calling, nodding my head, and the last I heard was, "I can barely read your transmission," and the radio pooped out. Later he told me he was yelling for me to shoot the canopy and bail out, and if I'd known I was on fire I probably would have. He came up close and I saw he was pointing like mad, trying to show me I was leaking fuel or something. He signaled with his thumb: "Let's get up." So we climbed. Altitude is a safety factor. The thinner air helps in case of fire, and if you get up another 10,000 feet you can glide thirty-five to forty miles if the engine fails.

Meantime, I had taken off my leg strap which holds the data for the trip. I was sure I was going to have to bail out. I'd gone off my hydraulic system. (When it's damaged it is safer to fly without hydraulics, even though you really have to wrestle that stick.) I got up to 18,000 feet and I could see frozen water on my right. Any minute I expected I'd have to bail out, and I always dreaded the prospect. It was the only real fear I had flying a plane, that if I had to bail out I wouldn't make it. Among other things, the cockpit is small. For a big guy, cramped in like I was, I thought I'd surely leave my kneecaps right in there.

Lieutenant Hawkins did a great job. He led me back to the field and called in to warn them. From the target to the base, flying time was about fifteen minutes. All of a sudden I was over the field. Not the same field we'd taken off from, but one nearer the target. It was a madhouse. Everybody was coming in at once, about sixty planes in from the mission, all low on fuel. But all I had eyes for was that tiny little field. I started to make my break on a fairly tight turn, when, *fffuummum,* a big explosion in the plane. One of the wheel doors had blown off. Now there was fire and smoke underneath the plane. Why a wing didn't go was just an act of God. The plane was still together, and flying, but I knew something bad was happening. All I cared about was getting on that deck.

I came in at about 225 miles an hour, twice as fast as you'd ordinarily do it. My approach was good and I'll never forget looking down and seeing a little Korean village near the field. With thirty feet of fire streaming from the plane, the villagers were running to beat hell. I pulled the emergency wheel latch, but only one wheel dropped down. I hit flush and skidded up the runway, really fast. No dive brakes, no flaps, nothing to slow up the plane. For

190

more than a mile I skidded, ripping and tearing up the runway, sparks flying. I could see the fire truck, and I pressed the brakes so hard I almost broke my ankle, and all the time I'm screaming, *"When is this dirty S.O.B. going to stop?"* Geez, I was mad, I always get mad when I'm scared, and I was praying and yelling at the same time.

Further up the runway the plane started sliding toward a second fire truck, and the truck tried to get out of the way, dust flying behind it. I stopped right at the end of the runway. The canopy wouldn't open at first, then I hit the emergency ejector, and the fire was all around me, everything on fire except the cockpit. Boy, I just dove out, and kind of somersaulted, and I took my helmet and *slammed* it on the ground, I was so mad. There were two Marines right there to grab me.

I came back and looked at the plane later, and it was burned to a crisp. They had doused it with foam, and the foam was all over it, and it was just cinders. The skid marks on the runway were 2,000 feet long.

Generally after a close call like that they ground you for two or three days, but we were hurting for pilots and I was back flying the next day. I was a little edgy, but it wasn't bad. We flew over Seoul at 20,000 feet, and what a mess that was, the whole town black and burned. One of the medical guys chewed them out for putting me back up so quick. It wasn't long before the cold and coughing got worse. My right wing got hit by flak one day, but by this time my resistance was so low I didn't much care.

I was really sick, the sickest I've been in my life. They flew me by helicopter to the hospital ship off Pohang, and I don't know how many days they had to feed me intravenously. I had pneumonia. I was on the ship three weeks, and when I got back my head was plugged up all the time. I couldn't hear the radio. I'd fly six or eight missions, then I'd have to see the doctor.

I was up to thirty-nine missions when they sent me back to Japan for treatment. They said they were going to have to do some work on the inner ear and the place for that was Hawaii. Once I got to Honolulu they said I might as well go on to Bethesda Naval Hospital in Maryland, and once I got there they said the hell with it and mustered me out. I had to sign a medical waiver because of my ears. One ear still bothers me. I catch myself yelling on the phone, "Speak up, speak up." A switch to the other ear and I'm back in communication.

Everybody tries to make a hero out of me over the Korean thing. I was no hero. There were maybe seventy-five pilots in our two squadrons and 99 per cent of them did a better job than I did. But I liked flying. It was the second best thing that ever happened to me. If I hadn't had baseball to come back to I might have gone on being a Marine pilot. The flying part came easy. From my early days in baseball I always had brand-new cars and I'd zip up the highways from Minnesota to Florida at eighty or ninety miles an hour, getting the feel for speed, and I know enough to realize it wasn't the greatest transition in the world to airplanes.

I was never a relaxed flyer. I was eager to learn, eager to understand conditions and circumstances in the air because I knew it was my ass if I didn't. Two things always scared me: 1) bad weather, because I knew I was a lousy instrument flyer, I wasn't well versed in it, and 2) the possibility of having to bail out. I was sure I would never get my kneecaps out. So I was always right on edge, watching everything. Good pilots are that way anyhow. But like anything else, you have to stick with it. I was up in a small plane with a friend not long ago. I hadn't flown in years. He asked me if I wanted to land it, and I said sure, and I had a hell of a time.

Well, I was out of the service, tired and half sick. When I got to San Francisco there was a call from Ford Frick, the commissioner. He said they wanted me in Cincinnati to throw out the first ball in the All-Star game. Everybody wants to know when I'm going to play. There's a lot of activity going on. Baseball's the big thing again. Then I got a call from Fred Corcoran. Fred had been my business manager, handling everything except my baseball contracts since 1946. He was strictly a golfer's agent until his brother John got us together and we made an agreement. John had the Ford dealership in Wellesley, Massachusetts, and I used to get my cars from him. I remember at that time I told Fred what I wanted him to do, then I said, "What do *you* get?"

"Fifteen per cent."

"Fine, fifty per cent."

"No," he said, "not fifty, fif*teen*." Boy, I thought I was getting a bargain. We've been close ever since. Fred Corcoran has been one of those guys in my life who was there whenever I needed him. I love him.

So now Fred is on the phone from New York and he says, "There's still two months left in the season. Everybody wants you back. I think you ought to try to play this year."

I said, "Hell, Fred, it's the middle of July. The Red Sox aren't going anywhere. I'm not ready to play baseball. Mr. Yawkey says I can do what I feel like doing. I feel like fishing. I'm going fishing."

"You're not a fisherman, you're a ballplayer."

"You've never seen me handle a fly rod. I'm the best there is."

"I'm serious, Ted. You've got to get started. It'll be the

best thing in the world for you. Work yourself in gradually, then be ready for a full season next year. Listen, baseball is your *business*."

That kind of got to me, and at Cincinnati the fans at the All-Star game gave me one of the warmest receptions I ever got, not a boo in the crowd, and that perked me up some more. It was a hot day at Crosley Field and I remember being so concerned for little Billy Pierce of the White Sox. Billy probably threw harder than anybody for a guy his size, he had a real big delivery, nice to look at, and he had overcome a lot. I understand he had had epilepsy, and I was really pulling for him. He was a nervous little guy, and here he was starting his first All-Star game in a bandbox park that's tough to pitch in, and against Robin Roberts to boot. Pierce held them in the palm of his hand that day. He threw the ball right by everybody.

Bob Lemon was there. He came over and said, "Boy, I'm glad to see *you* back." He knew he had handled me pretty well up to then. Later that season, before I got back into the lineup, Cleveland came to play us in Boston and some of the young guys the Red Sox had then—guys like Ted Lepcio and Dick Gernert and Billy Consolo and Karl Olson —were getting to Lemon pretty good. Base hits all over the lot. Really pounding him. I shouted out to the mound, "Hey Bob, these guys don't know who you are!"

I met Branch Rickey at the airport in Cincinnati after the All-Star game. I was heading back to Washington, and we sat and had coffee. I was always impressed with Mr. Rickey, the things he did for baseball, the strength he showed. He was very encouraging that day. He said I had been a credit to baseball and to my country, and that nobody could say anything bad about me in his presence. But the thing that impressed me most was when he said, "Ted, you've got five or six more good years left. I think you should play. I think you're going to be all right."

I went to Boston really getting the fever again, getting anxious to play, and my first day back I took some batting practice. Boudreau threw to me. Gee, it felt so good to be swinging a bat again. About the eighth or ninth pitch I hit one into the center-field bleachers. Cronin was watching. He said, "Ted, nobody's hit one out there all year." After I'd finished, we were standing at home plate and I told Cronin I thought the plate was off line. "Gee it couldn't be," he said, but he agreed to humor me. He got a guy to check it with a transit and sure enough it was off a fraction. Everybody made a big thing of this, a demonstration that the Williams eye was still intact, but if you had stood at that plate as often as I had you would know when it wasn't right.

Johnny Orlando had three brand-new uniforms with the old Number Nine on them pressed and hanging in my locker. He said they hadn't used the locker since I left. There were a lot of new faces. Boudreau had done a lot of trading, he had a youth movement going. I was thirty-five years old, the old guy on the club, but I didn't *feel* old. Being thirty-five didn't mean anything. I still felt I was the best hitter around. Boudreau made it clear he wanted me to play as soon as I was ready. That meant something to me. I had the feeling they all wanted me to play. And I have to believe the young guys were thinking, Hell, let's watch this guy, he might show us something.

I worked out with the Red Sox for about ten days. Claude Harmon gave me six pair of golf gloves to use so the blisters wouldn't get too bad. I finally got to pinch-hit in Washington, a pop-out. On the following Sunday we returned to Boston, nice sunny day, 27,000 fans in Fenway

Park, and another big ovation. In the eighth inning Boudreau sent me in to pinch-hit against Mike Garcia of Cleveland and on a 3–1 pitch I hit a low fastball over the right center-field fence. I had hit a home run the day I left and a home run my first day back. One of the writers asked Garcia if he grooved it.

After that it seemed like every pitch that came in was as big as a grapefruit. I think this will happen when you come in fresh like I did, because baseball is never quite as good at the end of the year, everybody is tired, the pitching isn't as tough. For the next thirty-seven games I hit .407, including thirteen home runs, a home run every seven times at bat. I had a slugging percentage of .901. Joe Cronin said I had set spring training back twenty years.

On the first day of spring training the next year I fell coming in for a line drive and broke my collarbone. I wasn't out there sixty seconds when it happened. I had driven up from the Florida Keys that morning, a four-hour drive, and was in uniform and on the field at ten. I was a little leg weary but that could be expected. The Red Sox were taking batting practice. I trotted out to where Jimmy Piersall was shagging in the field and I said, "Let's try to get together in the outfield this year, Bush, maybe do something right," and I had just turned around to face the infield when Hoot Evers hit a ball in my direction. I started in for it. It was sinking fast, and I speeded up, and when I realized I couldn't get it and tried to slow down I began to stumble, then I fell. I tried to roll on my shoulder as I hit, to cushion the impact, and I heard the pop. Piersall came running up to me. "I broke it," I said. "I'm sure something's broken."

The doctor right there was an old friend, Russell Sullivan, an orthopedic surgeon from Boston. We had been on the Keys together. They tried to put the collarbone together just by pulling the sections apart and working them back, but they couldn't. It was a serious break. They put it in a cast, and when I got to Boston Dr. Sullivan put it together with a stainless steel pin about four inches long and big around as a pencil. The pin is still in there. You can feel it through the skin.

Now I'm really down. First the elbow, then the Korean thing, and now when I feel like I might have some good years left after all, boom, broken collarbone. The whole thing haunts me to this day, because counting injuries and my service hitches, I lost six full seasons of baseball. The cost in dollars and cents is not as sad as the realization that it cost me one-fourth of my playing career.

This time I was out for six weeks—thirty-six games. In April I wrote an article with Joe Reichler for the *Saturday Evening Post*, announcing my retirement from baseball. I said I would quit as soon as the season ended. I meant it. I was hurt, I was tired, I was disgusted. Mad at the writers, mad at everybody. I had every intention of packing it in for good. My marriage break-up was part of it. Nothing sensational, nothing unusual. Doris and I had gotten on different paths, that's all. I hadn't lived in that house in Miami very long before I went to Korea, and I wasn't back three months before I moved out for good. I guess you would have to say that as my life away from home—my baseball—got bigger, my life at home got smaller. It happens.

Bobby Jo had come along, of course, and she meant a lot to me, but even there I wasn't as close to her as I wanted to be. I was gone so much I couldn't exert the influence I would like to have. I wanted her to go to college, but she didn't. She loved to fish when she was a little girl, we were great companions, but little girls grow up. I knew when I got back from Korea that Doris and I had had it. In May divorce papers were filed.

I got back into the Red Sox lineup on May 7, in Detroit, and went eight-for-nine in a doubleheader. The collarbone gave me some pain, I couldn't sleep on my left side, but it wasn't too bad, and the elbow was loosened up by the warm weather. It was stronger than it had been since the operation in 1950. I played every game after that, 117 altogether, and hit .345, which would have won the batting championship except they were walking me so damn much I didn't get the required number of official at-bats. It took 400 to qualify, I had 386. We weren't the hitting team we had been and the pitchers kept working around me. I led the league in walks for the eighth time. Lou Boudreau batted me second in the lineup for a while, trying to help me get enough times at bat, but I was still short.

Bobby Avila of Cleveland won the batting championship with .341. Casey Stengel said the 400-at-bats rule was unfair, that it was "never meant for a guy like Williams, it's for humpty-dumpties trying to steal a batting championship on half a season's work." I appreciated that, but it's funny, really. Some years later Tom Sturdivant came to our club from the Yankees. He said the Yankee pitchers had been told they weren't to give me anything to hit, and if I beat them in the seventh, eighth, or ninth innings it would mean a $50 fine.

In September I retired, but things had happened and were to happen that made me change my mind. First, I had met Ed Mifflin. We were at the train station in Baltimore, sometime in July, the first year the Orioles were in the league. I was sitting on one of the back benches alone, reading, waiting for the train to Boston. A fellow came up beside me and said, "You're not really going to quit, are you?"

I didn't even look up. "Yeah, I think I am."

"You're not going to quit with Greenberg hitting more home runs than you, with DiMaggio hitting more home runs. You're not even in the top ten yet. You got a chance to hit five hundred home runs. Only Ruth, Foxx and Ott ever did that. You could be in the top five in RBI's. You could get four thousand total bases. You don't have two thousand hits yet."

Gee, by this time I look up at this guy. He's telling me things that never dawned on me before. Never entered my mind. At the time I had about 320 home runs. I wasn't even thinking about 500. "Who are you?"

"I'm Ed Mifflin. I'm from Swarthmore, Pennsylvania."

"Sports writer?"

"No, just a baseball fan, a fan of yours."

I had never met Ed Mifflin, but he turned out to be a two-legged encyclopedia of baseball statistics, the kind of guy the *experts* go to for information. He's telling me I've got a chance to do this, a chance to do that. He's perking me up, getting me thinking, getting me interested. Every time I did something after that, every time I reached a milestone, Ed Mifflin would remind me of it. He'd write a letter: "You've got X number of total bases, that's only five less than Foxx." I'd score a couple runs and he'd send a wire: "You just passed DiMaggio." "Six more doubles and you'll pass Simmons. You just passed Heilman." "That's 494 home runs, one more than Gehrig, Ott's next."

I'd never been a guy to collect mementos. Plaques and things I always gave to somebody else to keep, and I never kept scrapbooks like Johnny Orlando. Half the pictures I had were washed away in a Florida hurricane one year. But I had always set goals for myself. I read not long ago where Carl Yastrzemski said he wouldn't set goals because it put an added strain on him. For me, I always had goals, but *realistic* goals: 30 home runs for the season, 100 runs batted in, .330 average. Sure, I was unhappy if I didn't reach them, but it gave me something to shoot for, something to keep my interest up over a long season, especially when we weren't in the pennant race. Professional basketball players do things like that to psych themselves up when they're tired. They pick out some guy who's been tough on them, or exaggerate some little slight and try to get a mad on. Sort of an artificial stimulus.

Well, with Ed Mifflin supplying the figures I began to have fun reaching these goals. Just like Mays when he hit his five hundredth home run. He said he hoped to pass Williams that year, and he did, and that had to be fun for him. I was stirred up again.

With my announced intention to retire, I didn't see any reason to go to spring training the following February. I just stayed down on the Keys fishing with Jimmy Albright, my guide, and reading Williams-Will-Be-Back and Williams-Won't-Be-Back stories. The year before I had signed a $100,000 contract, the biggest in baseball, but I was now just another unemployed fisherman. It was during the late summer of that year, just before this little limbo that I was in, that Joe Cronin and Mr. Yawkey said, "Why don't you manage the Red Sox?" Lou Boudreau had been fired in November. The team had plunged in the standings. Despite what some writers had implied, Boudreau and I never had problems, he always treated me right, but I think he lacked the ability to instill confidence in the team. So he was fired.

I said, "No, hell no, I don't want to manage. I'm a ballplayer. I can still hit in this league. If I stick around, it's going to be as a player. There's a big transition from player to manager. I'm not trained, I don't have the desire."

Cronin said, "We're going to have a lot of good young players. A good young pitching staff. These guys already look up to you. You'd be a good manager."

I said, "Joe, I don't even know how to make out the lineup card. I don't know enough about the subtle things, when to pull a hitter, when to make replacements, all that stuff I'd need help on."

He said, "I'll get you all the help you want. Get somebody to sit right beside you until you get your feet on the ground."

Well, it just didn't interest me, he didn't sell me a bit, and we left it. I could see myself getting right into a sling with the writers, and ending up like most managers do, with my ass fired. We had a doghouse team, going nowhere. Mr. Yawkey came to me again later and asked who I'd like to see manage the club and I said, "Mr. Yawkey, you've got a guy in Louisville who's been fighting his way up from the minor leagues." I was talking about Mike Higgins, who had played third base on our 1946 team. "He deserves it. I think Pinky Higgins deserves a chance to manage the club." Shortly after that Higgins was hired for 1955. In Boston they wrote that Ted Williams had wanted the job but Higgins got it instead.

On May 9, 1955, Doris won her divorce. It was in all the papers, nothing private: $50,000 and $125 a week, a $50,000 house. I won't tell you what I think of American divorce laws, because that would take some time, but I knew with that settlement I might as well forget about being a gentleman fisherman the rest of my life. I also knew from my record the previous season that I was still a long way from being the "out" man on the club. On May 13 I signed a $98,000 contract with the Red Sox.

For the third straight year I had missed spring training. They used to write that I "avoided" it. It wasn't that at all. I've always believed it to be necessary, but I also felt I had reached a point in my life where I could get in shape better on my own, doing what I knew had to be done. I was never far out of shape anyway. I was always an outdoors man. Fancy restaurants and night life and cocktail parties never fascinated me. I was never more than ten pounds over my playing weight.

I worked out for a few days, about ten or eleven, running hard to get my legs in shape and that year at the start I used golf gloves on both hands in batting practice so I wouldn't develop blisters. I was swinging a lot, trying to get ready in a hurry, and I couldn't afford to wait for the calluses.

I hit a home run my first day back. I hit .356 for the season. Al Kaline won the batting championship with .340. I wasn't even close, because I only got up 320 times. Even if they hadn't walked me so much (110 times) I probably would not have made it that year anyway, but the rules committee finally saw the injustice of it and changed the rules. Now a batter needs only 502 *physical* appearances at the plate rather than 400 official times-at-bat to qualify for the championship.

After that there was always something. A bad back, another case of pneumonia, lumbago, an injury to the arch of my foot when I slipped in the shower one day. In those days we wore those big wooden shower shoes and I was clumping around with soap under my feet and slipped off hard, jamming the side of the shoe into my arch. For two weeks I couldn't do a thing, just hobble around. I couldn't get up on my foot at all. My instep was like a boil. They had to shoot it with cortisone before I could get back in the lineup. Six more weeks wasted. Then there was another bad cold, the walking pneumonia, and I was out another month.

I seemed always to be coming back from something. The writers kept washing me up, and I kept jamming it back down their throats. Austen Lake said he was going to quit washing me up because I was making him look bad. But they weren't particularly exciting years. We were never in the pennant race. The closest we came in five years was third place. I conceded the pennant to the Yankees in June one year and oh, everybody made a stink out of that, but it was only the truth. I was tired a lot, mad a lot, bored a lot. One night I even tried some chewing tobacco just for something to do.

We were in Washington, a cold night, and Boudreau said I didn't have to play, so I was sitting the game out. Grady Hatton, a utility outfielder we had gotten from Cincinnati, was on the bench next to me. Hatton used to really load up. He had one of the biggest plugs in baseball, right up there with Snuffy Stirnweiss and Nellie Fox. The three of them were the worst I ever saw. Jim Tabor was another. We're sitting there and Grady's stuffing it in, and I'm looking at him, and after a while it's looking pretty good to me, the way he's savoring it.

About the third or fourth inning I finally said, "What the hell, Grady, give me some of that," and he tore me off a piece.

Right away the saliva started coming out of me like I had sprung a leak. I'd spit and every time I'd spit I'd swallow a little bit, taking in backwash. Now I'm beginning to feel a little queasy. I'm fighting vomiting. So I ducked into the clubhouse and got a 7-Up, and all that did was make it worse. I go back to the bench, and it's the seventh inning, two men on, and I get the word to go up and pinch-hit. I didn't know what I was going to do first, swing or throw up, but I swung and hit a line drive into right field for a base hit.

Actually I didn't mind the taste of chewing tobacco so much. If I ever took up tobacco in any form, that would be it. I still hate the smell of cigarettes, can't go into crowds without feeling like I'm in a smokehouse. I went to a football game in the Orange Bowl last fall and somebody had a cigarette going somewhere, not even close, and I could hardly breathe. I remember my third year with the Red Sox, 1941. We were coming back on the train from a pretty good road trip and I celebrated with a beer and my first cigar. I got so sick I had to stick my head out the window.

The years from 1953 to 1957 were so unhappy for me, with the spitting and gesturing incidents and my troubles with the fans and the writers, and us never doing very much. Fred Corcoran and Jack Sharkey were all the time trying to save me, trying to get me to make my peace with the world. Sharkey was the ex-heavyweight champion. He and I used to appear together at the Sportsman's Show in Boston, fly casting and demonstrating fishing equipment, and over the years we had become very close. Sharkey is the kind of guy who even if he didn't feel like fishing he would want to paddle the boat for you. Just a wonderful guy. But he is also an open book.

He would tell me stories about his troubles with the fans, how they'd boo and he'd stand in the middle of the ring yelling at them, "Boo, you sons of bitches, you're paying twenty-five dollars a head to see me fight." Then he'd tell me why he thought I had to be different.

"What if you get hurt," he'd say. "What if you can't play any more, what are you going to do? Be a high school coach? Sell fish? Nobody's going to give a job to a jerk."

He was always working on me. I'd be up there casting, and he'd be down beside the runway when somebody in the stands would make a crack—"Nice cast, Williams, too bad you can't use that thing at the park"—and I'd start to burn and Sharkey would whisper loud enough for the first ten rows, "Smile, chowderhead, *smile*, for Chrissake."

Corcoran took me to meet Bing Crosby one time and we

got to talking about getting along with the press. Crosby's advice was to play dumb. He said there was a time when Jimmy Fidler was saying some nasty stuff about him on radio, a lot of half-truths and innuendoes, things about his private life.

"One day I ran into Fidler at the Lakeside Golf Club," Crosby said, "and I gave him a big smile and said, 'Hello, Jimmy, how are you?' I said, 'Say, Jimmy, what are you doing these days?' Fidler kind of stammered around and said, 'Why, I've got a Sunday night radio show.' 'Gee, that's fine. I'll remember to listen next Sunday,' and I just walked away. He was flabbergasted."

But playing dumb and smiling like an idiot just wasn't in me. I was right back in the soup in March of 1956. It was my first spring training since before the Korean War. We had a bull session going around my locker, Charley Wagner had brought in some San Francisco reporters, and we were sitting there when somebody mentioned Johnny Podres. Podres had won two games in the 1955 World Series for the Dodgers and it had been announced afterward that he was being called into the service. His draft classification had been changed from IV-F to I-A.

I said it would never have happened if he hadn't won those two games and become a big star, because that probably got some phony politician wondering why a healthy boy like that hadn't been in the Army.

I must have been in top form, because I called the politicians gutless and the draft boards gutless and the sports writers gutless too because they weren't taking up for Podres.

I think I made at least one good point, though: I said that during peacetime it made sense to me that if a boy could get deferred to go to college, another boy who has chosen baseball for his career should be able to serve his military time in the off months. Those four years are important to the college boy, sure, but they're just as important to a ballplayer because his career has a definite time factor. Your income spirals if you're a lawyer, an insurance man or a doctor, but a ballplayer just has so many years and then his goes down. I said I thought the baseball executives could do something about it, too, but they were as gutless as the rest.

Well, that went hot over the wires and into the log as another demonstration of the Williams candor, and everybody's on me for it, yow, yow, yow. That was the year the spit started flying, and by the time the season was over I was exhausted. Yes, and dried out too. That year I won my annual race for 400 at-bats, I got 400 right on the button, but that was also the year Mickey Mantle hit .353 and beat me out in the last week.

I went to spring training in 1957 thinking it would be my last year. We played an exhibition game that spring in San Diego, the first time I'd been home in five years. My mother was going to be at the game but she got sick and couldn't make it. In all my career she probably saw me play only five or six times, never as a big leaguer. She was always so wrapped up in the Salvation Army. She did get to see a few television games and used to say what a great announcer Dizzy Dean was, because he always said nice things about me. Anyway, she missed this game, and I was sorry about that, and coming east we were in New Orleans and had a delay at the airport.

Hy Hurwitz, a Boston writer I always thought of as a troublemaker, brought this little guy from the New Orleans paper into the lounge at the airport. We were sitting and talking and somebody started in on the Korean War and about Johnny Podres being called back into the service. One thing led to another, and I started blasting everybody

—the politicians, President Truman, Senator Taft, drinking newspapermen I had known, the way you would do if you were a sailor on a ship grousing with your buddies about the damn admiral.

I said we hadn't half tried to win the Korean War, and when the guy told me he was an ex-Marine I had a few words to say about the Marine Corps, some of the crap they had to take, the lousy equipment. I had once posed for a Marine poster and they wanted me to do it again and I said I wouldn't, period.

I would say the same things again, because that was the way I felt, but I never dreamed this was any kind of formal interview. The reporter's name was Crozet Duplantier; he was the sports editor of the New Orleans *States*. I thought he was half drunk at the airport that day. He splashed that thing all over the paper, and I'm in it again. Wasn't that silly? To write what a ballplayer would say in casual conversation about a President or a senator?

But the next day when they asked me about it I wasn't in the mood to back down. I added a few words about the IRS and how they were taking advantage of Joe Louis, holding him up for back taxes despite all the things he had done for his country. They were hounding Louis, he would never be able to pay, he was stuck for life, but if he were some big-shot politician they'd let him pay two cents on the dollar.

I did send a wire of apology to the commanding general of the Marine Corps out of my loyalty to the guys I had served with, and Mr. Truman was great about it. He said he always enjoyed watching me play. He said he didn't see anything so bad in what I had said, and that he had said a few things himself in his day.

Well, I started the season mad and I finished mad, I didn't say two words to the Boston writers all year, and in between I probably had the most amazing season any near-forty-year-old athlete ever had. I'll never forget, I'd used a slightly heavier bat that spring, just trying to meet the ball a little better, and the bat felt so good I began the season with it. I think it weighed thirty-four and a half ounces, good wood, and I choked up about a quarter-inch more than I had.

And gee, the balls were just ringing off it, flying around, all over the lot—left field, center, right. On opening day in Fenway Park I got two hits off the Yankees, both to left field. I hit safely in the first eight games, the best start of my career. We were in Chicago one day early in the season and they were playing that tough shift on me, and I hit three bullets just to the left of second base, *pshew, pshew, pshew*. Next series, same thing.

The league started waking up—Williams is thirty-eight years old; it looks like he can't pull the ball any more. Everybody started opening up a little bit, spreading out, giving me some room. As early as April we went into Kansas City, Lou Boudreau was managing the A's then, and I looked up and—gee, no shift. They're playing me normal. I got three hits that day. And in June, when I always get rolling, I began swishing the bat like old times and the ball was whistling into right field. Except now there were *holes*. Every time I hit the ball it went through a hole. And there were home runs, big ones, even when I got tired.

I remember we went into Cleveland, and it was one of those cold, rotten nights. Early Wynn was pitching. I hit a home run the first time up and a home run the second time up and I said to Mike Higgins, "Come on, Mike, take me out." He said, "What for? You might hit another." Sure enough, I hit another one, setting a major league record; it was the second time that year I'd hit three home runs in one game. I had three off Bob Keegan in Chicago in May.

The only real "day" I ever had was just prior to my recall into the Marines in 1952. They gave me a book with the signatures of 400,000 fans. I gave them a home run my last time up to beat Detroit, 5-3.

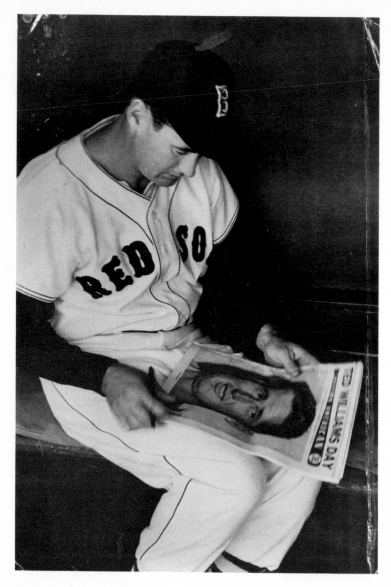

From that memorable last day (*above*) at Fenway Park to the war in
Korea (*opposite*) was a tough transition for a guy pushing 34. Above
right are the charred remains of the plane I brought in after being
hit by ground fire over North Korea.

If I looked sick and tired outside my quarters in Korea, it was because I was. I had had pneumonia, and I developed an ear problem that bothers me to this day. I was sent home.

At the 1953 All-Star game in Cincinnati, I was getting the itch to play again. Three Red Sox players were there: *(above)* George Kell, Sammy White and Billy Goodman. I was back in uniform before the season was out. Signing to play baseball was never hard for me, partly because of the greatest owner in baseball, Tom Yawkey *(below)*.

After Korea, the Red Sox teams I played on were never very good. My personal exploits got more and more attention from what I considered an unfair press (*above*). There were always so many of them in Boston. When the Braves left town, it seemed as if they just doubled up on the Red Sox. Evidently Boston writers never get fired.

I was said to be throwing a tantrum here *(upper left)*, but it was actually a bat I threw, and my reaction is on seeing the bat hit a lady fan. My spitting *(above, right)* became as famous as my hitting, but I finally clammed up *(lower left)* when I realized how the Boston fans really felt about me. The sign is an example.

Jim Thorpe *(above)*, a wonderful man, appeared with me at the Sportsman's Show one year and advised me on how to deal with the press. After winning my last batting championship (1958), I flew to New Brunswick for the closing day of the salmon season and caught this 20-pound hookbill *(below)*. No fish ever gave me a better fight.

The most miserable season of my career—1959—was the result of a pain in the neck. I pinched a nerve in the spring and for a time wore this cervical collar. For the season, I was below .300 for the only time in my big league career.

217

My last game, my last time at bat. The opponent was Baltimore, September 1960, Fenway Park. The picture series shows the final routine: waiting on the on-deck circle, taking a low pitch, then connecting for what every player dreams of hitting his last time up: a home run.

An older Ted Williams *(opposite, above)* can look back on a lot of pleasing things. One was knowing I had ranked with great hitters like Bill Terry, Rogers Hornsby and George Sisler *(opposite, below)*, and knowing, too, when I went out onto the field at Fenway Park for the last time *(above)* that no Red Sox player would ever wear No. 9 again.

In 1965, I was voted into the Hall of Fame with Casey Stengel *(below)*. I made my speech short to give Casey more time. He was always a candid spokesman for baseball, and his eloquence broke up Mickey Mantle and me *(above)* at the Senate anti-trust hearings.

Bagging my limit of grouse and woodcock (*above*) was plenty excitement enough in the years afterward, until I met Dolores Wettach, married her and came up with John Henry Williams (*below*), my son.

For a player, an emptying ballpark meant the game was over, and it was for me in 1960. As a manager, I look forward to the new game, knowing it will never be the same.

224

When they told me it was a record it surprised me. "You mean Ruth never did it? Gehrig never did it? Foxx?"

My daughter, Bobby Jo, saw me hit two home runs in one game that year, one of the few times she saw me play.

In September I hit four home runs in four consecutive times at bat to tie another record. I had just gotten over another cold, that heavy chest cold that was always knocking me flat. I was holed up in my room at the Somerset Hotel for seventeen days. Then I pinched-hit for a homer off Tom Morgan of Kansas City, then walked, then hit the only home run I ever got off Whitey Ford of the Yankees.

I have to say Ford was one of the five toughest pitchers I ever faced. Toughest for me. The others would be Bob Feller, for sheer stuff—he had more stuff than anybody; Bob Lemon, a great natural athlete, his pitches always moving, always sinking, always directed to a tough spot; Ed Lopat, who had the finest collection of junk you'll ever see; and Hoyt Wilhelm, strictly for his knuckleballs. Wilhelm had a sure-strike knuckler, then a real good knuckler, then with two strikes, a real bastard of a knuckler, dancing in your face. The closest thing to an unhittable ball I ever saw. I remember one time waiting for that knuckler, and darn if Wilhelm didn't throw a fastball. I said, "Well gee, here's a nice fastball." *Bow*, line drive into right field for a base hit. I had that much time. He never threw me another.

Ford, like Lopat, was a left-hander. He had that sharp-breaking curve, and he always got it in a good spot, away and down. Most of the hits I got off Ford were to center and left center. He made very few mistakes, a tough little guy, and smart. The home run I hit was a mistake. He threw a curve in the ninth inning of a game he was leading by seven runs, but he hung it high and I hit it into the right-field seats at Yankee Stadium. It was the only high curve Ford ever threw me.

225

The next day I was back in the lineup. I hit a grand-slam home run off Bob Turley, then the Yankees walked me three straight times. The Yankee Stadium fans didn't like that at all. They booed like hell. The next day Sturdivant walked me, then gave me something worthwhile and I hit the fourth home run. The next time up I singled.

This series of home runs was right near the end of what I think was the most phenomenal thing that happened to me that year. Counting walks and hits, I reached base safely sixteen straight times. That might be a record to last forever.

It was the kind of year where every move I made was a headline. I was out a couple days in Detroit. I had been getting on base so much I was worn out, my resistance was low, and Hy Hurwitz wrote that he had seen a medical report that said my condition was chronic and my career was finished. Another scoop for Hurwitz. Jim Bunning of the Tigers struck me out three times one day in June and it was a front page banner: "TED FANS THREE TIMES." Not the score, not who won, not whether there was an earthquake someplace or a war, but "Ted Fans." It was one of the few times I had struck out three times in one game in twenty years. (I got a little satisfaction in July. We went to Detroit and Bunning tried those high sliders again—unlike most sliders, Bunning's tended to rise, he kind of slung it sidearm—and I hit the first one on the roof of the upper deck and the second one into the right-field stands.)

We went into Cleveland one afternoon and I was about to ask Mike Higgins for a day off, when I picked up the Cleveland *News* and there's another big headline: "WILLIAMS VS. SCORE." Big match-up: twenty-year-old Herb Score, who could throw as hard as anybody I've ever seen, and tired old Ted Williams, age thirty-eight. That was the year the Red Sox offered a million dollars for Score, and if he hadn't gotten hurt he would have been worth it. He was as fast as Feller and Trucks, and they were the fastest. I didn't ask for the day off, I always enjoyed hitting against the best pitchers, so I played, and I hit a home run, but Score won the game, 7–1.

For the year I batted .388, five hits short of .400. I got hot in August and hit .453 over the last half of the year. The fans were pulling hard for me to hit .400 again. They almost rioted one night in Boston when I hit a liner off Harvey Kuenn's glove and the scorekeeper ruled it an error. The way they carried on I wouldn't have been surprised to see six or eight of them climb up the screen to get at the scorer. As it turned out, he later changed it to a hit. Everybody seemed to be for me. A politician in Boston tried to have the city change Kenmore Square to Williams Square.

I was the oldest player ever to win a big league batting championship. I hit thirty-eight home runs, the most I'd hit since 1949. Mantle hit .365 that year, *his* best, and beating Mickey had to please me a little, because he had won it the year before. I always set my sights on the guy ahead of me or the guy closest to me. I was *always* conscious of the other guy. Usually the guy was Joe DiMaggio. I had a slugging percentage of .731, my best since 1941. I hit better in Yankee Stadium than I ever had—.453.

In the standings, however, it was an old story. We were third, sixteen games behind the Yankees. I was second to Mantle in the vote for the Most Valuable Player. Mr. Yawkey got upset about it because a couple of the Chicago writers voted me way down, ninth and tenth, something like that. He called the voting "incompetent and unqualified," and Mantle himself said he was surprised. I wasn't. Mickey had a great year, the Yankees won.

As always, I went to Cronin after the season to talk about a new contract. He asked me, "What do you want?" Never

227

any arguments, just little discussions and it was over, bang, boom, bang. I said, "Joe, I'm going to quit after two years. I want a two-year contract for such-and-such. How does that hit you?" Fine. Simple as that. The biggest two-year contract in the history of baseball at that time. And gee, in 1958 I led the league again with .328, despite an ankle injury, a muscle pull in my side, a case of ptomaine poisoning from some tainted oysters in Washington, and a bad start. I didn't get above .300 until July. I beat out Pete Runnels on the last day of the season, my second change-of-life championship.

Runnels hit second in the Red Sox batting order that year, just ahead of me. We had gotten him from Washington in a trade. He was the kind of hitter who would have a great year, then a mediocre year, but he could slap the ball around. Real good bat control. From July on we were one-two in the batting race, and in the last two weeks I was half pulling for him to win it. I was thinking in my heart, I hope he wins it. I'm not going to give it to him, but I hope he wins it. Runnels had never won a batting championship. I had won five. We weren't in the pennant race. It certainly wouldn't make much difference to me at that point. I wasn't getting the kick out of it I had the year before.

I went nine for thirteen the last few days, and with two games to play we were tied at .322. We were in Washington for the last series of the year. First time up Runnels tripled and I walked. Then he singled to right and I did the same. Then he hit a home run to left, and I hit a home run to right. Now, fourth time up, he hit one deep to center field and Roy Sievers made a hell of a play to keep it from going in the stands. I got a hit and went ahead. The next day Pete Ramos pitched for Washington and he was always tough for me. But I got a single the first time up, then

Ramos threw me a little change up, I saw it coming and hit into the left-field bullpen. That broke Runnels' back. I wound up hitting .328 to his .322, and I told him after the game, "Pete, I wanted you to win it. I didn't give you anything, I tried all the way, but I was pulling for you to win."

Right after that game I got on a plane and flew to Boston, then to Bangor, Maine, late that night. The following day I was out on the Miramichi River in New Brunswick for the last day of the salmon season. I have come to believe over the years that fishing for Atlantic salmon is the greatest fishing there is. You're always in a beautiful spot, a nice stream, a nice little river, beautiful surroundings. It's a wonderful eating fish. It has a romantic life cycle; they know that a salmon spawned in a certain stream will live there four years, go out to sea and two years later come back to that same stream to spawn. It's an extremely game fish. It jumps. It's so hard to make it take sometimes you think it has been warned. You might be out on the river all day, making 400 casts, seeing salmon jump, seeing them roll, maybe getting a pull on your line, or seeing somebody else get one, and all the time you're enjoying the expectation that it's going to happen the very next cast.

I got on the river about two thirty in the afternoon. The season would be closed in two hours. The wind was blowing like a son of a gun, right down river, and I had to fish on the left side, casting to keep the fly away from me, picking it up slow and laying it down easy. And boy, I got hold of the fightingest salmon I ever caught, a twenty-pound hookbill, a beautiful fish. I've never had another like it. There was a guy fishing across the river and he came across and said, "I've heard what a hell of a fisherman you were, and I want to tell you you *are* a hell of a fisherman," and he took my picture with the fish. I've still got the picture in my den, me and my little beret and that big hook-bill. I wish now I had mounted that fish. I've tried ten years to get another like it.

I was so happy that night, there in my cabin on the Mira-michi. I felt, Gee, here I am forty years old and feeling like I could go on forever.

Then in the spring of 1959 I was sitting under the coco-nut trees with a bat in my hand, out back of my house in Islamorada on the Florida Keys, telling an old friend what I thought I was going to do that season, how good I felt. I got up and started swinging the bat, just swinging it as though it were a fly swatter. I didn't realize it then, but I hurt my neck that day. I'm sure of it.

The Red Sox were training in Scottsdale, Arizona, that year, and it was a lot cooler out there than it was in Flor-ida, actually cold at night, and right away my neck began to bother me. I couldn't bend my head. To turn my neck I had to turn my whole body. They finally took X rays and one guy said, "He's got a problem." Doc Fadden, the trainer, and the doctor there in Arizona agreed I should be sent right up to Leahey Clinic in Boston to see the ortho-pedic specialist, Dr. John Poppen.

I wound up in traction for three weeks. A pinched nerve. I remember being in that hospital, New England Bap-tist in Boston, feeling down, and getting a letter from John Glenn the astronaut. I'd been with him in Korea and he said he was writing to tell me he was going through the centrifuge, the weightlessness chamber, and I'd really get a kick out of it.

I took the letter into Mrs. Yawkey's room. She was in the hospital then for something, and between the hours I had to be in traction they let me walk around in a cervical collar and I'd visit Mrs. Yawkey. I told her about Glenn, that he was just the kind of guy who ought to be commandant of the Marine Corps. Then I threw the letter away. Just after that they announced the astronauts and John Glenn was the one from the Marines. I wish I had that letter.

I had never met any of the Kennedys until then. Ambassador Joe Kennedy asked Fred Corcoran if I would pose for a picture with John at the park in Washington the year before, this was prior to his announcing for the Presidency, he was still in the Senate then, and I said sure. But that was when I got sick on the oysters, and John Kennedy hurt his hand doing something, and we missed connections. Anyway, Ambassador Kennedy told Fred not to let them operate on my neck. "Ted will be through if he does," he said. Bobby Jones was supposed to have been operated on for a pinched nerve, and was in a wheelchair the rest of his life.

When I finally got out of the hospital and back with the team, I was no good to anybody. I had a miserable year. The worst by far of my career. I could barely turn my neck to look at the pitcher. I wasn't getting nearly enough of a look, and I thrashed around all year near .250. A lot of times I wouldn't even go to the dugout between innings if I didn't think I would get to bat. I'd just wait in the bullpen. I seemed to go from slump to slump. At one point I went to the plate twenty-one times without a hit, then almost did the same a few days later. As was pointed out to me by some of my friends in left field, I could spit farther than I was hitting.

I made my fifteenth All-Star game only out of the manager's kindness. In June, usually my best month, I was in such bad shape, Billy Jurges, who had taken over as manager from Higgins, had to bench me, the first time in my life I was ever taken out of the lineup for not hitting. I was absolutely miserable the whole year. The only relief I got was when the season ended, and then Mr. Yawkey called me in.

My two-year contract was up, but I sure wasn't thinking about quitting on a sour note like this. I went up to his apartment at the Ritz-Carlton, and he started talking and I could see what was on his mind. Finally he said, "What do you think you ought to do next year?"

And I came right back at him. "What do *you* think I ought to do?"

He said, "Ted, I think you ought to quit." Like that. He said, "You've had a great career. You were hurting this year and I don't want to see you hurt more. Listen, why don't you just wrap it up?"

Well, that kind of burned my ass. I remembered the draft thing in 1942, how everybody was pushing me the way I didn't want to go, and I just got burned. Sure, I was forty-one years old, forty-two before the end of the season, but what had happened in 1959 had nothing to do with age. I was hurt. I'd hit .345, .356, .345, .388 and .328 in the five previous years. Then .254. Clearly an injured man. I said, "Well, I'll tell you, Mr. Yawkey, I'm going to wait until next spring to decide. I still think I can hit. If I feel I can't do it by spring, I'll let you know."

But now I'm hearing some grumbling. I'm hearing a lot of grumbling that makes me think they're not so sure they want me back. I had this talk with Mr. Yawkey, and now I get word that maybe Dick O'Connell, the new general manager, doesn't want me back, and I'm hearing about this guy and that guy, and pretty soon I've had about all I can take. Screw this. If they don't want me, I won't play.

So I went up to see O'Connell. This was about the time of the Sportsman's Show in Boston and I used to make the trip do a double service, the show and the signing of my contract. I went up and I said, "Dick, if there are any doubts the club wants me back this year, hell, I'll quit. I think I can still play. I told Mr. Yawkey I'd go to spring training and find out. But I don't want to play unless the management *wants* me to. I can take that, too."

Well, he was nice as pie. "Aw, Ted, don't be silly." He pulled out a stack of papers. "I've got your contract right here, ready to sign, same figure as last year."

By this time, though, I had made up my mind on something else. I said, "Dick, look. I had a lousy year, the worst I ever had. I was injured and I suffered for it, but I don't deserve what I made last year. I've had the biggest raises a player ever had. I've gone up from nothing on this club to $125,000 a year. I want to take the biggest cut ever given a player."

So I signed to play my last year, 1960, for $90,000, a $35,000 cut, almost 30 per cent.

I was now an old, old man as far as baseball was concerned. Forty-two in August. Ty Cobb was out of baseball at forty-two. DiMaggio, Ruth, Hornsby, Foxx, Greenberg, they were through as players before they were forty-two. I'd always said when you're over thirty-five you're in on a pass. But I felt good that spring. Not The Kid from San Diego any more, all full of spit and vinegar, but not old either. I didn't hit any big home runs in spring training —in fact, I didn't hit any home runs at all—but I didn't have as much restriction in my swing either. The pain in the neck was still around but I could live with it.

Jurges started the season that year as the Boston manager, and I remember him saying the most he expected from me was a hundred games, and the least was pinch-hitting. I told him I'd quit if I couldn't help the club. I had no intention of just pinch-hitting. I played 113 games. Jurges got fired in June and Higgins took over again. First game of the season, first time up I hit a 500-foot home run straight up the middle of the diamond in Washington off Camilo Pascual, who was always tough for me. President Eisenhower was there that day. It was my four-hundred ninety-third, tying me with Gehrig behind Ruth, Foxx and Ott. Earl Battey, the catcher for Washington, and the umpire were still looking when I came around. The next day I hit another home run off Jim Coates of the Yankees. At one point I was hitting a home run every seven times at bat. For the season I hit twenty-nine, and my average was .316. Runnels won the championship with .320, so he got even for 1958. I only drove in seventy-two runs, but we were a seventh-place club, kept out of the cellar only by the incompetence of the Athletics. We lost eighty-nine games, the most in Yawkey's twenty-seven years as owner of the club.

The year went by in bits and bursts. I was tired a lot of the time, sore and stiff, and my neck still bothered me. I know I wasn't swinging exactly the way I wanted to all the time. But I was hitting home runs and I was staying well above .300. One night in Cleveland the weather was bad, rainy and cold. A couple days earlier I had hit my four hundred and ninety-ninth home run. In our lifetime there won't be ten guys to reach five hundred, but that night I went to Mike Higgins and said, "Mike, how about taking me out of the lineup. It's a lousy night. I could use the rest." He said, "Gee, Ted, I just handed the lineup card in. Go on and play tonight; I'll take you out tomorrow." I was thinking, What the hell difference does it make if he did turn in the card? He could take me out of the lineup as easy as he put me into it. But it never fails. The first time up I hit a home run to left field, my five hundredth.

The season moved into September. I hit a home run off Don Lee of Detroit. I had hit a home run off his father, Thornton Lee, twenty years before. I hit two home runs in Cleveland one night, Nos. 513 and 514, to pass Ott. *The Sporting News* voted me the Player of the Decade, and the next day somebody in Boston started a story that I had snubbed President Eisenhower at a reception in Washington, which goes to prove at least one of the Boston writers wasn't going to turn sentimental over my impending retirement.

They were trying to line up "days" for me in Detroit and other cities, but I didn't want to be bothered with days or anything else at that point. I mean I was just fed up with that part of it. I'd gotten criticized one year for not going to the Most Valuable Player banquet, when I was it, and I was just fed up with banquets and days and all of it. Besides, I didn't like to wear ties. They choke you, they get in your soup, they're a nuisance. I've always felt I was forty years ahead of my time about ties. I see now they're wearing those turtlenecks with jackets. Sports shirts will be next. I'll be in style at last.

We came into Boston for the last series, with Baltimore, and then it got down to the last game. The team still had a doubleheader in New York that weekend, but I went to Higgins and said, "Mike, this is the last game I'm going to play. I don't want to go to New York." He said, "All right, you don't have to go." Regardless of what I had done, this was it, I'd had it, I knew it. I knew the club was thinking about youth, it hadn't been in the pennant race since 1951. I knew there was a kid named Carl Yastrzemski coming up who was going to be a hell of a player. And in all fairness I have to say that I felt that a lot of people didn't want me around any more.

Well, like the .400 season, and the World Series, and the party I missed when we won the pennant, and the picture they took with Lefty Grove when he won his three hundredth game and I wasn't there, and the letters from Glenn and Dick Nixon when he was the vice president, that last game has gotten so much more important as the years go by. I wish I could remember every minute of it but I can't.

I don't remember if I arrived particularly early. I don't remember what was said in the locker room except I might have been aware of some feeling. You sense things. The players knew it was my last game. There was a headline in the paper that morning: "What Will We Do Without Ted?" I remember a guy from one of the magazines came in and I said, "What the hell are you doing here?" because I felt that gutless magazine had given me a bad time for years because I didn't show up for a banquet one time. Bud Leavitt, an old friend from the Bangor *Daily News,* was in the runway when I came out and we chatted. The photographers were crowding around. I didn't give them too much to focus on.

They had a ceremony for me at home plate. They gave me a silver bowl and a plaque. They retired my number, and the Mayor presented a $4,000 check to the Jimmy Fund for kids with cancer. I've been affiliated with the Jimmy Fund since 1947, getting a whole lot more credit than I deserve. It was just something somebody asked me to do and I did it. I went to a little field outside of Boston one night in 1947. They had an old wrestling ring set up, there were four wrestlers, and Frankie Fontaine the comedian was there, and the Jimmy Fund got started. Fontaine has been a great champion of kids' charities around Boston. He has about ten kids himself. A few years later the Red Sox joined in. Mr. Yawkey realized how important the work was, the children's cancer research, and the Red Sox have helped it grow.

I know I am just one of a multitude of athletes who have gone to see kids in hospitals, to see sick kids. People in the public eye are always asked to do these things and they do them gladly. I don't think you should get the Silver Star for it. It's something you *should* do without having people

236

rave over you. When they asked me, I went, that's all. No big deal. That kind of contribution is so overrated compared to what the people *in* these hospitals are doing. I have always felt it was just a twist of fate anyway that I was allowed to be on the outside, strong and healthy, instead of in there with them, maybe in a wheelchair.

Certainly I have seen some pathetic cases that stand out in my memory. Some pitiful, sorrowful things. I remember one kid had both his legs cut off by a train. Another one had suffered an electric shock and lost both his arms and legs. There was one boy who had to have his legs amputated after he got burned at the stake playing cowboys and Indians. The first kid I visited in Boston, a boy named Donald Nicoll, was dying of a stomach disease. I got a nice letter from his dad, saying they were fans of mine, asking me to visit the boy. They lived in West Roxbury. I still see the family. The boy made a great recovery and went on into the ministry. An awfully nice boy.

I promised one boy in Washington I'd hit a home run for him. Washington had a lot of pitchers who would try to buzz it by you, hard-throwing guys, and they could be hit, and I happened to hit one over the lights that night. But they always made more of my visits and what I did than they should have, and wrote a lot of things that just weren't true. Like being at the bed of an incurably sick child the night the team celebrated the 1946 pennant—when I was off tying flies for my fishing. A lot of crap like that.

I love kids, that's all, it's no virtue, and I don't see any reason to cash in on it. A guy likes kids, he has to hope their lives are going to be good, that they will avoid the pitfalls he had, that they will be appreciative of how lucky they are. I think one of the greatest things ever said is that a man never stands so high as when he stoops to help a kid. I think that is a hell of an expression.

237

Teddy Ballgame I got from a kid. A friend of mine, a photographer named Fred Kaplan, brought his little boy to a game at Fenway Park. He couldn't have been more than two years old at the time, but it made an impression on him. A couple years later Fred was going to the park again and the boy wanted to come, too. "Why?" Fred said. "Who do you want to see?"

"I want to see Teddy."

"Teddy who?"

The boy thought for a minute. "Teddy Ballgame."

Curt Gowdy introduced me at the ceremony as "controversial, but colorful," and called me "the greatest hitter who ever lived," which was a pleasing exaggeration. I thought about what I was going to say, but I don't know if it came out exactly right. I knew I was going to be brief. I had my hat off. I didn't tip it, I just took it off. I thanked them all, and I meant it, and I said, "Despite some of the terrible things written about me by the knights of the keyboard up there"—and I looked up at the pressbox—"and they *were* terrible things, I'd like to forget them but I can't, my stay in Boston has been the most wonderful part of my life. If someone should ask me the one place I'd want to play if I had it to do all over again, I would say Boston, for it has the greatest owner in baseball and the greatest fans in America."

I didn't take batting practice. It was one of the lousiest days you ever saw. The wind was blowing in—a dark, dreary, drizzly day, cold and threatening, a real doghouse day. And Baltimore was starting Steve Barber, a tough little sinking-ball left-hander. He never struck me out much, but he was hard to get hold of and his control was not too good.

Sure enough Barber was wilder than a March hare that day. And this is fate, it has to be. If I had had to face Barber four times that day I'd probably have gotten one good ball to hit, certainly not three. But Barber walked the first batter, walked the second, then he walked me on four straight balls. When he got behind the next batter, they pulled him out and Jack Fisher came in, another kid half my age. Fisher is a pretty good pitcher, too. He's been in the big leagues ever since. But he's a little easier to see.

The second time up I hit a fly to right center. Another day it might have gone, but the air was just too heavy. Jackie Brandt caught it easily. Then in the fifth inning I really got into one, high and deep into that gray sky, and gee, it just died. Al Pilarcik caught it against the 380 sign. I remember saying to Vic Wertz in the dugout, "If that one didn't go out, none of them will today."

I was second man up in the eighth inning. They'd turned the lights on by now. It was eerie and damp, and I had bundled up in my blue jacket in the dugout waiting for my turn to bat. Willie Tasby was up first, and I got my bat and went to the on-deck circle as soon as he moved out. This surely was going to be my last time at bat in baseball. Twenty-two years coming down to one time at bat. I remember how the fans were all up on their feet applauding when I went to the on-deck circle, and feeling the chills up my spine, and thinking how much I wanted to put one out of there—and knowing what the odds were.

The first pitch was a ball. Then, from the batter's box, it seemed to me Fisher humped up as if he were going to try to fire the ball by me. I *knew* he was going to try to pump it right past. And gee, here comes a ball I should have hit a mile, and I *missed* the son of a gun. I don't miss, *completely* miss, very often and I don't know yet how I missed that ball.

Fisher couldn't wait to throw the next one. He must have thought he threw the last one by me, and maybe he did, but all my professional life I had been a fastball hitter, and whenever I had an inkling one was coming it was that much better for me. This time I tried to be a little quicker, and I hit it a little better than the others that day. I had a little extra on it. It fought the wind, and it just kept on going into right center, toward the Red Sox bullpen, the one they put in in 1940 with the hope I'd hit a lot of homers out there. It kept going and then out.

There were only 10,454 people in Fenway Park that day, but they reacted like nothing I have ever heard. I mean they really put it on. They cheered like hell, and as I came around, the cheering grew louder and louder. I thought about tipping my hat, you damn right I did, and for a moment I was torn, but by the time I got to second base I knew I couldn't do it. Like I said, I was just fed up with that part of the act.

You can't imagine, though the warm feeling I had, for the very fact that I had done what every ballplayer would want to do on his last time up, having wanted to do it so badly, and knowing how the fans really felt, how happy they were for me. Maybe I should have let them *know* I knew, but I couldn't. It just wouldn't have been me.

I got to the dugout and went to the water cooler, then sat down, my head back against the wall, and gee, they were *still* applauding and calling my name, and players were pleading with me to go back out. "C'mon, Ted, give 'em your hat." I know they felt good for me too. Even Higgins came down and asked me to go out, and the umpire was looking over as if he expected me to. But I couldn't, and the inning ended, and Higgins sent me back out, I guess to give me another chance to acknowledge their cheers, because he had Carroll Hardy follow me to left field. When I got out there I had to turn around and run back in. From the early days I always tried to get in as fast as I could. No glad-handing, just *whhsssh*, right in. Bobby Doerr used to be that way too, like maybe he was a little embarrassed to be out there. I ran in with my head down, and the fans were all on their feet, clapping and clapping.

Celebrate? I don't remember celebrating. It was over, that's all. I was slow getting out of the clubhouse. I sat around for a while and had a beer and talked until there wasn't anybody else to talk to. Then I got dressed and sneaked out a side entrance to avoid the crowd. After that I don't remember what I did. I probably just went back to my room at the hotel, which was always a retreat for me, the place I'd gone back to so often after something bad had happened, something sure to get me in a wringer, something that started me thinking, God, here it goes again. That's when guys like Fred Corcoran and Owen Wood and Johnny Orlando would come around, to be with me for consolation when I was down. That's why they mean so much to me today.

I know I was relieved that part of it was over. The Red Sox didn't have anything exciting in store for me. Mr. Yawkey used to say, "What do you want to do, Ted?" And I'd say, "Well, I sure don't want to manage, but I don't want to be in baseball at all if baseball doesn't want me," and we'd leave it at that. I always felt close to Mr. Yawkey without actually being close, without hanging around his office like a lot of guys do. I never once went to him for anything unless I was called—the influence of my military training, I suppose. I think it always amazed people that I could adapt so well to military discipline and be such a single-minded civilian.

I thought for a long time the Red Sox wanted to keep me in some capacity, but as I look back I have to think there was a faction that didn't want me around, that kind of undercut me a little bit. Maybe there was some jealousy there, I don't know. I thought for a while it would have been nice to have helped with the coaching on the field, to do some scouting, watch some of the players, be able to give an intelligent opinion on some young guy coming up. Be able to compare him with another guy the club might want to trade for. Maybe go down and work with him and see if he's worth spending a lot of money on.

Sometimes I even think I should have stayed on the playing roster another year just to help Yastrzemski, and maybe do a little pinch-hitting. I'm positive I could have helped Yastrzemski be a better hitter. He had a terrible year that next season with the Red Sox, his first year up. I've worked with him some since then and it's usually just a matter of talking to him a few minutes. I know there are always guys in a farm system that could be better hitters. There have been times I thought I had a kid straightened out and he went somewhere and just tailed off, played under some manager who was a pitcher and couldn't tell him a damn thing about hitting. That's the best way I know to have a $100,000 prospect die on the vine.

But I never felt I was really wanted, so the hell with it. I'm not the type of guy who is just going to hang around. Hornsby and Cobb were like that, and Bill Terry, and that's why they weren't in baseball longer. Never yes-men. Always off-the-cuff, honest-to-God hard-nosed guys, really keen baseball minds, on top of it all the way. I don't say I have their quality but I certainly have their attitude. You could look at it another way, of course. If I had to frog around with baseball for the full season, I couldn't be fishing in June, I couldn't be fishing in September. That's the way I looked at it until I took this Washington job, and I'm still not so sure I was wrong.

Nobody knew this, but the Yankees tried to hire me to play one more year in 1961. Shortly after my last game

Fred Corcoran got a call from Dan Topping, the Yankee owner, and they met at the Savoy Plaza in New York. According to Fred, Mr. Topping said, "Would Williams play one year with the Yankees, strictly pinch-hit for us for what he's making now—$125,000?"

Corcoran told him I was still tied up with the Red Sox on a deferred payment setup, that he ought to call Tom Yawkey about it.

"I don't want to call Yawkey, I want to sign him as a free agent. Can he get his release?"

I'm sure if I had wanted him to Mr. Yawkey would have worked it out, but I wasn't interested in playing for the Yankees. What did New York have to offer? A lot of bad air and traffic jams. I told Fred to forget it, not to promote anything, I wasn't interested, I was never going to hit another ball in a big league park.

There was a time, though, that a deal was actually worked out between the Red Sox and the Yankees: Ted Williams for Joe DiMaggio. The feeling was that a right-handed power hitter like Joe was made for Fenway Park, with that short fence in left field, and I was better suited for Yankee Stadium, with right field so handy, and it was just fate that crossed us up. Mr. Yawkey and Mr. Topping met in a restaurant in New York and the way Fred Corcoran tells it they talked until two A.M. and shook hands on the deal.

The press got to sniffing around and almost got it right. The trade was on the verge of going through. Then the next morning Mr. Yawkey asked Mr. Topping to throw in that "little guy you've got in left field." The little guy was Yogi Berra. The deal fell through.

My last official act around a big league park was to cover the 1960 World Series—the Yankees against Pittsburgh—for *Life* magazine. I'll never forget, we were in Pittsburgh, sitting in a box seat near the field, and a woman in the next box reached over with a program and said, "Excuse me, Ted, would you mind signing this?"

"Certainly," without looking up.

"You know," she said, "you're one of my favorite players."

"Oh, is that right?"

"Yes. I'm Stan Musial's mother."

I told her she ought to be signing *my* program.

Right after that game, Fred and I were walking out of the park with John Fetzer, one of the Detroit owners, and he asked me if I'd be interested in managing the Tigers. I told him I appreciated it, but I had long since made up my mind that Boston was my first and last stop in the big leagues. By that time, of course, I had made my commitment to Sears, Roebuck.

The day after my final game I had received a telegram from George Struthers of Sears, Roebuck saying he wanted to talk to me about something important to my future. I had an idea what it was. On the following Saturday Struthers, one of the vice presidents, and Bob Anderson of Sears came to my room at the Somerset in Boston, and when we got through talking they knew my knowledge of hunting and fishing was extensive. I knew a lot about equipment. I had some ideas. I was impressed with them, and apparently they were with me. For nine years I have been chairman of Sears' Ted Williams Sports Advisory staff, giving my name to the top line of outdoor and recreation equipment, and baseball slowly ebbed from my life.

I was not bitter about it. I didn't think baseball owed me anything, and it had allowed me to have a lot. I'd been lucky. I wasn't a wealthy man, I didn't have things locked yet, but I was closing in on it. I was now at a point in my life where I could hunt, I could fish when I wanted to, I could pretty much go and come as I pleased. A big thing was made of it in Boston when I didn't go down for the 1967 World Series. They tried to get hold of me, I understand, to throw out a ball at one of the games, but that wasn't my show, I wasn't interested in making a big display. I watched the games on television. I didn't make myself available, because I didn't want to interrupt my fishing.

I keep a couple of phony-baloney clip-on ties in the drawer just in case, but I never dress up any more. The worst thing I can think of is to have to put on a coat and tie every day and go to work. The last time I wore a tuxedo was in 1940. It was a rental.

I know, though, that if I had it to do over I would start earlier to build a business. Build something to step into after my playing days were over. Maybe incorporate myself. I'd still be a ballplayer, hell yes. Baseball I loved, even with the heartaches. Everything I have I got through baseball. Nobody makes that kind of life out of something unless he loves it. But I would think more about the aftermath. I've done all right. I've made a few investments, gotten into some land, but I could have done better.

Sam Snead and I had a fishing tackle business in Miami for a while, but it didn't quite work out like we hoped. The Sears deal has been much better for me. I suppose, in any case, that I have appeared to be more aggressive than I think I am. I've always had the feeling I should be ten times smarter than I am. I've always felt I had nine million things going through my head, bothering me or worrying me, and I'm always hammering at myself to keep up.

I know any time I say anything, I kind of question myself as I say it. Is that right? What's the logic behind that? I'm that way with people. Jack Brothers, a fishing guide down on the Keys, made a remark about a tiger shark he had seen one day and we argued about where it was he had seen it. After a while I got my Wise *Fishermen's Encyclopedia* out and checked, and then I pointed out to Jack the error of his remark. "For Chrissakes, Williams," he said, "a guy has an argument with you and right away you pull an encyclopedia on him." I've done that a lot of times, gone back for more ammunition, because I want to know the answers. I want to know why. I think "why" is a wonderful word.

Because of the way I am, the way I've reacted to situations all my life, I can't pretend to be the easiest guy in the world to live with. I tried marriage again in 1961. A good-looking blonde named Lee Howard—the trim, modely type from Chicago. She'd been divorced too, and we both thought we'd try to settle down and give it another try. So we got married, and it wasn't long before we began having problems. We weren't suited. We couldn't get along. She finally got a divorce. I made up my mind I had given marriage a thorough test and found it undesirable, but a couple years ago I met a girl. She was in the seat across from me on a plane to San Francisco. I admired the way she looked, so I wadded up a note and threw it to her: "Who are you?"

She flipped back a reply: "Who are *you?*"

I wrote: "I am Mr. Williams, a fisherman who would like to meet you."

Her name was Dolores Wettach, a professional model who had been on the cover of *Vogue* and on a few television commercials, a pretty dark-haired girl from Vermont. She turned out to be a model who would just as soon tramp around the woods or sit in a boat with a rod in her hands. She loved the outdoors almost as much as I do. We finally got married, and now she is putting up with me and has given me a son. Already I can tell you he is the biggest thing in my life. I have named him John Henry for no other reason than I like the name. I know he's going to be taking up a lot of my time from now on. There isn't anyone around who could teach him to fish any better than his old man.

So baseball owes me nothing, and by the same token, I don't think I owe baseball anything. I gave it all I had when I had it to give. I gave of myself to things connected with the game—appearances, letter-writing, autographs. I would be less than honest if I said I was surprised when they voted me into the Hall of Fame, but I have to smile—I really thought a couple of my friends in the pressbox would try to keep me dangling awhile.

They held the ceremony in July of 1966. I hadn't been to Cooperstown since 1940, when we played an exhibition game against the Cubs and I hit a home run onto somebody's porch on Susquehanna Avenue. I thought that day how great it would be to have a career that makes you worthy of the Hall of Fame, and how much I wanted it. Just a boy and his dreams.

Casey Stengel and I were admitted on the same day, and I was pleased about that because I have always been a great admirer of Stengel's, the great manager that he was, the great strength of character he always showed. I don't think anybody contributed more to baseball than Casey Stengel. He ranks right there with Ty Cobb, Babe Ruth and Judge Landis. He was in baseball fifty years and caused as much copy to be written about the game and about himself as anybody. He was out of baseball the same year I was and the Yankees tried to say he retired and he said the hell with that noise, I was *fired.*

Nobody mentioned it that day, but if the Boston Braves had been a little more forceful I might have played for Stengel. When I was a kid ballplayer in San Diego he tried to get them to buy me. Casey was managing the Braves at the time, and was being treated with customary loving kindness by the Boston press. Dave Egan, the Colonel, said the cab driver who drove into Casey and broke his leg in 1937 ought to be voted man of the year.

I spent two nights in my motel room writing my speech for Cooperstown. I made it as short as possible because I knew Casey had a few things to say and he was always more entertaining than I was. I had on my best open-neck white polo shirt and a plaid jacket. When I got up on the rostrum somebody nearby yelled, "Egan ought to be here today!" and I made a face and said, "Yeah, that Egan . . ." and mumbled under my breath, carrying the joke out. Well, you could expect it: two Boston writers, Tim Horgan and Henry McKenna, wrote the next day that I used profanity in reference to Egan, that somebody had it on tape. Mr. Yawkey was there and knew I hadn't, he heard the whole thing, and he was mad as hell. I think he complained to the papers. It was one of the few times in my memory when I *didn't* use a few choice words to describe Egan. I was in too good a mood to let his memory spoil my day.

My speech was short enough to repeat the whole thing. I said:

"I guess every player thinks about going into the Hall of Fame. Now that the moment has come for me I find it is difficult to say what is really in my heart. But I know it is the greatest thrill of my life. I received two hundred and eighty-odd votes from the writers. I know I didn't have two hundred and eighty-odd close friends among the writers. I know they voted for me because they felt in their minds and some in their hearts that I rated it, and I want to say to them: Thank you, from the bottom of my heart.

"Today I am thinking about a lot of things. I am thinking of my playground director in San Diego, Rodney Luscomb, and my high school coach, Wos Caldwell, and my managers, who had such patience with me and helped me so much—fellows like Frank Shellenback, Donie Bush, Joe Cronin and Joe McCarthy. I am thinking of Eddie Collins, who had so much faith in me—and to be in the Hall of Fame with him particularly, as well as those other great players, is a great honor. I'm sorry Eddie isn't here today.

"I'm thinking too of Tom Yawkey. I have always said it: Tom Yawkey is the greatest owner in baseball. I was lucky to have played on the club he owned and I'm grateful to him for being here today.

"But I'd not be leveling if I left it at that. Ballplayers are not born great. They're not born great hitters or pitchers or managers, and luck isn't the big factor. No one has come up with a substitute for hard work. I've never met a great player who didn't have to work harder at learning to play ball than anything else he ever did. To me it was the greatest fun I ever had, which probably explains why today I feel both humility and pride, because God let me play the game and learn to be good at it.

"The other day Willie Mays hit his five hundred and twenty-second home run. He has gone past me, and he's pushing, and I say to him, 'Go get 'em, Willie.' Baseball gives every American boy a chance to excel. Not just to be as good as someone else, but to be better. This is the nature of man and the name of the game. I hope that some day Satchel Paige and Josh Gibson will be voted into the Hall of Fame as symbols of the great Negro players who are not here only because they weren't given the chance.

"As time goes on I'll be thinking baseball, teaching baseball and arguing for baseball to keep it right on top of American sports, just as it is in Japan, Mexico, Venezuela and other Latin and South American countries. I know

249

Casey Stengel feels the same way . . . I also know I'll lose a dear friend if I don't stop talking. I'm eating into his time, and that is unforgivable. So in closing, I am grateful and know how lucky I was to have been born an American and had a chance to play the game I loved, the *greatest* game."

And baseball *is* the greatest game, great enough to survive the raps it takes and the raps it deserves. Certainly it is easy to criticize. I think of Ty Cobb and how he used to criticize me and how I thought he was an old crab, and now I find myself being critical too. I don't think baseball in the big leagues is as good as it was. I'm not going to back off on that. By the same token I don't think it is going to fold its tent tomorrow either. But things could be done.

Expansion, surely, has hurt the big leagues. It has been done too quickly. It has killed off the minor leagues, and it has put guys on big league rosters who wouldn't have a prayer otherwise. Most of the expansion clubs are *still* on the bottom, and now they're about to expand some more. It all seems to be inevitable—every big city wants a big league team—so they will have to adjust in other areas. Make cosmetic changes. Spruce things up. A lot of owners used to be critical of Bill Veeck with his pinch-hitting midgets and wild stunts, but he got people interested.

My thinking, though, is more in terms of the game itself, not of nylon giveaways and exploding scoreboards and silly-looking uniforms. For one thing, I think baseball should adopt the football specialist. A guy who would do nothing but hit. I hate it when I see a pitcher up there with the bases loaded, some half-athlete who swings like an old maid, rear end flying, can't run a step, gets about one hit a year. Why not have a specialist who could bat two times a game for weak hitters like that? Then great hitters like Mantle or Mays—and I would damn sure rather see them at the plate than 99 per cent of the pitchers—could stick around longer, could continue to play as specialists when their legs are gone. I was pleased to see "specialists" used this past spring, if only as an experiment.

I think a 140-game schedule makes sense, cut a week or so off each end of the season, get away from some of that bad weather. The owners won't do it without cutting salaries, which would get everybody mad, so forget that. But they're worried now about the lousy hitting. I know for a fact you don't hit as well in cold weather. It doesn't matter so much to a pitcher. He would just as soon not be losing all that liquid he sweats off on a hot day anyway.

Speed up the games? Everybody talks about it, nobody lifts a finger. I think they ought to play seven-inning second games of doubleheaders, and in the spring cut a batter down to three balls, two strikes. There'd be a lot more swinging, a guy would get ready quicker. A pitcher should be required to walk *briskly* to the mound. The catcher should be out there waiting. Batters should be in the batter's box on penalty of a forfeit strike. Once he's in that box, except for injury, he should be required to stay there.

The pitchers are the worst. As a breed they're the lesser ballplayers, which is the game's fault, because most good athletes who go into baseball gravitate to pitching, start off as pitchers, then get pampered to death until they become less than what they were. They forget how to bat, they learn to do everything short of going for a nap to slow up a game. Picking around, looking at the sky, playing with the resin bag. I used to hate it, so I'd just stand right in the box and let the umpire get after them.

Batters do it too, of course. They're up there picking their nose, fooling with their cap, dusting themselves off, doing everything but getting ready to hit. A pain in the ass. Rocky Colavito used to be like that. Carl Yastrzemski is another one. He has about forty-two things to do before he gets into the batter's box.

Because it's the hardest game to play, takes more skill, more dedication, more determination, more practice, more everything, baseball isn't getting the best young athletes like it used to. They find they can do something in sports that's easier. And in professional sports, something that is more lucrative. Here's a baseball player. He has to have good eyesight, good legs, a good arm. He has to hit against a ball that can hurt him. He has to play day and night, travel all over the damn country at crazy hours, and for more months out of the year.

Now, here's a golfer. He makes a big deal out of having to play thirty tournaments a year. He doesn't have to have great reflexes. He doesn't have to have good eyesight. He doesn't have to be fast afoot. He doesn't have to be young. Golfers win major tournaments into their fifties. In the history of baseball, only Satchel Paige was still effective at that age and he was a pitcher.

You can win a lot of money in golf without ever winning a tournament. You never hear a boo in golf. You don't have a pitcher throwing curves and sliders and knuckleballs, and if he doesn't like you, maybe a fastball at your cap. There is nothing to hurt you in golf unless lightning strikes or somebody throws a club. And gee, there's that golf ball, sitting right there for you to hit, and a flat-faced club to hit it with. My friend Sam Snead would argue that you have to play your foul balls in golf, you just can't watch them go into the stands and forget about them, and that an emotional guy like me would have a tough time making a dime at golf. But listen, thousands of guys play par golf. Young guys are flocking into the pros like lemmings. How many guys hit .300 in the American League last year?

I think without question the hardest single thing to do in sport is to hit a baseball. A .300 hitter, that rarest of breeds these days, goes through life with the certainty that he will fail at his job seven out of ten times. If John Unitas completed three of every ten passes he threw he would be the ex-quarterback of the Baltimore Colts.

I know as I get into managing I will be called a hitter's manager. I said at Cooperstown that hitters are made, and I know at my baseball camp in Lakeville I always got such a kick out of seeing a boy with talent, wanting to help him, wanting to be available to help him. Boy, I love that. But if he doesn't have the interest, if he's not willing to practice, to sacrifice, I don't want to waste my time with him. I will expect that of my players in Washington.

Baseball is crying for good hitters. It's the most important part of the game. Where the big money is. Where much of the status is, and the fan interest. But in 1968 the major leagues scored fewer runs per game than they had since 1908. The combined batting average (.236) was the lowest since the turn of the century. Everybody had been saying it was a sacrifice the fan had to make to see the big hits, the home runs, but the theory did not hold up. There were fewer home runs hit per game (1.23) than there had been in twenty years. Meanwhile, the averages keep falling. From 1931 to 1940, the batting champions of the American League averaged .366. From 1941 to 1950, it was down to .349. Take away my .406 in 1941 and it drops to .342. From 1951 to 1960, the average was .343. Without my .388 in 1957, it falls to .338. From 1961 through 1968, the batting champions averaged .324.

There are a lot of factors for the decline in hitting, and I won't go into them all. Some of the obvious things are the logistics: the increase in night games, the expanded season (everybody's getting tired), the size of the new parks

(Chavez Ravine in Los Angeles is a hell-hole for a batter compared to cozy old Ebbets Field). Night ball is here to stay, no doubt about that, but the ball doesn't travel as well in the heavy night air. It's more difficult to see at night, no matter how good the lights. You're playing on a disturbed routine, eating different hours, sleeping differently. You get tired and sluggish.

Certainly the size of the new parks is a factor. I think a ball hit 420 feet should be a home run anywhere, any time. You've really crushed one when it goes that far. You deserve more than a long fly out, just as you deserve less when you pop one over an unusually short fence, like left field in Fenway Park or down the right-field line in Yankee Stadium. I think a reasonable uniformity of playing fields is important. In established parks this could be difficult to achieve, but if you can't move the fences out you can certainly bring them in so that no ball hit 420 feet is an out.

Recently the rules committee lowered the mound from fifteen inches to ten inches, and decreased the strike zone at the top by about four inches. It remains to be seen how the umpires call them, but even if they adjust accurately how much has been done to help the hitter? Not as much as baseball people would think.

In the first place, much of the pitching angle from the mound is an illusory one. It looks more overpowering than it is. Say the average pitcher is six feet tall, throwing six to eight inches above his head and down to a point midway in the strike zone, or about three feet off the ground. On a fifteen-inch mound, the angle of the pitch's trajectory from a six-foot pitcher throwing three-quarter arm is only about *three degrees*.

The illusion is created by the slope of the mound, and by the pitcher coming forward. But he is also bending as he throws, reducing the height of his release, and he is coming *down* the mound. He is never at the top of the mound when he releases the ball.

Lowering the mound to ten inches decreases that angle of pitch no more than a fraction of a degree. It's no big deal. The mounds were low when I first started playing on the sandlots of San Diego, and as I went up the ladder to the big leagues they got progressively higher. There was no effect on me as a hitter. On the contrary. I got better, not worse.

As for the strike zone, lowering it from the top is of little consequence to the hitter. Even unchanged, a high strike is still a lovely ball to hit. There are not many hitters —not *any* hitters I know of—who would argue that point. Pitchers don't give you that strike. They're not that dumb. In my twenty-five years of baseball, for every pitch I got above the belt there were eight or ten below it. With few exceptions, pitchers always throw low to the good hitter.

The low strike is the one that hurts you. The pitch down around the knees, the out pitch, the real bastard to hit. That's the one they should do something about. Bring the strike zone up a couple inches *above* the knee. Make it an easier pitch for the umpire to call, and an easier pitch to get a bat on properly, and to swing at properly.

All right, somebody asked me, "What would *you* do to bring hitting back if you were the commissioner of base-ball?" And before anybody reads anything into this, I do *not* want to be commissioner of anything except my fishing boat. Period. But I'll answer the question. The first thing I would do to help the hitters—and there is no doubt they have been hurt by circumstances beyond their control—the first thing would be to appoint a committee of three men, all former players, former *hitters*, guys who knew some-thing about what it takes to be a hitter.

The committee would study every ball park in the big

leagues. Survey them all. Check the lights, the backgrounds, the playing areas. Any distraction, any inconsistency, any inferior equipment they found would be corrected or eliminated. That's the first thing I did when I visited the Washington park for the first time as manager.

Some hitters, a *lot* of hitters, aren't smart enough to realize it, but any distraction at that plate is a detriment to good hitting, no matter how small. I remember a recent World Series. Don Drysdale of the Dodgers beat the Yankees in Los Angeles, and after the game Mickey Mantle said he couldn't see the ball because of the background at Dodger Stadium. Isn't that a hell of a note? World Series. Big new park. Great hitter against a great pitcher. Thousands of dollars riding on the outcome. The hitter deserving of at least an equal chance—and he can't even see the ball.

If it were left to me, I would make sure no pitch in any park could come to the plate from a bad background, out of somebody's white shirt in the center-field bleachers. Not even if the pitcher is a glandular case throwing way over his head. I'd go further. I'd establish an angle from home plate to the center-field bleachers, applicable to any park. The seats that fell within the extensions of that angle would be closed off, there'd never be anybody there to distract the hitter.

You say, "Yah, that damn Williams, real quick to spend somebody else's money." But what would it mean? Maybe six hundred fifty-cent seats. Big deal. We're talking about improving the most important gate attraction in baseball. Six hundred seats is peanuts.

If there's bad background beyond the bleachers, shields should be erected. I remember when Baltimore came in the league. There was a white schoolhouse the trees did not obscure. It was a distraction. I don't think scoreboards should be in center field. Baltimore has one there. The background at Kansas City is bad. I'd much rather play in Kansas City at night. The center-field stands in Yankee Stadium can be distracting.

Certainly they could use lights better. Shadows disturb a hitter. Late in the game, or late in the season, they creep out toward the mound. A pitch thrown from the sunlight might come into the shadows. I think any time you've got a shadow like that the lights ought to be turned on. I think if a shadow even hits a part of the pitcher's arm, like they do coming off the light towers, something ought to be done. I think a batter ought to have the right to say, "Turn on the lights." Or the manager of the team at bat. I don't care if it's eleven o'clock in the morning. If he wants them on, turn them on.

I was watching the Red Sox play Cleveland on television last season. In Cleveland the stands are high, like they are at Yankee Stadium. By the sixth inning, there was a shadow a third of the way to the mound. I could see the pitcher, but I couldn't see the pitch, and I could barely see the batter. It made me sick looking at it. I shut it off.

Now, there might be tons of lights in a ball park, but if they're not right they can throw a hitter off, too. I played twenty years in Comiskey Park in Chicago and there was a light on the roof in right center field that *always* bothered me. Ordinarily I cocked my hat to the left, giving my right eye (the one nearest the pitcher) a little more exposure. But that light in Chicago made me bring the brim down over the right eye. It threw me off. And isn't that an awful thing to have to say? That with all this money, with all this technology, with all the sophisticated equipment available, the parks are still bad, the lights are still bad. Naturally, I make a statement like that and somebody else is bound to turn around and say, "The lights *are* good." But I was the guy who was supposed to have the great eyesight and I say they were lousy.

After you've corrected the ball parks, which is the easy part, you move on to correcting the hitter. Here's where it gets tough. They've been saying the last few years that the ball is dead. The ball's not dead. The hitters are, from the neck up.

Everybody's trying to *pull* the damn ball, to begin with, trying to hit home runs. They don't protect themselves with two strikes—they don't shorten up with the bat, they don't think about hitting through the box, getting wood on the ball. They're still up there swinging from their rear end. They think about that big, powerful swing, but not about being quick with the bat. They don't do their home-work—on the pitcher, on the situation, on the game. They're not selective. They swing at bad pitches, and that's the first rule in the book: *Get a good ball to hit.* Most of all, they don't have any idea what that little game between pitcher and hitter is all about.

I remember a conversation I had with Rico Petrocelli of the Red Sox a couple of springs ago. I said, "Rico, have I ever told you anything about hitting?"

"No."

"You know why? Because I can't. You've got a wonder-ful style. You hit pretty near every pitch well. You've got good power. In a jam, I'd as soon see you at the plate as anybody. But you know what, Rico? I'm beginning to think you're stupid. You don't even have the vaguest idea what is going on at the plate. Just yesterday a guy threw a fastball right by you on a three-and-one pitch." What I meant was that here was a kid who with two strikes could very well hit as tough a pitch as you could throw, but when he had the pitcher in the hole at 3-and-1 and the pitcher *had* to come right in there with it, he did not realize he could really rip, really take advantage. He was up there looking for the tough one when he could have been taking pickings.

I have to laugh. Rico said, "You know, Ted, you're right. I'm stupid."

A hitter can't just go up there and swing. He's got to *think*. Listen, when I played I knew the parks, the mounds, the batters' boxes, the backgrounds. I studied the pitchers. I knew what was going on at that plate. It used to kill me to strike out, but when I struck out I knew what it was that got me and what I was going to try to do about it. I'd venture to say that of all the times I struck out there were only two or three occasions when I didn't know what the pitch was. If I asked a teammate what he had hit, or missed, and he didn't know, I couldn't believe it, I was mystified. The pitcher was out there taking the food right out of his mouth and he didn't even know how it was happening. Bobby Doerr was great for that. He'd even hit one out of the park and couldn't tell me what he hit.

I was watching a game on television between the Tigers and the Orioles one afternoon after a morning of bonefishing on the Florida Keys. I'd just turned the set on when Boog Powell of Baltimore hit one of those gargantuan home runs. I didn't see the pitch. The next time Powell got up, there were two on, and the pitcher was really working on him, giving him those big bloopy curves. But Powell's still swinging from his rear end, and he dribbles one to second base.

Now it's the fifth or sixth inning, Powell up again, same pitcher, same situation, tight game. I made the comment to a friend who was watching the game with me, "Boy, he's really got to be looking for that crap now."

But Powell's still got that big swing going, and here's another bloopy curve, and damn if he doesn't dribble another to second base. He wasn't ready, that's all. I realize young guys make mistakes, but here is a guy who has been in the big leagues four years, a big powerful guy who can handle a bat, and he didn't have an inkling.

That same inning Al Kaline got up for Detroit. First pitch, he took a fastball strike like it was batting practice. He barely moved. He knew exactly what he was doing. I said to my friend, "He's waiting for the breaking stuff. He knows he's going to get it." Sure enough, here comes a curve, and Kaline rips it into left field. There's the difference.

There's no doubt that a smart pitcher is always after an edge. The hitter has be smart to beat the edge. I remember the 1949 All-Star game in Chicago. Lou Boudreau was managing the American League team, and Lou was an astute guy. The National League starter that day was Larry Jansen. He threw a slow curve, I pulled it foul; another curve, pulled it foul. Then he busted one right in on the fists and I took it. Strike three.

I'd been wearing out Cleveland that year, even with the shift, and Boudreau didn't know what to do with me. After the All-Star game, they had a meeting. Jim Bagby, who had been traded from our club to Cleveland, told me about it later. Boudreau told him to try Jansen's method. They came into Boston, and first time up Bagby threw me a slow curve, I pulled it foul. Another curve, foul. Now a fastball inside, and I hit it four miles. When Bagby got to the bench, he said to Boudreau, "That is *not* the way to pitch to that son of a bitch."

I consider some of the guys playing today great hitters, however, so it's altogether possible that the hitting cycle overall is down and the pitching up. Certainly the slider is having an effect. We began to see sliders in the league around 1946 or 1947, and by 1948 all the good pitchers had one. Before that there were pitchers whose curves acted like sliders. Hank Borowy threw his curve hard and it sank and didn't break too much, so it acted like a slider. Johnny Allen's was the same way. Claude Passeau's fastball acted like a slider.

The big thing the slider did was give the pitcher a third pitch right away. With two pitches you might guess right half the time. With three your guessing goes down proportionately. All hitters have trouble with the slider—Mays says it's the toughest pitch, Hank Aaron says it's the toughest. I say it's the greatest pitch in baseball. It's easy to learn, easy to control. It immediately gives a pitcher a better repertoire.

But the pitch that creates all the hysteria today, the one everybody complains about, is the spitball, and it's the biggest piece of fiction I know of. All a batter has to do is have the umpire look at the ball, because to be an effective spitter, the ball has to be loaded up good. I played under Frank Shellenback for two years in San Diego, the greatest spitballer in the minor leagues. He threw spitters *all* the time, and I know he had to get the damn ball gobbered up with that slippery elm. The more he got on it the better it was. You can't just wet your fingertips and throw a spitball. And you can't control it unless you throw it a lot. I defy any pitcher to show me he can do it just wetting his fingers.

Everybody said Lou Burdette threw spitters. I hit against Burdette. If he threw spitters, they didn't look like spitters. They'd sink, or fade a little. They certainly weren't *good* spitters. Mike Garcia threw one to me one time and the spit came up and hit me in the eye. The umpire threw the ball out.

As far as the fear hitters have of getting conked with the ball, all hitters go through it, and they have to accept terror as a pitcher's legitimate weapon. A pitcher puts a hitter through those test periods. Start wearing down the fences and they start giving you a look. Then they find out if you can hit from the prone position. I remember we had one pitcher on our club that Bill Skowron had been murdering. He said, "The next time that Skowron gets up I'm going to hit him right on the NY, right on the insignia of his cap." Bang, next time up he hit Moose right on the helmet. Sounded like a rifle shot.

A good hitter knows that sort of thing is part of the act; the thing he must do as long as he plays is fight to stay in there, because once he starts bailing out, the pitcher has him beat. I remember Ed Chase, who pitched for Washington. He had forearms like a milkman—he *was* a milkman, and still is. He had a hell of a curve. Hell of a fastball. But he was wild. One day he got me to 3 and 2, two men on, and threw a big sharp curve and I took it. Fooled me. Strike three.

I got up again in the fourth inning, bases loaded, count 3 and 2, and here comes another, and I'm hanging in there, waiting, waiting, and I don't think I moved until the ball was right by my ear. It hit the brim of my cap and spun it on my head.

Well, there are hitters and there are hitters. It is probably my misfortune that I have been and will inevitably be compared with Joe DiMaggio. We were of the same era. We were the top two players of our league. In my heart I have always felt I was a better hitter than Joe, which was always my first consideration, but I have to say that he was the greatest baseball player of our time. He could do it all.

He was a better fielder than I was. A better thrower. Everything he did was stylish. He ran gracefully, he fielded gracefully, he hit with authority and style. I suppose that is what separates him from Willie Mays in my mind's eye— that even when Joe missed he looked good. It is also true, of course, that in his thirteen years with the Yankees they won the pennant ten times. That has to be a factor.

If I had to pick an All-Star team of those players that I played with and against, limiting it to the American League, DiMaggio would certainly head it up. With him in the outfield I would go with Mantle and Al Kaline, though they both should have been even better. Mantle was a great athlete —great speed, great power—but he made a career of swinging hard at every pitch. I remember I gave Kaline a rubber ball to squeeze when he came up his first year, trying to help him strengthen his arms—if I had it to do over, that's one thing I'd concentrate on, getting stronger—and gee, his second or third year Kaline hit .340 and looked great. He hasn't done nearly as well since.

Jimmy Foxx would be my first baseman, just a hair's edge over Hank Greenberg. Foxx could run better. Next to Di-Maggio, he was the greatest player I ever saw. Second base would be the toughest position to make a choice. I saw Bobby Doerr and Joe Gordon, how good they were. Gordon would have the edge for power at bat and range afield, but I would still consider Doerr his equal, with Nellie Fox a close third. Charley Gehringer was over the hill when I saw him. There was no questioning his greatness, but he was just a little past it. You can't underrate that Fox. He was always blunking or blooping one to win the game in the ninth inning. I think every time he bunted against us for five years, *brrrupppp*, a base hit. It got to be a damn joke.

I think of shortstop as essentially a fielding position, so I would probably choose Luis Aparicio of the White Sox, with due respects to Phil Rizzuto. Against us, Aparicio had the greatest range, a good arm, and he was very fast. Rizzuto was probably a better playmaker, but Aparicio would get a ball Rizzuto might not reach. Aparicio was also a better hitter. Of course, if you're talking about hitting alone, Vern Stephens, Joe Cronin and Luke Appling were the best I saw.

Brooks Robinson of Baltimore, for hitting *and* fielding, was the best I saw at third, ahead of George Kell and Kenny Keltner. Yogi Berra was the all-round catcher—a good hitter and a worker behind the plate. Bill Dickey was a hitter-type catcher who could do everything. Berra didn't quite have the ability to receive that Dickey had, but Berra was smart behind the plate. He knew the little things that make the pitcher great. You have a great catcher to go with a great pitching staff, boy, you've got 75 per cent of it made. You get a lumberhead back there and he'll ruin your pitching. Berra had it. He knew how to work with the pitcher.

Of course, Jim Hegan of Cleveland was the real stylish catcher. He wasn't the hitter Berra was, but for handling a pitcher nobody could beat Jim Hegan. Billy Goodman was telling me just the other day how he was never able to steal one of Hegan's signs. Never. I remember when Hegan first came up, about 1947. He got me out on a couple pitches that really fooled me, and when I got back to the bench I told Cronin, "That damn Hegan has to be the smartest catcher in the league. Right now he's the smartest."

A couple innings later, Cronin said, "You know who's calling the pitches don't you?"

"Who?"

"Boudreau." He was right. Boudreau was calling the pitches from shortstop. He'd touch his knee for a fastball, or straighten up for a curve, do something, and he was relaying the signals to Hegan. But it wasn't long before Hegan could very well handle it alone.

Talk about stealing signs. I was stealing Berra's from first base one day. He was getting kind of careless with his right knee, and I was taking a pretty good lead off first so I could see him flash the signs. I'd pass it on to Del Baker coaching first, and Baker would relay it to the batter. When I got up the next inning, Berra was fuming. "Boy, what a bunch of dumb-ass pitchers we've got," he said. "Baker knows what they're going to throw every time."

I've already named the five toughest pitchers for me to hit: Ford, Lopat, Lemon, Feller and Wilhelm. I've been exposed to pitchers all my life, making a living off their dumbness, off their mistakes, but these were five pitchers who were never dumb. Even after he lost his best stuff—and he had more than anybody—Feller was able to win on smartness. I remember we were playing the Yankees in Boston one day, facing Lopat, and our first man up got a line drive hit, the second man hit a hell of a shot that the left fielder made a nice play on, then I got up and hit one off the center-field fence to drive in a run. We didn't get another hit the rest of the game. Two hits the first inning and that was all. The Yankees won, 2–1. One of the writers questioned Lopat after the game, asking how he had pitched so well after such a shaky start.

Lopat said, "Well, I want to tell you, I was warming up on the sidelines and I felt so good I made up my mind I was really ready to powder the ball. So I powdered the ball that first inning and those guys hit nothing but line shots. I said to myself, Nuts to this, and I went back to my barnyard stuff."

The best pitchers all had good deliveries. They weren't stereotyped. Lemon would vary his delivery, cross you up by coming from a different angle. The best pitchers never conceded to a hitter. Three and one and they'd still give you tough pitches. The trouble with the average pitcher is his hardheadedness. He has too inflated an opinion of what he's got. Say it's a fastball. He thinks he can throw it by you any time, any place, anywhere. If you hit it, he gives it to you again.

John Rigney was like that. He would put it in there, and you would ride it out. Robin Roberts stayed with his fastball almost three years after he had lost it—then he learned to pitch on control, like Feller did. All the great hitters could hit fastballs, no matter how fast the pitcher was. The average pitcher doesn't spend enough time studying the hitters, he doesn't work hard enough on getting his breaking pitch over in a tough spot.

Well, I could name twenty outstanding pitchers I have seen. I could name thirty. I suppose right behind those five, though, would come Hal Newhouser, Virgil Trucks, Dizzy Trout—all of Detroit—Allie Reynolds and Vic Raschi of New York and Herb Score of Cleveland, and every one of them challenged you. *Stuff* pitchers, fast, hard-throwing. It just so happened that I had better success against them because I was always a fastball hitter and they were all a little stubborn about their fastballs. (Trucks was my all-time favorite. I hit twelve home runs off Trucks.) When I am relaxed in the bow of my boat off Islamorada, enjoying the Florida sun and the fruits of a career of hitting fastballs, I am always grateful for stubborn pitchers.

Now, of course, I am temporarily out of my boat and back into baseball as the manager of the Senators. I don't know for how long—if you were hoping for a short term, though, I've got a five-year contract. I am back for two reasons: the price was right (there's a price for everything), and the man who offered it was the smartest guy I ever met. I couldn't refuse him. I kept saying "no" until I heard myself say "yes." Bob Short is the guy, the new owner of the Senators. He called me once, just after I'd had a nice day of fishing off Islamorada, and I said thanks very much but no thanks. He called again. He got Joe Cronin to call. "C'mon, Ted," Joe said, "this guy needs you. *Baseball* needs you." Short called me again. I kept saying no, but he must have sensed I was weakening, or that the fishing was getting lousy.

We seemed to talk for hours, at his expense. He began to outline what he had to offer. It was becoming clear that if I was ever going to get back into baseball this was the way to do it—on my own terms, with a chance to own part of a club, with a long-term contract that would give me the time to find out once and for all if the things I had been saying about baseball, and about hitting a baseball, were true. I suppose when you get right down to it a fellow can get his fill of hunting and fishing if he does it to the exclusion of all else, year-round, eight years in a row. I have to admit it has been fun putting my baseball theories into practice rather than just bouncing them off the walls.

I finally met Bob Short face to face in Atlanta last February. I had to go to South Carolina for Sears and he met me halfway in his Lear Jet. He was not only dynamic, but he was imaginative about baseball, though he had never been involved in it before, and he was damned persuasive. I had the feeling we could grow together in Washington and that he would be the kind of guy you would want to be associated with over a long, tough haul. He offered me a five year contract, with an option to purchase 10 percent of the club. I would be manager and vice president, and if I didn't like managing I could kick myself upstairs to do whatever I saw fit to help the club.

As I said at the beginning, I don't know where this new course will take me. I still feel that managing is essentially a loser's job; managers are about the most expendable pieces of furniture on earth. Try to keep count of how many get fired every year and you'll get dizzy. But I think I've learned a few things in my years of exile, learned things about people, about myself, and I would hope that the fans in Washington find me a little more accommodating, a little more to their liking than they may have been led to expect. For myself, when I look back on *this* experience I hope to be less bitter about it.

I don't know how a man wants to be remembered, other than for his achievements. I just haven't thought about it. I believe I am a compassionate man. I believe I'm concerned with people. I don't think I was as concerned or as compassionate in those early days as I am now. Why the hell should I have been? Why *would* I be then? I was worried about Theodore Samuel Williams. I was worried about hitting, I was worried about my career, I was worried about money. Why the hell would I be? Maybe that's wrong, but that's exactly the way I felt.

I know this. I was and am too complex a personality, too much a confusion of boyish enthusiasm and bitter experience to be completely understood by everybody, so forget that. I know what has been right in my life and I know what has been wrong. If you put it all down, I feel in my heart I would have more on the right side than the wrong. I think, however, that the Kid who made the sports page jump was never the same person to himself as he was to the reader, and maybe not the same even to the people who knew him. I think it is natural that I regret that deception.

It's funny, really, and I have to laugh. I was going down to Florida to fish one winter. In those days I used the name "G. C. Luther" when I traveled, because it made for less attention. How do you doubt a name like G. C. Luther? I signed in at this motel in Fort Myers, and the manager looked at me and looked at the signature and said, "Gee, for a minute I thought you were Ted Williams."

I said, "Yeah, a lot of people say that. I think Williams is actually a much older man."

We started talking—about fishing, about how long he'd lived there, about where to eat—and after a while I started to leave. He said, "I have to admit, I had my doubts when you signed in, Mr. Luther. I thought you really were Ted Williams. But I can see you're not. You've got a much nicer disposition."

Put it in capital letters and run it on page one.

Appendix

*Ted Williams' records at the conclusion of his career**
Theodore Samuel Williams
(The Kid, the Splendid Splinter and the Big Guy)
(Johnny Orlando, Red Sox equipment manager, is credited
with being the first to call him the Kid; the Splendid Splinter
from his younger height and slimness, and the Big Guy by all
American League players as his mark of No. 1 rating.)

Born August 30, 1918, at San Diego, California. Height
6'4". Weight 198. Greenish-brown eyes, brown hair.
Throws right and bats left-handed.
Hobbies: hunting and fishing.

Led American League in 1941 with .406 batting average to
become the first major leaguer to hit .400 or more in a decade.
In winning his fifth batting crown in 1957, Ted at thirty-nine
years of age became the oldest player in the history of the
majors to win a batting crown; won again at forty in 1958.

* Reprinted from *The Baseball Register*, published by The Sporting
News, St. Louis, Missouri 63166.

271

Holds major league record for most consecutive playing years leading in runs scored (5), 1940, 1941, 1942, 1946, 1947 (in military service 1943–1945); also holds major league mark for most consecutive playing years leading in bases on balls (6), 1941, 1942, 1946, 1947, 1948, 1949 (in military service 1943–1945). During the six-year span previously listed Williams received 100 or more bases on balls each season, establishing record for most consecutive playing years 100 or more bases on balls.

Holds major league mark for most successive times reaching first base safely (16): September 17 (hit homer as pinch hitter); September 18 (walked as pinch hitter); September 20 (hit homer as pinch hitter); September 21 (homer and three bases on balls); September 22 (homer, single and two walks); September 23 (single, three bases on balls and hit by pitcher) —1957.

While George Herman (Babe) Ruth is unofficially credited with as many as eighty intentional bases on balls in a season, Ted Williams holds the official record for most intentional bases on balls, season (33)—1957.

Tied major league record by hitting three home runs in a game twice during the 1957 season, May 8 and June 13, 1957; also hit three home runs in a game July 14, 1946 (first game); tied major league record for most home runs in consecutive times at bat (4): September 17, 20, 21, 22—1957. (Bases on balls received in this span do not count against "consecutive" mark.)

Tied American League record for most total bases in fewest consecutive times at bat (22): September 17, 20, 21, 22, 23, 24—1957. (First two times at bat. Eight at-bats, five home runs.)

Led in total bases 1939, 1942, 1946, 1947, 1949, 1951. Led in bases on balls 1941, 1942, 1946, 1947, 1948, 1949, 1951, 1954. Led in slugging percentage 1941, 1942, 1946, 1947, 1948, 1949, 1951, 1954, 1957. Led outfielders in double plays 1951.

Hit for cycle, second game, July 21, 1946; has lifetime slugging percentage of .645.

Named Most Valuable Player in American League in 1946 and 1949, and lost to Joe DiMaggio of New York Yankees by one point in 1947.

Named as outfielder on *The Sporting News* All-Star Major

League Teams 1939, 1940, 1941, 1942, 1946, 1947, 1948, 1949, 1951, 1953, 1955, 1956, 1957, 1958.

Named Top American League Player by *The Sporting News* in 1957.

Named Major League Player of the Year by *The Sporting News* 1941, 1942, 1947, 1949, 1957.

Named Player of the Decade by *The Sporting News* 1960.

MINOR AND MAJOR LEAGUE TOTALS

Year	Club	League	Pos.	G	AB	R	H	2B	3B	HR	RBI	BA	PO	A	E	ERA
1936	San Diego	P.C.	OF	42	107	18	29	8	2	0	11	.271	64	5	2	.972
1937	San Diego	P.C.	OF	138	454	66	132	24	2	23	98	.291	213	10	7	.970
1938	Minneapolis	A.A.	OF	148	528	130*	193	30	9	43*	142*	.366*	269	17	11	.963
1939	Boston	Amer.	OF	149	565	131	185	44	11	31	145*	.327*	318	11	19*	.945
1940	Boston	Amer.	OF-P	144	561	134*	193	43	14	23	113	.344	302	15	13	.961
1941	Boston	Amer.	OF	143	456	135*	185	33	3	37*	120	.406*	262	11	11	.961
1942	Boston	Amer.	OF	150	522	141*	186	34	5	36*	137*	.356*	313	15	4	.988
1943–45	Boston	Amer.							(In military service)							
1946	Boston	Amer.	OF	150	514	142*	176	37	8	38	123	.342	325	7	10	.971
1947	Boston	Amer.	OF	156	528	125*	181	40	9	32*	114*	.343*	347	10	9	.975
1948	Boston	Amer.	OF	137	509	124	188	44*	3	25	127	.369*	289	9	5	.983
1949	Boston	Amer.	OF	155†	566	150*	194	39*	3	43*	159†	.343	337	12	6	.983
1950	Boston‡	Amer.	OF	89	334	82	106	24	1	28	97	.317	165	7	8	.956
1951	Boston	Amer.	OF	148	531	109	169	28	4	30	126	.318	315	12	4	.988
1952	Boston§	Amer.	OF	6	10	2	4	0	1	1	3	.400	4	0	0	1.000
1953	Boston§	Amer.	OF	37	91	17	37	6	0	13	34	.407	31	1	1	.970
1954	Boston	Amer.	OF	117	386	93	133	23	1	29	89	.345	213	5	4	.982
1955	Boston	Amer.	OF	98	320	77	114	21	3	28	83	.356	170	5	2	.989
1956	Boston	Amer.	OF	136	400	71	138	28	2	24	82	.345	174	7	5	.973
1957	Boston	Amer.	OF	132	420	96	163	28	1	38	87	.388*	215	2	5	.995
1958	Boston	Amer.	OF	129	411	81	135	23	2	26	85	.328*	154	3	7	.995
1959	Boston	Amer.	OF	103	272	32	69	15	0	10	43	.254	94	4	3	.957
1960	Boston	Amer.	OF	113	310	56	98	15	0	29	72	.316	131	6	1	.993
	Major League Totals			2292	7706	1798	2654	525	71	521	1839	.344	4159	142	113	.974

* Denotes led league
† Tied for lead
‡ Suffered fractured left elbow when he crashed into the left-field wall making catch in first inning of All-Star game at Chicago, July 11, 1950; despite injury he stayed in game until ninth inning. Williams had played seventy American League games up to the All-Star affair, but appeared in only nineteen more contests with the Red Sox for the rest of the season.
§ In military service most of the season

PITCHING RECORD

Year	Club	League	G	IP	W	L	Pct.	H	R	ER	SO	BB	ERA
1940	Boston	Amer.	1	2	0	0	.000	3	1	1	1	0	4.50

WORLD SERIES RECORD

Year	Club	League	Pos.	G	AB	R	H	2B	3B	HR	RBI	BA	PO	A	E	FA
1946	Boston	Amer.	OF	7	25	2	5	0	0	0	1	.200	16	2	0	1.000

ALL-STAR GAME RECORD

Year	League	Pos.	AB	R	H	2B	3B	HR	RBI	BA	PO	A	E	FA
1940	American	OF	2	0	0	0	0	0	0	.000	3	0	0	1.000
1941	American	OF	4	1	2	1	0	1	4	.500	3	0	1	.750
1942	American	OF	4	0	1	0	0	0	0	.250	0	0	0	.000
1946	American	OF	4	4	4	0	0	2	5	1.000	1	0	0	1.000
1947	American	OF	4	0	2	1	0	0	0	.500	3	0	0	1.000
1948	American	PH	0	0	0	0	0	0	0	.000	0	0	0	.000
1949	American	OF	2	1	0	0	0	0	0	.000	1	0	0	1.000
1950	American	OF	4	0	1	0	0	0	1	.250	2	0	0	1.000
1951	American	OF	3	0	1	0	1	0	0	.333	3	0	0	1.000
1954	American	OF	2	1	0	0	0	0	0	.000	2	0	0	1.000
1955	American	OF	3	1	1	0	0	0	0	.333	1	0	0	1.000
1956	American	OF	4	1	1	0	0	1	2	.250	2	0	0	1.000
1957	American	OF	3	1	0	0	0	0	0	.000	2	0	0	1.000
1958	American	OF	2	0	0	0	0	0	0	.000	1	0	0	1.000
1959	American (both games)	PH-OF	3	0	0	0	0	0	0	.000	0	0	0	.000
1960	American (both games)	PH	2	0	1	0	0	0	0	.500	0	0	0	0.00
All-Star Game Totals			46	10	14	2	1	4	12	.304	24	0	1	.960

Photograph Credits

Index